# For Our Consideration
## Food for the Christian Mind

### Jeffrey A. Klick

All rights reserved.
No part of this publication may be reproduced, stored in a retrieval system, or transmitted in any way by any means—electronic, mechanical, photocopy, recording, or otherwise—without the prior permission of the copyright holder, except as provided by U.S. copyright law. Requests for permission should be made in writing.

Nothing in this book is intended to constitute or replace legal advice but is given as general information. Any legal or tax issues addressed are done with the understanding that those issues should be discussed with competent professionals. In addition, the web links referred to within the text were all working when the book was published. Given the fluid nature of the Internet, some may no longer be functional.

Scripture references marked ESV are from The Holy Bible, English Standard Version, Copyright © 2001 by Crossway Bibles, a division of Good News Publishers.

Scripture references marked NIV are from New International Version, Copyright © 1973, 1978, 1984 by International Bible Society.

Scripture references marked NASB are from the New American Standard Bible, Copyright © 1960, 1962, 1963, 1968, 1971, 1972, 1973, 1975, 1977, 1995 by The Lockman Foundation.

Scripture references marked KJV are from The Holy Bible, King James Version, Public Domain.

Scripture references marked HCSB are from Holman Christian Standard Bible, Copyright © 1999, 2000, 2002, 2003, 2009 by Holman Bible Publishers.

Scriptures not marked are from one of the above translations.
2017 Copyright ©Jeffrey A. Klick

# Comments from Others

I had the privilege to sit underneath Pastor Jeff's teaching and preaching for nearly five years. Week in and week out, his preparation, devotion to God's word and his practical experience greatly impacted those willing to listen and apply God's word to their lives. As a co-conference speaker and co-author of two other books, I can personally attest to Jeff's skills and abilities when it comes to taking the Word of God and breaking it down into bite size chunks that allows the average person to consume and digest God's word.

*For Our Consideration* is like buying an album of a famous band's greatest hits. In this book, Jeff pulls together decades of studying the Word of God, couples that with "all the comes" with being a pastor for 35 years, and then he adds his own life's experience into the mix. Rich, applicable, and insightful are all good words to describe the contents of this book, but perhaps the best description is "Food for the Christian Life." Eat, drink and grow from this wonderful collection from a man after God's heart.

**Glenn A. Miller, CEO, Miller Management Systems, LLC**

Wow! What an encouraging book! *For Your Consideration* by Dr. Jeffrey Klick takes us on a journey down the path of everyday challenges in the Christian life – each time bringing us to the horizon where we can clearly see the Way of the Son! The witty style, countless stories, touching illustrations and biblical application in this eclectic work make it an excellent resource for family devotions and other discipleship settings. Dr. Klick's book should encourage any true believer as the Scriptures ripple through each chapter, validating the amazing truths of the gospel. As I read through the chapters I was often impressed with an alternate title to the book: Too Good to Be True! Yet, praise God, it is!

**Eric Burd, President – Household of Faith Fellowship of Churches**
**Pastor – Vancouver Household of Faith Community Church**

Dr. Klick's devotional, *For Your Consideration* is a practical help for anyone looking for a quick read to start his day. Each entry is solidly biblical, encouraging, and easy to understand. The book will make you think, sometimes make you laugh, and mostly help you rejoice in the One who made you!

**J. Mark Fox, author of A Faithful Man and Real Life Moments: a Dad's Devotional**

Dr. Klick has done it again. He's provided his readers a thought provoking devotional that will be read and reread again and again. Each chapter contains inspiring insight into true Biblical knowledge that will help guide the reader as well as motivate him/her to put in practice the Bible truth discussed.

Each devotional contains encouraging words from the Bible and examples of folks who live life just like you do. At the end are questions to not only help the reader retain what was read but to further discuss the subject with God in prayer. A great book for individual devotions or group Bible studies.

**Brian Whiteside – Pastor, author, and radio show host**

*For Our Consideration* is the culmination of Jeff's years of service to the church and study of God's word. These pages are rich with insight and inspiration sure to enrich your mind and strengthen your heart.

**J.R. Miller, Professor of Applied Theology and Leadership at Southern California Seminary & author of Elders Lead a Healthy Family.**

While reading Dr. Klick's new book, *For Our Consideration*, I realized that I found myself re-enjoying many of these devotionals. I try to read Dr. Klick's social media and blog postings as often as possible because his writing is always on point and gives my spirit a lift. At times, his writing will seem as if Jesus had him write that particular devotional just for me. It will hit me right in the heart in just the way to wake my spirit and allow me to feel the convictions of God.

If you are a spouse, a parent, and/or a child of God, this is a must read and something to be instituted into your life and walk with our LORD and Savior Jesus Christ. After reading it through once, you will want to start from the beginning, over and over.

**Shawn D. Savage, M.A.T.S. and Caroline R. Savage, D.M.**
**Savage Ministries International, Ambassadors for Christ Radio**

# The Purpose

The gracious people that call Hope Family Fellowship their church home see the title of this book nearly every week. My sermons end with a list of questions or statements intended to provide additional "homework" for the listeners under the heading "For Our Consideration."

A sermon is only as good as it is relatable and practical. A message should make us think, pray, repent if needed, feel encouraged, be saturated with Scripture, and always draw us nearer to our Lord and Savior Jesus.

The following thoughts are written to assist each one of us to do what my sermons intend. Each article that follows should provide some food for thought, and perhaps aid discussion around the dinner table or within a small group setting. The articles and studies can be used in any order desired and are not presented in any predetermined sequence.

Many dads have confided in me that it is hard to find something to use for family devotions. These articles, and the questions that follow each one might help in your quest to lead your family in a spiritual discussion.

Some articles are short and others may take a bit longer to read, but each one will help you think and open many avenues of discussion. Agreement with what is written is not required. My point in sharing is to help each person return to the Book of all Books and seek out what is true and life-giving.

I pray that you will be blessed as you study to show yourself approved by the Lord and live a life worthy of the marvelous grace we have received from Him.

# Contents

*Food for Thought* ............................................................. x

Beyond the Whoosh ....................................................... 1
Lavished Grace ............................................................... 3
Do Not Be Anxious .......................................................... 5
What Cannot Be Told ...................................................... 7
Don't Waste Offenses ................................................... 10
The Nobody Club ........................................................... 13
Who Are You? ................................................................ 16
A Subtle Deception ........................................................ 21
Direction not Perfection ................................................ 24
God Is Not Finished ....................................................... 27
God's Own People .......................................................... 31
New Life ......................................................................... 34
10 Ways God Provides Resources .................................. 37
Looking with Hope Through Troubled Times ................ 40
Two Are Better Than One .............................................. 47
We All Stand on Something ........................................... 51
Why Complicate the Simple? ......................................... 55
God's Expectations ........................................................ 60
Motive Matters .............................................................. 63
Boasting is Just Fine ...................................................... 66

*Discussion Starters* ..................................................... 71

Mr. Frustration .............................................................. 72
Christian Tension .......................................................... 75
Is there a Gift of Criticism? ........................................... 78

A Case of Mistaken Identity ........................................ 81
Be Given to Hospitality ............................................... 84
Death to Self? ........................................................... 87
Grace vs. Works ........................................................ 92
Heart Battles ............................................................. 95
Who Ya Listening To? ................................................ 99
Have We Lost Something? ........................................ 104
Holiness, Sin and other Offensive Words ...................... 108
What about Them? ................................................... 112
Christian Sensuality ................................................. 116
It Ain't Judging If You Are Sinning .............................. 121
Is Education Evil? ..................................................... 126
Three Essentials ...................................................... 130
Living for what Matters............................................. 133
Suffering and Faith................................................... 137
The First Sin? .......................................................... 141
What is Forgiveness? ................................................ 145
If - A Huge Word ..................................................... 149
How Should a Christian "Dress"? ................................ 153
I'm Balanced, but I am not so Sure about You! ................ 156

## ___Family ............................................ 160

Generational Ripples ............................................... 161
Generational Faith Impartation ................................. 165
Choose Your Friends Wisely....................................... 170
Is God in a Hurry? .................................................... 174

Family Forgiveness ................................................. 178
The Second Biggest Decision...................................... 182
The Second Biggest Decision – Ladies' Version................ 187
A Challenge to My Fellow Grandparents ....................... 193

## ___Marriage................................................... 199

Living Words, Killing Words ....................................... 200
Does Your Marriage Have a Prayer?............................. 204
God is Pro-Marriage ................................................ 209
Intense Fellowship .................................................. 214
Why Should I Stay? ................................................. 219
How's Your Prayer Life Guys? ..................................... 224
Different is Good .................................................... 229
Marriage and Mind Reading ....................................... 234
Marriage: The Perfect Tool for Spiritual Growth ............. 238

## ___Section Two................................................. 243

One Another.......................................................... 246
Discipleship Thoughts .............................................. 251
Practical Family Discipleship Tools .............................. 271
A Bible Study on Authority ........................................ 288
Parental Authority .................................................. 308
Called to War – A Spiritual Warfare Discussion............... 318
Spiritual Incrementalism Part One............................... 332
Spiritual Incrementalism Part Two .............................. 339
Spiritual Incrementalism Part Three ............................ 345
Fatherhood Part One A Calling ................................... 351

Fatherhood Part Two God's Idea.................................. 354
Fatherhood Part Three Love Your Wife ......................... 358
Fatherhood Part Four Love Your Wife - What in the World does that Mean? ...................................................... 362
Fatherhood Part Five Priests and Prophets?..................... 366
Fatherhood Part Six What Am I Supposed to be Doing Again? 370
Fatherhood Part Seven Take the Next Step ..................... 374
Biography......................................................... 377
Dr. Klick's Other Books............................................. 378

# Food for Thought

"You can never get enough of what you don't need to make you happy." – Eric Hoffer

# Beyond the Whoosh

As my car went crashing through the guardrail the thoughts of a flaming death filled my mind. Would it hurt? What if I just laid there broken but not dead? The ground was far, far away. Miles, it seemed. I frantically tried to call my wife, but she didn't answer. I quickly sent her a text telling her goodbye and that I loved her. Death was approaching.

The fall was amazing. In fact, it felt like the video I just watched about skydivers. The ground was still way off and yet, I knew the end of my life was near. This experience had happened dozens of times before. No, I'm not the world's worst driver, just a frequent dreamer of falling.

But this time, it was different. In all my previous dreams, somehow the car, and I, always seemed to survive the crash. A ramp would appear out of nowhere to redirect the car, or suddenly a grassy hill would arise and I would land just perfectly to coast down it to safety. Not this time.

As the ground was rushing up into my view, suddenly there was a man next to me in the passenger seat of my car. Somehow, I knew he was not human, but he simply sat there smiling calmly. He casually said, "You are not going to survive this one, are you ready to leave?"
I said, "Yes," and whoosh, we went out the windows flying like a blur to the light. Then, I awoke. Bummer. Not that I didn't die in the car crash, but that I didn't get to see beyond the whoosh.

As I lay there processing what just happened, peace descended upon me. If death is like that, then I'm good to go! No fear, no worries, nothing but a smiling companion who asks, "Are you ready to go?"

For Our Consideration

Death's sting has been removed for those that know the One that defeated it.

I would have liked to stay asleep and view what others have seen beyond the Light. Paul stated that he knew a man that was caught into the third heaven and saw things we simply cannot know just yet. John the Beloved was given a Revelation of the risen Christ that I read and reread often. We get a glimpse of what is next, but not the full picture.

I didn't get the picture beyond the whoosh, but I did receive great comfort regarding the process of getting there, and for that, I am very grateful. In fact, I can't wait to go to bed and see what happens next.

## Questions to Ponder or Discuss:

1. Have you ever dreamed about flying or falling? Did you crash?

2. What is your view of death?

3. As you read Revelation, do you get excited about heaven? Explain.

4. Why does God give us glimpses into the next life?

# Lavished Grace

Is God conservative? Not politically, but regarding His natural resources? Grace is sometimes defined - "of the merciful kindness by which God, exerting his holy influence upon souls, turns them to Christ, keeps, strengthens, increases them in Christian faith, knowledge, affection, and kindles them to the exercise of the Christian virtues."

> In him we have redemption through his blood, the forgiveness of our trespasses, according to the riches of his grace, which he lavished upon us, in all wisdom and insight making known to us the mystery of his will, according to his purpose, which he set forth in Christ as a plan for the fullness of time, to unite all things in him, things in heaven and things on earth. Ephesians 1:7-10

Lavished - means poured to overflowing, filling to where it is running over and spilling out in abundance!

Once we are In Him, we have redemption because of what Christ did on the cross. Our trespasses and sins are forgiven, not simply covered over, but removed as far as the east is from the west. This was accomplished according to the riches of God's grace, His merciful kindness which He lavished upon us!

God does not have any limits or lack of resources at His disposal. God does not run out of grace or forgiving power. Our loving heavenly Father is not a miser with His forgiveness or grace, but pours it upon us, lavishes it. As His children, we are invited to swim in His love,

For Our Consideration

grace, and forgiveness. Our world may run out of natural resources someday, but not our God.

I sometimes think that I have used up my measure of His grace and forgiveness that is available from Him, then I recall these wonderful words from Paul. "In Him, we have redemption, forgiveness, and in a measure given according to His riches, and God lavishes upon me His forgiveness and grace."

God's plan includes pouring out His grace on His children, empowering them to further the work of His Kingdom, His plan includes uniting all things to Christ in the fullness of time, and that includes those of us that swim in His lavishly poured out grace.

God does not have shortages and He delights to overwhelm His children with His love, grace, and forgiveness. If you have sinned or feel far away from the Lord, run to Him, He is waiting to lavish upon you His grace at this very time, and He has plenty to go around.

## Questions to Ponder or Discuss:

1. Have you ever felt like you out-sinned the grace of God?

2. How would you define lavished grace?

3. What does the kindness of God mean to you?

4. Reread the story of the Prodigal Son in Luke 15:11-32? How do grace and forgiveness fit into it?

# Do Not Be Anxious

> Do not be anxious about tomorrow, for tomorrow will be anxious for itself, Sufficient for the day is its own trouble. Matthew 6:34

Tomorrow is often something that we fear or worry about, but the truth is tomorrow never shows up. We only have today. Jesus told the large crowd that had gathered to listen to His teachings to not be anxious about tomorrow for it will all work out, you'll see, it will be good. Do we really believe that sentence?

How much emotional energy do we waste on fretting about tomorrow? How much time do we invest in worrying about something that we can do nothing about? Today is yesterday's tomorrow and today is what we have. I can learn from yesterday and plan and pray about tomorrow, but I can only live in today.

Jesus said not to worry or be fearful, and the Apostle Paul told us that all things would work out for good for those who love the Lord in Romans 8:28, but we struggle believing these truths as the realities of life crash into our day.

Our minds tend to interfere with our faith. We know the truth of God's word but our minds fight against our faith. I know all will eventually be well, but my mind sees the trouble, problems, failures, and wages war against my faith. The minute by minute struggle involves taking my thoughts captive to the obedience of Christ and making my mind a servant to my faith!

We know the end of the Bible and as we read we see that all will be well! Jesus is the Victor. Satan and death are defeated and a new

For Our Consideration

heaven and earth await the believer. The journey between this reality presented in the Scripture and what we endure during our days is where the struggle exists - we are not to fret, worry, or be anxious about the process, and this takes faith and the power of the Holy Spirit!

Like reading the last chapter of a mystery book first, or watching the ending of a suspenseful movie before the beginning, we know how it will all work out. If we would view our life from the end promised in the Scripture, we would learn how to enjoy the plot twists along the way as we journey through the daily struggles.

Jesus said, do not be anxious because He holds the keys to life and death. The end has already been written and it is excellent for those who love Him. Regardless of the trials, hardships, and unexpected twists along the journey of our life, we know the ending and it is Jesus, no wonder He said do not be anxious. We will be with Him and like Him, and that is an excellent ending!

## Questions to Ponder or Discuss:

1. Is worrying and being anxious a sin? Why or why not?

2. What is the difference between planning and being anxious?

3. What is the difference between being cautious and taking preventative measures and being anxious?

4. How does knowing the end of the story help us as we live our lives day by day?

# What Cannot Be Told

I have some friends (The Downing Family) that sing bluegrass and on one of their recent CD's, there is a line that sticks in my brain

> **"Can you imagine what awaits the redeemed?"**

No, I can't even begin to comprehend or dream what is ahead but think about this verse for a moment:

> But, as it is written, "What no eye has seen, nor ear heard, nor the heart of man imagined, what God has prepared for those who love him" 1 Corinthians 2:9

I have a pretty good imagination and yet, whatever awaits those of us that love Jesus, is beyond what our brains can dream. In fact, Paul, or some other guy, (I will let others fight about who it really was) had an amazing experience:

> I know a man in Christ who fourteen years ago was caught up to the third heaven—whether in the body or out of the body I do not know, God knows. And I know that this man was caught up into paradise—whether in the body or out of the body I do not know, God knows—and he heard things that cannot be told, which man may not utter.
> 2 Corinthians 12:2-4

## For Our Consideration

Don't you wish that he could have told or uttered! Wouldn't you have loved to sit and have a cup of coffee with that man shortly after his experience? So many questions could be instantly answered. Well, he didn't say what he saw or heard, so we can't know, at least completely. We get glimpses in the Book of Revelation and hints here and there in Scripture, but only a glance, and through a "mirror dimly." (1 Corinthians 13:12)

But, think about that man who did see and hear for a minute *after* he had the experience. Do you think that he ever worried about anything ever again? Do you think that anything on earth would draw him away from what he saw and heard? Do you think he would ever forget?

Would money matter to him any longer? Would he care if someone was talking about him or if he was not part of the "in crowd"? So, what if his 401(k) tanked or favorite sports team came in dead last. Would he be prideful of anything accomplished on earth? Would anything temporal hold his first love any longer? I doubt it.

Once he had tasted of the eternal, what is quickly passing away would not really matter too much anymore. God has prepared for us things that we cannot even grasp with our human mind, and we have a God-given longing for eternity! We know (or need to be reminded) what we see is temporary, a mere vapor. (James 4:14)

Jesus told His disciples not to worry, He was leaving, but He would return to take them to be with Him. In fact, He told them that He was preparing a place for them. (John 14:1-3) Perhaps this man saw a room or two of his dwelling place (mansion KJV). Maybe he only caught a glimpse of the streets made of pure gold or the huge pearls that are the doors to the city. Maybe he heard a trumpet or angel choir. Who knows, but we *can* imagine.

And, we can long for the eternal while we await our blessed Savior's return. In the early church, they would often greet one another with the word Maranatha – O Lord come or come quickly Lord Jesus. Living under extreme persecution, the brethren placed their hope in the return of Jesus. We too can look for our Lord's return. Whether He returns to meet us in the air, or we meet Him at death, Maranatha!

We are to be busy about our Master's work until we meet Him again, but we must never lose sight of the eternal in the face of all our temporal surroundings. We all can dream, and we should. Can *you* imagine what awaits the redeemed?

## Questions to Ponder or Discuss:

1. Spend a few minutes describing what you think heaven will look like. Then add a description of the new earth.

2. How would getting a glimpse of our future home help us today in our current condition?

3. Is our life reflective of an eternal perspective? Why or why not?

4. Is there one thing we can change considering living with an eternal perspective?

For Our Consideration

# Don't Waste Offenses

It is inevitable that offenses will come to us. Someone somewhere at some time will say or do something that will bother us. Perhaps they will be rude, speak evil of us, not appreciate our efforts or intentions, or worse, assign us evil motives when we really meant well. I am not a prophet or son of a prophet, but I can almost guarantee you that offenses will happen to you. This is especially true if you are in any sort of leadership position.

We have multiple options when someone hurts, wounds, disparages, or betrays us:

- We can seek revenge.
- We can attempt to protect our reputation.
- We can return evil for evil.
- We can tell everyone we know how badly we were treated.
- We can become defensive.
- We can become a martyr.

I'm sure there are other responses that would fit in this vein of reaction to being hurt. For the record, none of these are productive or Biblical.

There are a couple of other responses that I believe would be preferable to the list above. First, we can simply overlook the offense. What a novel concept in our instant communication, selfie-posting world. We can let the hurt go realizing that we have hurt others by our words, actions, and inaction.

This is a Biblical response:

> Good sense makes one slow to anger, and it is his glory to overlook an offense. Proverbs 19:11

If we would really take a good, long look at our own lives, we would realize how often we have been less than perfect in our dealings with others. We do not have any stones to throw at others for their failures.

We have said foolish things. We have been hurtful in our actions, words, slights, opinions, the exclusion of others into our circles, and probably a host of other relational type sins. We have not been perfect and it is imperfect of us to expect perfection from other people. We can simply understand that everyone makes mistakes.

Even if the slight, hurt, or wound was intentional, we can still overlook it. Proverbs states that it is to our glory to do so! We are commanded to love those that hurt us. Jesus went so far as to say we must love our enemies and those that persecute us. We are never instructed to return evil for evil, but grace and a blessing instead.

The second response we can have in order not to waste an offense is to learn from it. We can observe how we feel amid the pain and learn not to repeat the action that causes such wounds. If we were treated badly by someone? Let's not do that to others. If we are excluded from the in-group, let's reach out to others so they don't experience the same pain. Did we enjoy being talked about behind our back? Let's not do the same with someone else's.

We have the option to learn from the pain we are feeling. I am not denying that it hurts; simply that we have redemptive options of dealing with *that* hurt. We can overlook it realizing that we too have failed. And, we can learn not to do unto others what we hated being

For Our Consideration

done to us. By implementing these two understandings into our lives, we can learn not to waste an offense through bitterness, anger, or self-pity.

I'm not saying it is easy to do, or even the only two options, but I am saying that these are something to prayerfully consider the next time we are offended.

## Questions to Ponder or Discuss:

1. When was the last time you were offended? Describe the event and think through your response.

2. What was the result of your response?

3. When was the last time you realized that you offended someone else?

4. How could either the offense received or one that you provided for someone else be used to further growth in your life?

# The Nobody Club

A.A. has the famous greeting when introducing a new member, "Hi, my name is Bob, and I'm an alcoholic." After the greeting, everyone says, "Hi Bob." It's more like, "Hiiiiiii Bob." A long, drawn-out greeting of recognition and acceptance.

If I ever started a club it would go more like, "Hi, my name is Jeff, and I am a nobody." Everyone would respond, "Hiiiiiii Jeff." Many of us feel more like a nobody rather than a special somebody. As we are bombarded with the accomplishments of the popular, gifted and special people, it is easy to believe we are charter members of the nobody club.

Most of us do not impact the nations, have huge audiences that hang on our every word or must fight off the paparazzi every time we walk outside. We are nobody special. For preachers, if the truth is told, it is sometimes hard to have your weekly listeners tell you how inspired they were by whoever is the popular radio, TV or internet preaching sensation. Who am I to compete with those almost mythical, gifted, story-telling marvels? I am nobody special.

This is also true for authors, athletes, and non-actors. Our books don't sell millions of copies. We are not professionals that make their living from sports. We do not look like those that grace our screens. When we compare ourselves and what we have done to those that have the fame, we are nobody. "Hiiiiiii Jeff" rings in my ears.

This feeling of being a nobody is true. It is also false. While we may be nobody special to everyone, we are most special to the One that matters. We are created in the image of God. We are His dearly loved

## For Our Consideration

child. If no one else finds us special, our Father does. In fact, He says this about us:

> For we are his workmanship, created in Christ Jesus for good works, which God prepared beforehand, that we should walk in them. Ephesians 2:10

The word workmanship in this verse includes the understanding of masterpiece. A proper way to quote this verse is to state that we are His masterpiece! For the record, our Creator does not create junk. Nor does He fail. Nor does He do useless. Everything He does is for a purpose, and that purpose is perfect.

In addition to God, we are important to others. There may not be many, but there certainly is someone. Maybe they are not even born yet, but there are those that we will impact. Even if we don't know who they may be, God does. Behind every famous person stands an entire army of people whose names we do not know. This is true in Scripture, and it is true in our world today.

Most of us have families that love us. We probably hold a job of some sort and there are people that rely on us. We have an impact on others, even if we don't recognize it. We really do matter, and probably to a great deal more people than we can imagine.

If by some strange chance, you are an orphaned, single, unemployed adult, and still can't think of anyone that would care if you lived or died, consider the last part of the verse I shared above. God created each of us for good works. There is someone, somewhere, that is just waiting for you to do what God intended for you to do.

Food for Thought

We do not belong in the nobody club, but the masterpiece club. We need to say, "Hi, I'm Jeff, and I am a masterpiece." And the response will be from other masterpieces, "Hiiiiiii Jeff." We have good works to do, so let's go get busy and do them my fellow, former, nobodies. You have value, you are a somebody, and you are a masterpiece in process.

## Questions to Ponder or Discuss:

1. Do you ever feel like a nobody? Are there events that bring this feeling on, or is just a regular state of mind?

2. Why is it unwise to compare ourselves to others?

3. On the other hand, why it is wise to understand what our Creator thinks of us?

4. How do you feel about being called a masterpiece? Why?

For Our Consideration

## Who Are You?

Now there is a question that must be answered. Many will say what they do - their occupation or family position - I am an accountant, or an author, or a doctor. I am the second born child, stepchild or adopted child.

Some will say what they have been told - I am worthless, pretty, ugly, fat, skinny, freckled, smart, or good for nothing. Perhaps you were always unfavorably compared to your sibling, "Why can't you be more like your brother or sister?" Maybe you have been told you were an accident, a mistake, unloved, unwanted, a bother and an inconvenience.

Maybe you would say it is based on what others' opinions (real or implied) are of you - again, usually tied to behavior - angry, insensitive, harsh, uncaring, unfeeling, too sensitive, too loving, gullible, cynic, negative, positive, optimist, pessimist, successful, failure, brave, cowardly, strong, weak, fearful, full of faith, worry wart or seemingly unaware of fear or danger. How about a failure?

What have you been told - good or bad? What have you been called over and over? Who are you?

To properly answer this question, we must visit Pilate's famous question directed to Jesus - "What is truth?" Each of us has some outside of ourselves standard of truth. We all learn to have a value system from where our worth arises - both personal and societal.

We either adopt that of our parents, friends, our social circle, peers, the worlds, or something beyond. Many seek answers in the spiritual realm. Most of us would believe that there is only one standard of truth - the Word of God.

Our search to determine who we are should begin and end in the Scriptures. Others, even important to us others, may share things about and to us, but what God says should carry the most weight.

My associate pastor Dennis and I have discussed at length about how hard it is for those we talk to, our family members, church folks, even each other, to make a critical distinction - there is a vast difference between saying we don't like or approve of a behavior vs. saying we don't like or approve of you.

You did something bad, which does not mean *you* are bad. You said something wrong, that does not mean *you* are wrong. You made a mistake, which does not mean *you* are a mistake. You failed or messed up, that does not mean *you* are a failure or a mess. It is hard to receive correction, but being reproved does not mean you are a failure, loser, or unloved or unwanted, you just did something wrong.

This is not some power of positive thinking view, but an attempt to make my thoughts align with the Scripture. Who am I, who are you? If you are in Christ, born again, saved, then you are at least the following according to God's Word:

> Therefore, if anyone is in Christ, he is a new creation. The old has passed away; behold, the new has come.
> 2 Corinthians 5:17

We are something totally different than we were when we did not believe Jesus died for our sins and is our Lord. Everything is new after we do.

For Our Consideration

> Therefore, we are ambassadors for Christ, God making His appeal through us. We implore you on behalf of Christ, be reconciled to God. For our sake He made Him to be sin Who knew no sin, so that in Him we might become the righteousness of God. 2 Corinthians 5:20-21

We are both an ambassador for Christ and now the righteousness of God in Him.

> I am writing to you, little children, because your sins are forgiven for His name's sake. 1 John 2:12

We are completely forgiven in Christ.

> So, if the Son sets you free, you will be free indeed. John 8:36

We are free in Christ, no longer slaves to sin. We are now free to obey our Lord without hindrances.

> Beloved, we are God's children now, and what we will be has not yet appeared; but we know that when He appears we shall be like Him, because we shall see Him as He is.
> 1 John 3:2

God is my Daddy and I am His child! Whose child, are you?

> So, you are no longer a slave, but a son, and if a son, then an heir through God. Galatians 4:7

Food for Thought

I am family and therefore entitled to an amazing inheritance as an heir.

> For we are His workmanship, created in Christ Jesus for good works, which God prepared beforehand, that we should walk in them. Ephesians 2:10

I am a work in progress under the watchful eye of the ultimate Master Who does not make junk or mistakes!

> But you are a chosen race, a royal priesthood, a holy nation, a people for His own possession, that you may proclaim the excellencies of Him who called you out of darkness into His marvelous light. 1 Peter 2:9

I am part of something new, royal, holy and dearly loved! I am a light dweller.

> But our citizenship is in heaven, and from it we await a Savior, the Lord Jesus Christ, Philippians 3:20

I am simply passing through this country because I belong somewhere else.

The Bible certainly says more about who we are in Christ, but not less! Because of these truths about my identity, I can withstand the criticisms of others. Because these are true, I know who I am and whatever someone else may say to or about me, these verses remain true. Because I know these realities, I will live a life that has meaning and purpose. I am a dearly loved child of the King!

For Our Consideration

So, what or who are you going to believe about who you are - humans, the devil, your own mind, or God's Word? Who is going to determine your viewpoint and your worth? Who should? What is your basis of truth? What should we believe regarding who we are? I believe the above from God's Word, how about you?

## Questions to Ponder or Discuss:

1. What name is on your mind regarding who you are? Why?

2. What does it mean to you to be a child of the King?

3. What does it mean to you to be completely new in Jesus?

4. What does it mean to you to be an ambassador for Christ?

# A Subtle Deception

Has the devil ever lied to you? Have you ever lied to yourself? Have you ever felt very strongly about someone only to find out later that you were wrong? Most of us are wrong at some time or another in our lives! Often, this error involves looking at someone else and includes what we think of them. One error usually goes like this...

Everybody else is so spiritual but I am a clod. Everybody else's family is almost perfect and mine is a wreck. Everyone else's marriage is wonderful and I am stuck in this one. Everyone else's children are so well behaved and mine are so wild, etc. etc. etc. The truth is everyone has problems. If you could spend time in anyone else's home, you might just be surprised. Sure, everyone looks good on Sundays, but hey, so do you!

We have a hard time imagining anyone else being as "bad" as we are. Herein lays one of the biggest lies of the devil. The Bible tells us not to compare ourselves with others; for if we do this, we are foolish (2 Corinthians 10:12). The only accurate standard is our obedience to the Lord. What has God told you to do? If you are obeying the revealed will of God, then you are on the correct path. When you try to compare yourself, your marriage, or family to others you are using the wrong measuring stick.

If you could open a window into other people's lives and observe what is going on, you would see many rough areas just like in yours. Couples who you thought never had a harsh word for each other do disagree sometimes. Children who look so neat and obedient on Sunday mornings have an old nature and need the rod just like your children do on Monday! I do not believe I have ever met a couple who

## For Our Consideration

did not disagree or argue (I did meet one once who said this, but I think they were lying!). I have never met a perfect child, husband, wife, or family, for we all are being changed from one degree of glory to the next degree of glory (2 Corinthians 3:18). Sometimes it is an ugly process!

The devil's main weapon against us is deception. He whispers into our minds that we are not worthy, or we are not good enough. We do not pray enough, read enough, or fast enough. We are just not spiritual enough. And you know something, he is right! However, it does not depend on us. Our performance is not the basis on which we are judged. We are judged on our obedience. Jesus is the author and finisher of our faith. He began a good work in us and He will complete it! We are all masterpieces in process. Ever see a painting half done? How about a statue that was not finished yet? It's not always pretty looking. But wait until the master finishes it! Then it will be something to look at!

We are all in different stages of completion by our Master. The enemy loves to whisper into our minds, "Look at all those others. See how far you must go. You are not as far along as them. You are not even good enough to be in the same room as them." And we believe him! The devil's strategy usually works. He wants us to get our eyes off the Master and place them on each other or worse yet, ourselves!

People should group together by vision, purpose, and goals, not on whether they are worthy or not. Who is worthy to stand before the Lord? Who has arrived? Who has all wisdom and truth? Only the Lord Jesus! We all stand based on faith and by the grace of God, not based on our works.

A wise man will keep companionship with other wise men but a companion of fools comes to ruin (Proverbs 13:20). It is a good thing to be around families you want to be like, but do not listen to the enemy's voice as you do. We are all on the same path of trying to obey the master. Some days we do better than others, so do not compare yourself with anyone else, for it is always a trap.

We all struggle; you are not the only one. The devil lies to all of us, but praise God for His infinite grace and mercy! Let us believe God and quit listening to the lies of our enemy!

## Questions to Ponder or Discuss:

1. What was the last lie from our foe that you believed?

2. Why is it unwise to evaluate others by what we see?

3. Why is it important to have good friends that can freely share with us?

4. How does the Scripture teach that we should battle the lies of the enemy?

For Our Consideration

# Direction not Perfection

Be completely humble. Esteem everyone as better than yourself. Die daily to your desires and seek to be a servant of all. Watch every word that comes out of your mouth for you will give an account of it on the Day of Judgment. Take every thought captive and make sure it is in obedience to Christ. Guard your eyes to avoid evil and let your light shine before everyone. No pressure huh?

If you add to that the commands to love your friends and even your enemies, do not return evil for evil but bless instead, feed the hungry, clothe those without, give freely to those that ask, and redeem the time for the days are evil, our days are pretty much full. And, we are destined to fail. What are we to do?

We walk in grace. Moment by moment we live, move and have our being in Christ. Jesus Christ lived a perfect, sinless life fully pleasing to His Heavenly Father. We are not Jesus and so we will never arrive at total perfection this side of eternity. On our best day, we still fall woefully short of perfection. Even if we did everything we should have, countless things were left undone. We fail but we are not failures. We are works in progress.

When we fall, and we all fall, we fall in the right direction. We are called to walk on the Highway of Holiness following our Lord and Master but that does not mean we do not slip and fall. We walk in His footsteps but we are often entangled and we stumble. We are not perfect, we are recipients of grace from the One that is. If we could be perfect then Jesus did not need to come and live a sinless life. One of the wisest humans outside of Jesus wrote:

# Food for Thought

> For the righteous falls seven times and rises again, but the wicked stumble in times of calamity. Proverbs 24:16

We fall but we get back up. We fall multiple times but we get up and keep on walking by the grace given by our Lord. We are not perfect but we are heading somewhere and it is perfect. We are not yet clothed with immortality and perfection but we will be someday soon. We do not yet look like Jesus but we shall in eternity. What a glorious day that will be!

In the meantime, we walk. We fall, get up and keep on walking. We cry, repent, forgive others, ourselves, and we walk. We have a cloud of witnesses that if we could see and hear them, would be shouting out encouragement to us! "Keep it up, you're almost there. Don't quit now, you are so close. Come on, get up, shake off the dirt and filth, be cleansed in the blood of Jesus, and keep on walking."

How do I know they are saying such things? Consider whom the writer of Hebrews was probably referring to when he wrote that famous passage in 12:1. If we were to go back and study each of the lives of the people in chapter 11, we would see a direction, not perfection. None of those mentioned were perfect. In fact, most of them were people that failed and fell. But, they got back up and kept on walking. So, must we. These people looked to God for forgiveness, strength, and direction, and so must we.

We must be those that lay aside the sin that so easily entangles us and look to Jesus, the author, and finisher of our faith. As we consider Him, we renew our minds, regain our strength and we walk on towards the prize.

For Our Consideration

We are not perfect, but we know Who is and we are those following Him. Someday soon, we shall see Him and be like Him. In that day, we will only fall at His feet, and that is the proper direction to fall.

## Questions to Ponder or Discuss:

1. Can perfection be achieved this side of death? Explain your answer

2. How does God look at our repeated failures? Why?

3. Does it help to consider that those listed in the Scriptures (Other than Jesus of course!) failed? Explain.

4. Do you agree that we all stumble and fall? If so, what should we do when this happens and why should we do it?

# God Is Not Finished

I know God rested after creation and Jesus said, "It is finished," but God is still working. Paul states in these two verses a truth that we can bank our souls on:

> For I am confident of this very thing, that He who began a good work in you will perfect it until the day of Christ Jesus. Philippians 1:6

> For we are His workmanship, created in Christ Jesus for good works, which God prepared beforehand so that we would walk in them. Ephesians 2:10

God is not finished with us yet. On July 25, 1973, Jesus began a good work in a desperate sinner named Jeff. He will complete it. Over these years Jesus' workmanship has been chiseled, heated in the fire, spun on the potter's wheel and received an abundance of grace. I am not complete but I am not the same piece of clay as in the beginning...at least I am not in the same shape.

In an instant, everything was changed. Before that blessed day, I was lost, separated from Life, and dead in my sins. After that day, I was a new creation in Christ, the righteousness of God, washed in the precious blood of the Lord Jesus Christ and a work was started that will be completed. I have that on good authority, it will be accomplished.

Being a bit older helps to bring perspective to this life we live here on earth. Time has a way of providing insight to the many adjustments the Master allows, or causes, in His masterpieces. Jesus does not make junk and He will complete the work He began. Many times, the process seems painful and disconnected, but the Master knows what He is doing.

The Master knows how much heat to apply. He knows how hard to hit the block of marble and how many spins it takes to mold the clay. These word pictures point to the same conclusion - there is a Master Craftsman and He will complete His project. Why? Because God is not finished yet. Jesus began the work and He will finish it.

As December 5th passes each year, I am reminded of another tool the Lord has used in this piece of clay's life. In 1993, my world was turned upside down by events that I had no control over. My employment/ministry earth shook violently and the storms came crashing down on my foundation. Would it stand? Was God in control? Was the Master still working on this block of marble? (Notice I did not say, blockhead.)

Like many others before me, I knew the verses shared above but they really had not been tested. Oh, there had been some mild trials and stresses, but not a direct blow of this magnitude. Would my faith stand and would my God provide and prove His Word? By God's grace, I am grateful to say, "yes" to all questions.

God used the events of that year to spin this piece of clay out of his comfort zone. Tears, fears, and stress of the unknown pressed this masterpiece in progress into a closer relationship with my Lord. Forgiveness was learned at a deeper level. Many actions endured proved to be the foundation of a learning process so I would not do the same things to others. Change and growth came.

God had a plan and every event was carefully observed under His personal attention. Out of the fire came a wonderful church and some sharp edges sanded off its pastor. God has been good, is good, and will always be good, no matter what happens in my life. I know this and I rejoice in it.

The fire is hot and the pounding often hurts. Spinning around like wet clay in supernatural hands sometimes makes me dizzy, but I know the work will go on and it will produce what the Master desires. He promised to complete the work and He will not fail. Why do I know this? Because God is not finished with me. Or you. He is still working and He alone knows when the masterpiece is just the way He wants it.

God alone will determine when His work is complete. God alone knows exactly what He is doing with each one of us. God alone has the blueprints and final picture in mind. Therefore, God alone is the One that determines the value and effectiveness of each life. God will not fail and He does not lie. Jesus began a good work and He will complete it. Jesus is the author and finisher of the work in our lives and He will bring us to completion.

As we spin around on the potter's wheel or have some more rough edges chiseled from us, or spend some time in the fire of affliction, we can look to the Master and learn to enter rest. God does not make mistakes and He will not fail; that is not possible and this eternal truth extends all the way down to each one of His works in progress. Rejoice!

For Our Consideration

## Questions to Ponder or Discuss:

1. Do you believe that God can finish what He began in you?

2. Why does God allow trials and hardship in our lives?

3. What is your picture of being on a potter's wheel and how it relates to walking with God our Father?

4. What does resting in God and His work mean to you?

# God's Own People

> "But you are a chosen people, a royal priesthood, a holy nation, a people belonging to God, that you may declare the praises of Him who called you out of darkness into His wonderful light. Once you were not a people, but now you are the people of God; once you had not received mercy, but now you have received mercy." 1 Peter 2:9-10 (NIV)

As believers, we are unique in the entire world, for only Christians can claim a personal relationship with God; an intimate family type one with our heavenly Father. All other religions of the world, Buddhism, Hinduism, Humanism, Islam, etc. focus on what we must do; only Christianity focuses on what God has done.

God, in His infinite wisdom, chose to become a personal God and He did not have to! He does not "need" us, for God has no needs; but God desires to be in a relationship with us. He is not some far-off deity that cannot be reached; He is always near. Longing to be in fellowship with each of His children. God is a personal God who desires to be known by His children.

Have you ever noticed how many times in Scripture the phrase "Your God" is used?" Or, "My God." Count how many times God says, "You are my people." I call these the "ownership" verses. You will be amazed! Here are just a few:

- I will take you as my own people, and I will be your God. Exodus 6:7

For Our Consideration

- Do not fear, for I am with you; do not be dismayed, for I am your God. Isaiah 41:10
- So, you will be my people, and I will be your God. Jeremiah 30:22
- You my sheep, the sheep of My pasture, are people, and I am your God, declares the Sovereign Lord. Ezekiel 34:31
- You will be my people, and I will be your God. Ezekiel 36:28b
- There remains, then, a Sabbath-rest for the people of God... Hebrews 4:9
- Love the Lord your God with all your heart and with all your soul and with all your strength and with all your mind and, love your neighbor as yourself. Luke 10:27

Our God is a personal God! He created us with the express purpose of spending time with us. From the beginning, God has been taking walks in the cool of the garden, and He still desires this type of relationship with each of us today.

We may be alone sometimes, but we never should be lonely, for God is always with us and available for fellowship! If you are not able to find another living soul in the entire world, God is still there. Moreover, He is waiting to fill the void in your life. He desires to be your God, your friend, your companion, your source, and your life.

We are the people of God. Our walk with God is not based on a set of rituals, but on a relationship. God desires for us to know Him.

This term "know" is the same word that was used about the marital relationship. It implies total intimacy, no secrets, nothing at all hidden. God is, of course, beyond our understanding. Nevertheless, He wants to reveal Himself to us. He does this through His Word and His Spirit.

Just like a human relationship, intimacy develops as we spend quality time together. Everyone talks about quality time, but you cannot make it happen! Quality time always happens within the context of quantity time. Some of the best quality time with our spouse or children happens when we least expect it. You cannot schedule quality time! Relationships must be worked at. The same is true with our God. We must spend quantity time with Him to know Him better.

Have you spent time with your Father lately? Hurry, He is waiting and longing for you to come and spend time with Him.

## Questions to Ponder or Discuss:

1. Why do you think that God chose to reveal Himself in a personal fashion?

2. What does being in the family of God mean to you?

3. What does spending time with God look like in your life?

4. Do you believe that God wants to spend time with you? Why or why not?

For Our Consideration

# New Life

Our friends I mentioned before, we have known for many, many years. In addition to being nice people, they play bluegrass music. Frequent guests at music festivals and Silver Dollar City, the Downing Family are talented musicians and produce some excellent tunes. As a disclaimer, I am not a paid spokesman and do not receive any compensation for my writing. :)

Their latest CD includes several songs that really speak to me. The truth is, I am not even a big bluegrass fan, but their music always touches my spirit. I enjoy all the songs on the *You've Gotta Rest* CD, but two are ministering to me every time I listen to them.

One song is entitled, "*The Half That's Not Been Told*," and is a glimpse into heaven. If we really knew what was ahead we would live our lives in a way that mattered here. In addition to the beautiful harmony in the song, is a musical description of what we as believers all long for - heaven. Every one of us wishes that we could catch a glimpse of eternity. Just seeing what is described in this song would help us endure what we must on this side. Come quickly Lord Jesus and reveal what You have for Your children!

While I am enjoying meditating about heaven, my life continues this side and that is where the second song comes into play. "*The Story of Your Life*," is one that brings me to tears every time I listen to it. The lyrics are excellent and if we would simply follow them, our lives would come into focus. Consider these thoughts:

> I will write your story again, if you will give your life to Me, I'll give it back to you. I am the One Who makes everything new,

> I'll rewind the years and redeem the time, and I'll rewrite the story of your life...

Who among us has not wished for this to be true? Who has not regretted bad decisions, harsh words spoken, broken relationships, sinful behavior, and lost days, months, and even years? As humans, our life is populated with joys but also sorrows, heartache, tears. Good days and miserable ones. We have wonderful relationships and some that are not so much. Our earthly life is made up of a mixture of laughter, crying, longings, rejections, fears, pleasure, friendships, enemies, intimacy and being alone.

Our story is written each day as we live our lives. But, and it is a huge, gigantic, wonderful word, God is in the redeeming business. When we go to our Father and run into His arms, He pours His love upon us. God can and does rewrite the story of our lives. When we fall at His feet declaring how unworthy we are of His love, He picks us up and hugs us. He gently says, "I love you. I will make everything new. I will use what you have done, or what has been done to you, in ways you cannot even imagine."

Is this just a fantasy or is it reality? Paul the apostle was a persecutor of the Church. Before Christ, he was full of murderous hatred. Even after Christ, Paul had some serious issues. He argued with Peter, broke fellowship with The Son of Encouragement (Barnabas) and I believe had a fiery temper. This same imperfect man wrote this passage:

> And we know that for those who love God all things work together for good, for those who are called according to his purpose. Romans 8:28

For Our Consideration

God is in the redeeming business and I believe loves doing so. Whatever our lives have been up to this point, if we will but run to our Father, He will redeem the time, rewrite our story, and make everything new. Good can and will come out of our darkest days under the loving hand of our Father.

I am not saying there will be no more pain or consequences from our previous actions. What I am saying is that God loves His children. God is the One who knows all, understands all, and will redeem for His glory. God can make something good even out of the worst situation and the worst of people. He did it for me, and He will do it for you.

If you will give your life to Him, He will redeem and make all things new. Why wait? By the way, here is the link to the Downing Family website if you are interested: http://www.thedowningfamily.net/

## Questions to Ponder or Discuss:

1. Is God able to rewrite the story of our life? Why or why not?

2. What does God's redemption mean to you?

3. Can God really make all things work for the good for those that love Him? Explain.

4. How big is your God? How great is His mercy? How much love does He have? Explain.

# 10 Ways God Provides Resources

Many years ago, my wife and I were touring the then famous Crystal Cathedral. During the experience, we entered a beautifully decorated room and encountered the ORGAN. This beast was multiple stories high and I have no clue how someone would ever play it. The tour guide explained to us that someone had donated one million dollars to purchase the instrument. That still is a good chunk of change and was even more so in the early 1980's.

Next, the very enthused guide explained, that since the organ cost so much to maintain, the same person gave them another million dollars to hire people to keep the organ in tune and running.

I had an epiphany at that moment - there is no lack of money for God's work. If someone would donate two million dollars for an organ, then if God was leading me to do anything for His Kingdom, money could and would be provided. Lack of money is never the issue; finding God's will always is.

This understanding resurfaced as I was reading one of G. Campbell Morgan's sermons recently. The title of the message is, "*Jubilation in Desolation,*" and I would commend it to you. The salient point of the message is:

**God can supply all that is needful from resources of which we know nothing.**

For example, God had made:

- Everything to begin from nothing in Creation
- Water to flow from a rock

For Our Consideration

- Manna to appear daily for years
- Shoes to not wear out for 40 years
- Quail to fly to the desert to feed millions
- Moses survive without food or water for 40 days, not once, but twice
- Ravens feed a prophet
- A widow's flour and oil not run out until another provision was available
- Poison stew and undrinkable water healed by flour and a stick
- Hundreds of gallons of excellent wine from water
- Bread and fish multiply to feed thousands, twice

I know that list is more than ten, but you get the idea - God can create resources, command nature to provide them, and change us physically so we don't even need them. God is never limited in fulfilling His will.

The key to provision seems to be discerning what God wants, how He wants it done, and in what fashion. The famous saying is still true - God's will done in God's way will never lack God's provision. Do we really believe this?

To be honest, many times I don't. I believe that I must teach, work, sell, organize, lead by example, follow the latest fundraising guides, and use every tool available to me to accomplish God's will. None of these are wrong, and in fact, we should be trying to do the best we possibly can, but the results are not mine to control.

For every successful fundraising campaign, there are multiple failures. Every perfectly organized meeting does not produce fantastic results. Teaching, leading and selling sometimes fail miserably. Does that mean we are failures? Not at all. We may simply be seeking something other than what God desires and therefore we do not have His provision.

If we really believe that God is able, and we should, then we need to move to a position of faith and rest. We do our best and trust the One that can do anything for the results. Is there a need? God can supply all that is truly needed from a vast store of resources that we are completely unaware of. We ask, wait, and walk in obedience to what He commands.

God is able. God is willing to fund whatever He directs us to attempt. If we lack funds, perhaps the issue is not asking for more money, but asking if what we are doing is what God really wants. There is nothing wrong with asking for money; but seeking the Kingdom first is what is commanded in Matthew 6:33.

## Questions to Ponder or Discuss:

1. Does God have any shortages of funds? Explain.

2. Explain how God's will interconnects with funding needs from your point of view?

3. How do we discern what God really wants?

4. How does timing work into the above discussion regarding God's provision or does it at all? Explain.

For Our Consideration

# Looking with Hope Through Troubled Times

Is God Finished with America? At a time when pollsters say the United States is fast becoming a "post-Christian" nation, international evangelist Reinhard Bonnke believes God has a different vision for the future of America.

Bonnke – whose ministry, Christ for all Nations, has recorded 72 million people responding to the call of salvation in Africa and elsewhere – claims God spoke to him in a dream last year saying, "America will be saved!" I heard this man in KC one time...very powerful.

I wonder did people who are my age now look at the world when I was sixteen and think the end of the world was near. *Leave it to Beaver* and *Father Knows Best* were being replaced with Tied dye clothes, VW Vans, rampant immorality and long-haired hippies.

*But God...* Two words that change everything. Joseph was sold into Egypt, But God had other plans, we were dead in our sins and trespasses, but God being rich mercy saved us. Epaphroditus was close to death, but God saved him, Lazarus was dead, but Jesus raised him.

*Suddenly,* yet another word that is often associated with God and His moving. Earthquakes to free prisoners, heavens ripped open to display reality, when there was no way, suddenly there was. God is like that.

God is in charge - it is time yet again. My hope is in God for God is, and we must never forget these truths.

Food for Thought

The Bible is a grand sweeping portrayal of a faithful God and an unfaithful people. A God of mercy and a people in desperate need of it. A world full of lost, dying sinners and Life Himself entering to redeem them. God is able, "but God" and "suddenly" still apply today!

But even if there is not a mass revival, we can be part of reviving our lives. We have a sphere of influence that is directly under our control - our personal walk with God, our marriage, our fellowships, and those we touch. I may not be able to change the course of nations, but I can be part of shaping the future of those under my care.

Yes, there are challenges but troubled times are nothing new to God's people and we know Who holds our times in His hands. We have a job to do, a mission to fulfill, a destiny to walk out. We have work to do, and most of it is right before our eyes and readily available to be accomplished.

Sin is not new. Man being power happy, politically corrupt, sensually dominated, morally impure, and twisted is not new. Read the Law as the Children of Israel were freed from slavery after 400 years. Why did God have to tell them such basic things? They simply did not know. Weird laws, page after page of minute details. How to treat the poor, how to treat your family, what to do with your animals and what not to do. How to treat your neighbor's wife and property. Even how to plant. Why? They did not know.

We live in a sick society dominated by sinful man. So, did they. We live in a morally relativistic culture, so did those in Jesus' day. Rome and Greece before her were perverted, sensual, corrupt down to how they treated children. Corinth was known for what again? Baal worship, temple prostitution, child sacrifice. Sin abounds, yet God's grace shines.

For Our Consideration

Depravity knows no boundaries and is not is limited to any period in history. The current onslaught of technology produces both good and evil. Opportunities of the Kingdom and fuel for our foes. Man has been corrupted from the Garden and only Christ can change that.

So, wickedness abounds. The future can be scary and the world is a mess. Even though many have walked through times like these before, what should we focus on in our day? Are we in the last days? The end times? The final rage of Satan before judgment? I don't know, I will let others answer those questions.

What I do know, is this is our time. I am alive now and God expects me to do something for Him. I was created for good works that He has prepared for me to walk in, so says Ephesians 2:10.

Yes, evil abounds and the darkness is thick. Praise God! The darker the dark the brighter the smallest light. Our personal testimony, our marriage, our family are all lights that must shine in the darkest of times.

Our society will throw at our children advances and perversions we have not seen yet, but in their roots, it is all sin. The sickness has the same cure regardless of how it is packaged. We are light dwellers and containers, therefore, Matthew 5:16 is even more important - let our light shine as we have been commanded!

We must train. We must model. We must stay diligent on guard. Yes, we have a foe, but we have the Lord. Yes, we have an adversary that seeks to devour, but we are in the service of the King. Our Daddy is God. My Daddy can and will beat up your daddy if he is the devil.

Where sin is abundant, grace abounds. Our world is sick and lost, but we have life and hope. We invest in our homes because we know the answer lies in demonstrating the power of God where we live.

Our marriages and families represent a lighthouse in dark days. Stable, strong, enduring, loving. These words become even more important when we see everything crumble around us.

Is God finished with America? I don't know. God has not told me and it is not my jurisdiction. My reality involves my wife, children, grandchildren, my church, friends, book writing, blog sharing and whatever else my hand finds to do to share the Truth of the Life-Changing Gospel.

Others are charged with purifying the entire church, holding at bay the sins of a nation, changing a political party, reaching the lost overseas and a host of others areas, which are only objects of prayer for me. God has called others to work in those fields; I am called to be faithful in mine.

Here's a freeing word for you - so are you. Jesus said He would build His Church and He will. God is sovereign and He is. I am not, and neither are you. We are called to be faithful stewards of the grace we have been given. God is the One that determines the value and ultimate impact. We are not to compare, envy, or judge one another in such matters; we are called to be faithful.

In fact, I will go even stronger. If you were to leave your home, go to the mission field and God had not called you there, you are rebelling. You are doing a good work in the wrong way and not walking in your obedience, so, therefore, you are wrong. Don't envy others, obey what your Father commands you to do.

God is waiting to say, "Well done, good and faithful servant. You were faithful in what I have you to do, now I will give you more." Don't envy another's servant, you don't even know what his or her Lord has told them. Be faithful, be obedient, and finish well. Accomplish what is at hand.

## For Our Consideration

Let YOUR light shine where you live. Your family has a realm of influence unlike anyone else's.

Jeff, do you really believe that focusing on our homes can really make a significant difference? Yes, I do, thanks for asking.

Much of counseling time is absorbed by dysfunctional family relationships. Marriage problems, parent to child, child to parent and child to child. If a significant percentage of dysfunction could be changed into function, what would logically happen? I will tell you, an explosion of ministry.

In fact, I would challenge those in paid full-time ministry to study out Ephesians 4:9-16 where the job description of a pastor is explored. A key component is often overlooked here. Much of our work as pastors/elders is to help fix what is broken. The word, "equip" which is our primary job description means to repair what is broken, put back into proper working order, as in mending a broken bone.

The family, the primary building block of the church and society is broken. If we directed our efforts to mend this broken institution, a ripple effect would sweep our nation. But we all know this, so let me move on to some examples of how it can work.

These are simply given to explain how light can impact the darkness not to bring glory to men.

Our church just gave away $5,000 of someone else's money. In fact, that someone else wants us to do it every year from now on. They are not believers, at least not strong ones, yet they live by one family in our church that would be a typical family - large, drive a van, dress weird and have kids that are nice to their parents and to each other - in other words, very different from the typical American family.

These folks were so impressed with this family that they wanted to set up a scholarship fund to help kids go to college or post-high school training. They said, if these kids are any picture of the other kids at your church, we want to help. So, young people applied for grants and the $5k was given away. Some towards college, some towards a young lady going to the Philippines to learn midwifery, and others to various post-high school type training.

We have a few young ladies that are in their late teens, early 20's that love to help poorer, public school families with clothing. So, they began a clothes closet. Once a year, on back to school events they go to where the poorest parents can be found and invite them to come shop for free. Last month over 300 came to get free clothes.

Missions trips, hospital outreaches, neighborhood service projects, some young men that have a lawn care business reached out to a widow who is Catholic. She was so enthralled with them she has been coming to our services for a few months now. Ministry is only limited by the imagination when function replaces dysfunction.

What would happen if thousands or even millions of families began to do the same in our country? What would happen to the impression the darkness has of the light? If it can happen on a small scale, it can happen on a larger one.

"But God," and "suddenly" are still actions God takes. Our job is to be faithful, observe those around us that need help, and let our light shine in a dark world.

For Our Consideration

## Questions to Ponder or Discuss:

1. Is it possible to have hope when there is so much evil around? Why or why not?

2. Do you have any "but God or suddenly" type moments in your walk with God? Explain.

3. Are there areas that you are concerned about that simply are not yours to be involved in? Explain.

4. Is God sovereign and able to take care of everything? Why or why not?

# Two Are Better Than One

The wisest man who ever lived, (other than Jesus) stated:

> "And though a man might prevail against one who is alone, two will withstand him—a threefold cord is not quickly broken." Ecclesiastes 4:12

In life, work, play, and just about everywhere, two are better than one. Most of us like some alone time, but in general terms, hardly anyone likes to be alone all the time. I know, there are hermits, but most people reading this are not one. I also wonder if the hermit types began that way, or ended up choosing the lifestyle after living with other people, but that thought is for another time.

The advantages of being with others outweigh the disadvantages, at least most of the time. Being alone makes us vulnerable to deception. We need others to bring a perspective that we do not have. I do not really think any two people process everything alike in every possible situation no matter how close they align with someone else. We all have a perspective, and we all need others to help balance us out. Jesus did not need balancing out because He was perfect. We are not Jesus.

We will learn a great deal about ourselves by being with others. If we are alone all the time we may think we are wonderful people. However, if we spend time with others, they may not share our opinion. By our self, we do not possess enough facts to see the picture we present to others. As we learn how to interact with those around us, clarity comes.

For Our Consideration

Our flesh sometimes reacts to another's flesh. "Why are they so self-focused?" we ask. Of course, what prompted that thought was that they were getting the attention we wanted, but we will not go there. "Why do they think they are always right?" we whine. Here is a news flash, they probably do not, and we are not always right either. They might just disagree with us, and that rubs us wrong.

On the positive side, if we learn how to embrace the differences we will grow and be stronger. Not everyone thinks like we do, and that is a good thing because we are not always correct. We need others. We need someone that is different to help us see the situation from another point of view. Together we will see clearer and make a better decision than alone. This is Biblical:

> Without counsel plans fail, but with many advisers they succeed. Proverbs 15:22

> Plans are established by counsel; by wise guidance wage war. Proverbs 20:18

When the early church was struggling, a council was called. Acts 15 gives us some insight into how the meeting proceeded. Through discussion, prayer, acceptance of something totally outside the current understanding, God's will was made clear. Godly men listened to other godly men and a great victory was achieved.

Most churches and businesses have some sort of plurality of leadership structure. Why? Because we all know that someone by themselves, will not make as good of decisions, as someone making them in agreement with others. None of us possess all the wisdom or experience to assure that we are correct all the time.

For this concept to work, it takes humility and an environment for freedom of expression of opinions. Husbands that refuse to listen to their wives are cutting off a huge supply of God-given wisdom. Pastors that will not accept advice or insights from the other leaders are destined to have an audience of one. Business owners that will not adapt, or allow their employees to have input rarely keep them.

I believe it is by Design that we are meant to live in community and in personal relationships. The hermit is the one that is outside the norm, not the person that wants to be around others. God said, "It is not good for man to be alone." He met that need through a companion. We are created with the need for others. Pride, arrogance, and ego often keep us from learning how much we need one another.

Solomon knew this principle. By our self, we will be overcome easily. If we join with another, it is much harder to take us down. If we tie ourselves with many others we will have what we call the Church, and the gates of hell will not overpower us. That is a promise from Her Builder.

For Our Consideration

## Questions to Ponder or Discuss:

1. When was the last time you left a relationship? Why did you? What can you learn from that experience?

2. Do you believe that other people make good mirrors to expose our own faults? Why or why not?

3. Why is a plurality of leadership a good idea?

4. How does pride and humility play into this discussion?

# We All Stand on Something

> If the foundations are destroyed, what can the righteous do?
> Psalm 11:3

The Psalmist David asks this question and it is worth exploring. Most of us do not have to think too hard to realize that our society is in big trouble. Marriages are being destroyed, all manner of hideous crimes are being committed by even young children, moral restraint is almost unheard of, and evil seems to be winning the day. The daily news via TV or online outlets is mostly a depressing gathering of stories revealing that the foundations are cracked and ready to crumble into a pile of dust! What can the righteous do is indeed an excellent question.

A good beginning for our reply is to recognize and address the root problems. "Why" is a question that needs to be asked. Why are we in this condition? Why is marriage falling apart and being rapidly replaced with cohabitation and alternate lifestyles? Why are young children becoming violent and callous? Why is the Church seemingly ineffective?

One of the benefits of getting older is that we realize that we no longer have, or need to have all the answers to every question. It is true that there are many possible answers to the questions posed, and any simple response will be incomplete. However, that does not mean we should not attempt to look at these questions and pursue a different course of action currently being followed. Even though we cannot do, or understand everything, we should do something!

## For Our Consideration

Many individual lives fall apart because storms hit (death, disease, divorce) and they are unprepared or never dreamed that tragedy would happen to them. History shows that nations (made up of individuals) often reject God and replace Him with other gods like mammon, power, humanism, and a host of other idols. Each of these false gods pretends to provide a solid foundation but the storms test their ability. What can be shaken will be and that is a promise from the one, true God.

> At that time, his voice shook the earth, but now he has promised, "Yet once more I will shake not only the earth but also the heavens. This phrase, "Yet once more," indicates the removal of things that are shaken—that is, things that have been made—in order that the things that cannot be shaken may remain. Therefore, let us be grateful for receiving a kingdom that cannot be shaken, and thus let us offer to God acceptable worship, with reverence and awe.
> Hebrews 12:26-28

Rain, wind, and floods come to everyone but destruction is tied to our foundation. If we are building upon The Rock, we will stand. If we build upon the foundation of any other god, we will fall. "Other gods" come in many shapes and disguises. I already referred to money, power, and human reasoning. How about greed, selfishness, false religion, pride, judgmentalism, legalism, secularism, having a temporal focus, to name a few more. Building our lives and marriages upon these foundations of sand will not stand the test of storms.

We do not want to build on these false gods so what should we build upon? Part of the answer resides in two passages that I already quoted. There is a kingdom that cannot be shaken and Jesus said that if His words are heard, and acted upon, we would stand at the time of the storm.

Simply put we must be those that obey Jesus and have as our main desire, the furthering of His Kingdom. Most of us are very familiar with these words and concepts, but walking them out is a different matter. Let us consider two very important passages:

> But seek first the kingdom of God and his righteousness, and all these things will be added to you. Matthew 6:33

> Whoever has my commandments and keeps them, he it is who loves me. John 14:21

If we are "seeking first the kingdom of God" then whatever else there may be in our life must take a lower place. There cannot be two first places. Seeking God with all our heart, all our soul, and our entire mind, as we are commanded in multiple places, suggests that this pursuit must be all encompassing. We proclaim the Jesus is Lord, and this is good and right. How often have we stopped to consider what that really means?

Lordship is an exclusive title and claim. There cannot be two supreme lords ruling in our lives at the same time for one must take preeminence over the other. Jesus said we cannot serve God and money and we cannot have two lords sitting on the throne of our life either.

Who sits as Lord in our homes? Who is Lord over our marriage? Who is Lord over how we train our children? If Jesus is not the foundation of our home, whatever we attempt to build will be rocked

For Our Consideration

by the storms of life and will collapse. If Jesus is the Chief Cornerstone, then what we built will stand on the day of testing. What foundation are we building upon?

The good news is that each day is new and provides an opportunity for change! If we have not been building properly, we still can. Don't waste the new day. Begin to build something that will endure in the face of trial, wind, and storm. They will come, but destruction is optional. Build wisely.

## Questions to Ponder or Discuss:

1. Why do foundations matter?

2. Why does God allow shaking in His children's lives?

3. What does seeking first the Kingdom of God mean to you?

4. What does Jesus being Lord of your life really mean?

Food for Thought

# Why Complicate the Simple?

Discipleship is all about relationships. We enter the Kingdom of God via a personal encounter (relationship) with the Lord Jesus Christ. We accept His perfect atoning sacrifice and we are now in a restored relationship with our heavenly Father. Our sins are forgiven and we are redeemed. We now can have as personal of a relationship with our Creator as we desire.

After we are born again, we become part of a huge family called the Body of Christ. This Body is made up of all those who have also been redeemed by the sacrifice of Jesus. While salvation is accomplished in a one on one transaction between our Maker and us, discipleship is accomplished in a multiple relationship setting. We are saved alone, but if we reside on this side of eternity, we will be in many relationships with God's other children.

Like a family, the Body of Christ has members that are older and those that are younger. Those who are older have a responsibility to assist and help those that are younger. The members of the Body of Christ that have more experience are supposed to share that experience with those who are younger. The experience may be positive or negative but both should be freely shared for both have value. We may feel all our mistakes are wasted but they won't be if we share them with others so they don't have to repeat the same ones.

There are many tools available to assist the discipleship process but the reality is that it will still all be about personal relationships. Like the Ethiopian eunuch that had questions about what he was reading, (Acts 8) new believers will have questions about their faith. Philip asked a powerful question - "Do you understand what you are

## For Our Consideration

reading?" The wise Ethiopian man answered, "How can I unless someone guides me?" These questions and the answers given are at the heart of discipleship. The older helps the younger gain wisdom and understanding.

We live in a social media world. There are smart phones, iPads, notepads, webcasts, the internet, and a plethora of books being published daily. These are powerful tools to assist the furtherance of the Gospel and can greatly enhance the discipleship process. They cannot, however, replace the relationship aspect of it. New believers will still ask, "How can I unless someone explains it?" and they will be correct in asking. Those who are older will still have to explain to those who are younger what they are reading and seeing, even in our high-tech world.

Discipleship is all about relationships. It always has been and always will be. Two or more people talking and sharing information that leads to growth. Of course, this can be accomplished on other sides of the globe via technology, but the people will still need to talk. Questions abound and answers are available but those answers are always connected to a relationship of some sort. It is by God's design.

God designed us to need human interaction to grow and mature in Him. Human relationships reveal many aspects of our character that would not otherwise be exposed. God is the One that first brought up the whole, "It is not good for man to be alone," thing in Genesis 2. For the record, the man was not alone; he had an intimate, personal relationship with his Creator! Yet, the Creator thought it best for Adam to have someone else to share his life with, thus Eve was created.

Our Christianity is lived out with others and that is by God's design. Discipleship will only fully be effective when we live in on-going relationships with other disciples. Classroom instruction can be helpful, as well as six or eight-week lessons, but the reality of discipleship occurs as we walk in long-term relationships with others. I would also add that for discipleship to really make much of a difference, relationships must be at the center of any discipling effort. Jesus simply could have thrown down His word from heaven, but a great deal would have been lost. Jesus modeled relationships.

Some verses to consider considering the relational aspects of discipleship:

> Iron sharpens iron, and one man sharpens another. Proverbs 27:17

> Faithful are the wounds of a friend; profuse are the kisses of an enemy. Proverbs 27:6

> Likewise, you who are younger, be subject to the elders. Clothe yourselves, all of you, with humility toward one another, for "God opposes the proud but gives grace to the humble." 1 Peter 5:5

> Do nothing from selfish ambition or conceit, but in humility count others more significant than yourselves. Philippians 2:3

While there are hundreds of verses we could consider, these four provide plenty of material to point us in a relational direction. We need each other to become sharp, to be honest with one another, even when difficult, to learn humility, and to help us die to our selfishness daily. Spending time with someone else will eventually lead us in to conflict, wounds, a choice to submit and humility. Almost none of these take place without the personal interaction with another person.

The relationship aspect of discipleship will help everyone involved to mature in Christ, and that is, after all the goal. The older teacher learns to grow in patience and the younger student experiences humility and growing pains. As delicate issues are addressed, faithful wounds are given and the sharpening process deepens. Yes, relationships are messy, but without the potential struggle there is little growth, and with the relationship difficulties maturity follows.

We tend to overcomplicate discipleship, but when it is all said and done, relationships must be formed and growth will come because of people walking together in their mutual pursuit of Christ. This is certainly not all that can be said about the topic, but this at least must be considered when discussing discipleship. The Kingdom of God is relational in all aspects.

## Questions to Ponder or Discuss:

1. What do you think the best process is for making disciples?

2. How important are relationships in the Kingdom of God?

3. Do you think we need others in our lives to fully understand the Lord and the Body of Christ? Why or why not?

4. Was there someone in your life that helped you grow in your Christian walk? If they are still alive, have you thanked them recently?

For Our Consideration

# God's Expectations

Every believer at some time or another probably wonders what God really wants of them. God knows all, possesses all, and doesn't need anything, so what could I possibly do for Him? What can you give to someone who has everything that they want or desire? You think shopping for your mate is hard, what can you give to God?

There are perhaps many answers, but I know of at least one thing God wants from every one of His children - faithfulness.

In the parable of the Talents in Matthew 25:21, the punchline is:

> His master said to him, 'Well done, good and faithful servant. You have been faithful over a little; I will set you over much. Enter into the joy of your master.'

It really didn't make any difference the number of talents given, what seemed to matter to God the most was the faithfulness (or not) of the receiver. Be faithful in a little, and you will be set over much later.

Let's consider another couple of passages:

> One who is faithful in a very little is also faithful in much, and one who is dishonest in a very little is also dishonest in much. If then you have not been faithful in the unrighteous wealth, who will entrust to you the true riches? And if you have not been faithful in that which is another's, who will give you that which is your own? Luke 16:10-12

> Moreover, it is required of stewards that they be found faithful. 1 Corinthians 4:2

God states that how we handle His money is both a little thing and something that matters a great deal. We are to be faithful with what we have been entrusted with, and again, it really does not seem to matter much whether it is a lot or a little. The issue is faithfulness.

Paul instructed his young disciple Timothy in this key passage:

> ...and what you have heard from me in the presence of many witnesses entrust to faithful men who will be able to teach others also. 2 Timothy 2:2

Why was Paul telling Timothy to make sure he found faithful men and didn't say spiritually gifted or highly talented men for example? Why did Paul expressly state faithful men?

Finally, Jesus in His glory explained to John how important faithfulness is in this passage:

> Do not fear what you are about to suffer. Behold, the devil is about to throw some of you into prison, that you may be tested, and for ten days you will have tribulation. Be faithful unto death, and I will give you the crown of life. Revelation 2:10

Be faithful unto death - it seems that the God of the universe expects us to be faithful even when death is on the line. (Princess Bride tone intended) He gives us the Holy Spirit, and His Word to assure us that

## For Our Consideration

we can learn to be faithful, and there are eternal rewards directly tied to how we perform the tasks we are given.

I am not so sure it matters what we do for the Lord as much as how we do it. We are commanded to be faithful and provided with little comment about the relative value of what we do. So, any believer, who is walking in daily obedience to the Lord, can know that if they are faithfully doing what God has asked them to do, they will give a wonderful gift to our Heavenly Father and will reap eternal rewards as a direct result. Perhaps we can give something to the Someone that has everything after all.

As a final (I know I wrote finally above, but I didn't mean it) note...if you have been unfaithful, there is still time, grace and opportunity. Repent and receive forgiveness and empowering grace to change. God will provide you additional opportunities to learn to be faithful - He is just like that! God wants you to succeed and He is faithful to continue providing the opportunities until you do.

## Questions to Ponder or Discuss:

1. Why did God give different amounts of talents to the three men?

2. Why is faithfulness such a big deal to God?

3. Should we really work for eternal rewards? Why or why not?

4. Is there hope for those that have been unfaithful in some fashion? Why or why not?

# Motive Matters

Motives are tricky things. Many years ago, I heard a speaker ask a question – "Why do we do the things we do and who do we do them for?" Okay, I know that is really two questions, but do not tune me out over a detail.

Both of those questions are in my mind on a regular basis and prompt many more questions.

- Why do I do what I do?
- Why did I do what I did?
- Whom am I really thinking about when I did what I did or do what I do?
- Am I as noble-minded and selfless as I have deceived myself into believing?
- Do I not care what someone thinks about me or is that a lie?
- How much of my self-worth is tied up in others' opinion of me?

The list could on for a while, but I will spare you the pain of having to run through my thought life.

In every relational type situation I encounter, there are multiple wills playing out. There is, of course, my will. There is someone else involved and they have a will. There is our enemy's will and there is God's will. I know we are to seek God's will in everything, but do I? Yet another question I ask.

It seems to me that many times I want what I want when I want it and God's will, or anyone else's for that matter means very little to me. Shocking isn't it? Why do I do the things I do and say the things I

## For Our Consideration

say? Is God's will really at the forefront of my words and actions. That question makes me squirm.

After over forty years of walking with God and thirty-five years of being a pastor, I still struggle with my motives; daily. Dictionaries define motives as the reason we do what we do.

Here is another question – do my motives line up with these words of Scripture?

> Do nothing from selfish ambition or conceit, but in humility count others more significant than yourselves. Philippians 2:3

> I therefore, a prisoner for the Lord, urge you to walk in a manner worthy of the calling to which you have been called, with all humility and gentleness, with patience, bearing with one another in love, eager to maintain the unity of the Spirit in the bond of peace. Ephesians 4:1-3

> Put on then, as God's chosen ones, holy and beloved, compassionate hearts, kindness, humility, meekness, and patience, bearing with one another and, if one has a complaint against another, forgiving each other; as the Lord has forgiven you, so you also must forgive. Colossians 3:12-13

To be honest, no. The desire is often there but my flesh is not always in agreement with my brain. So, what do we do, quit? Of course not. We see where we fall short, ask and receive grace and we walk on with our Lord. We learn from our mistakes and failures, and we walk on. We repent of our sin, and we walk on. We fall, get back up, and we walk on. If we have hurt someone, we ask for forgiveness and walk on. If we need to make restitution, we do so, and we walk on.

Why am I writing this? What is my motive behind it? As far as I can tell, it is to help myself, and anyone who reads it, to think deeper. But really, only God knows the deep recesses of our hearts.

Jeremiah stated centuries ago that the heart is desperately sick (Jeremiah 17:9) but thankfully he didn't stop there, in verse 10 he also states that the Lord searches and knows our hearts and mind, and for that, I am very grateful. My Lord loves me, accepts me, empowers me, and is changing me for His glory and purposes. If my motives need changing, my Lord will see to it that they are changed. I can, and do, rest in that truth.

## Questions to Ponder or Discuss:

1. Why is it hard to know our true motives?

2. Why does God care so much about His children being humble?

3. If my own motives are difficult to discern what does that tell me about assigning a motive to others?

4. What does Paul mean by living a life worthy of our calling in Christ?

For Our Consideration

# Boasting is Just Fine

Many of us grew up in homes where our parents told us not to brag and boast. This is, of course, correct, but there is a proper time and place to boast and not be considered arrogant. Paul, the apostle, encourages us to boast, for he clearly states, "Let the one who boasts, boast in the Lord." We boast in Christ, and what He has accomplished, not in ourselves.

> For consider your calling, brothers: not many of you were wise according to worldly standards, not many were powerful, not many were of noble birth. But God chose what is foolish in the world to shame the wise; God chose what is weak in the world to shame the strong; God chose what is low and despised in the world, even things that are not, to bring to nothing things that are, so that no human being might boast in the presence of God. And because of him you are in Christ Jesus, who became to us wisdom from God, righteousness and sanctification and redemption, so that, as it is written, "Let the one who boasts, boast in the Lord.". 1 Corinthians 1:26-31

When I was a much younger man, around sixteen or seventeen years of age, I worked at a gas station. We called them service stations because you received, well, service.

Back in the days before self-serve and credit card readers, one would pull their car up to the pump and someone ran out of a building and filled up the tank for you. At the better stations, this same person would wash the windows, check the oil and even fill up your tires. Gas was also selling for 27 cents a gallon. Those days are long gone.

At most places today, you use a credit card, pay a buck for air, and if you do wander inside the convenience store, you speak to someone behind a 3-inch thick piece of glass that acts like you are bothering their reading. After wiping the tear from my eye, we can go back to the story and leave that short trip down memory lane.

One day there was a carload of thieves making the rounds to the local gas stations. These hoods would drive up, distract you with dozens of questions, and then try to steal money from the cash register that was right inside the door. Our little building had a back room in it as well as the typical displays of oil cans and antifreeze containers outside the door. The cash register was visible from where the cars would drive in for fuel and it would have seemed like easy pickings to this gang.

What was not known to them was that in those days word traveled quickly by phone, not as quick as tweets, but close enough. We had been notified that the thieves were around and sure enough, they showed up at my door. What this gang of thugs also didn't know was that Glenn was in the back room.

As the car pulled in and the guys started fast-talking to me, I held up my finger and said, "Wait a sec, I will get Glenn." Glenn was a huge guy. In fact, after he left high school he became a starting lineman for the Washington Huskies football team. Glenn was over 6'5" and close to 275 lbs., which was big in those days.

As Glenn filled the door and ducked a bit, I wished camera phones had been invented back then. The blood drained from the punk's face and it must have flowed to his right foot for he burned rubber for quite some ways as they sped out of the parking lot. To complete the picture,

## For Our Consideration

I weighed 125lbs ringing wet and was about as muscular as a beanpole, but that didn't matter, Glenn was big enough for both of us.

Now, I could boast about how I scared away the crooks but that would not be accurate or honest. What would be true is my boasting in Glenn. Any boasting that we can do is because of the Lord. Even Glenn could not take the credit for his size; you should have seen his parents! God blessed Glenn with size and speed, and so even his boasting would have to be in the Lord if he was going to be honest.

Paul reminds the Corinthians to think about what they were before Christ, and this is an excellent process for us as well. I was a lost, pleasure seeking, self-centered, smelly, hippy that was on the highway to hell and didn't even know it. My prospects were bleak and future was assured. I was weak physically, couldn't put together two coherent thoughts, and certainly was not of noble birth. I also was low and despised. Yup, I fit Paul's description to the max. And if the truth is told and embraced, so does everyone else before they know Christ.

I have read interviews of the rich and beautiful and both described the lost, hopelessness of their life. Money, beauty, endless pleasure, popularity, gifts and talents, physical abilities, man's wisdom in abundance, and just about anything else you can name, does not fill the God-size hole in the human heart. We need Jesus, and we need Him desperately. Everyone does.

After we meet Christ, everything begins to change. Paul states that we are in Christ. By being in Christ, God begins to use the weak, low and despised to put to shame the strong and the things that are in this world. We, who were nothing in the world, become a treasure in God's eyes and kingdom. We, who were rejected, considered expendable and unnecessary are precious to the Sovereign King of the universe.

In fact, after salvation, we are adopted and become a part of God's family and plan. We become righteous and are invited into the throne room of heaven any time we desire. We really do become royalty and possess noble blood!

Jesus makes a clear appeal to this reality in the following passage:

> For you say, I am rich, I have prospered, and I need nothing, not realizing that you are wretched, pitiable, poor, blind, and naked. I counsel you to buy from me gold refined by fire, so that you may be rich, and white garments so that you may clothe yourself and the shame of your nakedness may not be seen, and salve to anoint your eyes, so that you may see. Revelation 3:17-18

Before I met Jesus, no one could convince me that I was poor, blind and completely exposed. What was readily apparent to everyone else was not seen by my unseeing eyes. I thought I was cool, part of the in-crowd, and something to behold. Under the burning gaze of love from my Savior, the scales dropped out of my eyes and I came into agreement with Jesus' assessment of my condition. I was wretched, pitiable, poor, blind and naked. I desperately needed help for I had the fatal disease of sin, and Jesus was the only cure.

Today, I can boast again. Not in my strength, wisdom or accomplishments, but in the Lord. I am the righteousness of God in Christ. I am a new creation in Christ. I am sanctified in Christ. I am being changed from one degree of glory to the next in Christ. I am loved by my Father and headed to spend eternity with my Family in Christ. Let him who boasts, boast in the Lord.

For Our Consideration

May we become very good at boasting in, and about Him, and not ourselves or accomplishments.

## Questions to Ponder or Discuss:

1. What credit can we take for God's grace, mercy and salvation?

2. If God is for us then does it matter how big the enemy may be? Why or why not?

3. How does boasting in the Lord and fleshly pride compare?

4. What does sanctification mean and why do we care as believers?

# Discussion Starters

"The future is something which everyone reaches at the rate of 60 minutes an hour, whatever he does, whoever he is."
C. S. Lewis

For Our Consideration

# Mr. Frustration

For many years I lived with Mr. Frustration. This fiend, not friend, visited uninvited and often overstayed his welcome. As a pastor, this obnoxious intruder showed up on Sunday afternoons and stayed well into the following week. Around Wednesday or Thursday, I would finally kick him out.

My guest was uninvited, however, I often left the door open for him to enter a room in my mind. After struggling with this nuisance for decades, I finally figured out how to shut the door in his face. I am not always successful, but the visits have slowed down and sometimes, Mr. Frustration never even shows up and seeks an entry.

In my case, Mr. Frustration came disguised as discouragement with trying to evaluate the results of my work. Many seem to struggle with this battle, at least some that I have talked with over the years. Questions like:

- Does my life matter?
- Would anyone miss me if I suddenly disappeared?
- Why do people sleep every week? I must be really boring, not like _____.
- I don't seem to be making any impact with my messages?
- Nothing seems to be changing?
- Why bother, my life is insignificant?

Perhaps you have never struggled along these lines. God bless you. Many have shared with me that they have and still do, asking, "does my life matter and how can I tell?" It seems we want to know if what we do has any value or long-term impact on anyone else.

My process of shutting the door in this intruder's face is to answer this question – Did I present, to the best of my ability, what the Lord wanted me to say? If I did, then I can rest.

Now, everyone can seek to refine and improve techniques and skills, and we all should continue to improve in performing whatever job we have, but I'm talking here about a fundamental issue – did I do what the Lord asked me to do?

If the answer is yes, then I can rest in that fact. If the answer is no, then I need to change that to a yes, the next time. Here is the key for me – I do the best I can in walking in obedience to the Lord and He will take care of the results. This is freeing if we embrace it.

I am not responsible for the results, only my part in the process. Also, I am not in the proper place to evaluate those results for I do not have a large enough picture of reality; only God does. Only God can see what is really going on in someone's heart, mind, and know the outcome of their life. Only God. Not me. Not you.

Our job is to walk in obedience to the revealed will of God and we let Him take care of the results of our obedience. If we can't see the results, and I guarantee you most of the time we cannot, that does not change our primary calling – obey the Lord. God will watch over His word and He is more than able to accomplish what He desires.

If we embrace this truth, Mr. Frustration may come knocking, but we do not have to open the door to him. We are all called to walk in obedience to the Father, and if we are doing our best, we will hear, "Well done good and faithful servant," and that is not frustrating in the least.

For Our Consideration

## Questions to Ponder or Discuss:

1. Do you have a Mr. Frustration in your life?

2. How do you evaluate your accomplishments and effect on others?

3. Do you agree that we are not responsible for the results of our efforts, only our work? Why or why not?

4. Can you name five ways that your life matters?

Discussion Starters

# Christian Tension

A one-winged bird will not fly straight. In fact, it probably will not fly at all. The bird needs both wings to soar and the imagery is applicable to us. The Bible is full of tensions (two wings) that help keep us airborne in our faith. For example:

- If you want to be great in the Kingdom of God, learn to be a servant of all.
- We are saved by grace alone and not by works, yet our faith is proven by our works.
- God is the Sovereign Lord of the Universe yet we are told to act in certain ways and given a choice to obey or not.
- God knows all things yet we are told to pray to make a difference.
- We are told to love the sinner yet hate the sin.
- The devil is a defeated foe yet we are told to resist and overcome him.
- We are free in Christ yet we limit our freedom for the sake of love.

Those seven are enough to make my point and I am sure you can think of many more. In fact, I found one recently during my reading time:

> And because lawlessness will be increased, the love of many will grow cold. Matthew 24:12

Interesting. One wing that is often exalted is love, grace, and freedom in Christ. We are saved by grace, live in grace, and are under

## For Our Consideration

grace, God is love, we are free from guilt, and any mention of obedience, works, or human effort invites a verbal beating.

Those on the other side (wing) shout, "Lawlessness" as the danger of overemphasis on grace and God's love. They continue, "What about obedience, grieving the Holy Spirit, holiness, and overcoming temptation and sin?" Picking either wing at the expense of the other will result in erratic flight patterns.

Over the last four decades or so, I have observed many that have shouted, "Grace, I'm free in Christ!" They are of course correct. However, many times this revelation has resulted in sinful excesses because of that truth. We are warned by Peter:

> Live as people who are free, not using your freedom as a cover-up for evil, but living as servants of God. 1 Peter 2:16

Jesus said that because of lawlessness love would grow cold. Interesting. Most people that use grace as a cover for all manner of sin do end up despising anyone that asks for deference or holiness. Perhaps Jesus was right after all. Lawlessness eventually turns love cold.

On the other wing, those that go down the path of law, endless rules and man-made standards of holiness will end up despising everyone that disagrees with them. Sounds like Pharisee thinking to me and Jesus never accused those guys of demonstrating love.

If love is our calling card to the world, and it is, we must learn how to fly with both wings intact. We need grace without lawlessness and obedience without bondage. In other words, we need to be people who know and obey all the Scriptures, and not just our favorite doctrines.

Discussion Starters

## Questions to Ponder or Discuss:

1. Revisiting the seven tensions listed, are there any covered that you disagree with? Why?

2. Where do you land on the grace vs. lawlessness arguments? Why?

3. Is it possible to have obedience without bondage to the law? Explain your answer.

4. How do we learn to love those that disagree with us?

For Our Consideration

# Is there a Gift of Criticism?

Some of us seem gifted in pointing out the flaws, failures, and problems we see in others. In an eyeblink, we can spot the speck in our brother's eye. If you don't know of any faults, simply ask us and we will be glad to inform you of many you may have overlooked.

I wondered what the Bible had to say about the gift of criticism. Since I tend to so often excel in it, I figured it must be God-given and therefore easily confirmed through the Word of God. I opened my computer program and began to search for the word criticism in my ESV Bible.

What I found was "no entry." However, the program did refer me to this Scripture:

> Let no corrupting talk come out of your mouths, but only such as is good for building up, as fits the occasion, that it may give grace to those who hear. Ephesians 4:29

Nobody likes a smart aleck Bible program! Not deterred, I entered the word "critical," to see what would appear. Again, "no entry." Also, again, the program added a free verse for my consideration:

> The ear that listens to life-giving reproof will dwell among the wise. Proverbs 15:31

Seems like my program has a problem with me and my attitude! Sure, it's okay to be given life-given reproof, but not okay to be critical.

We help each other by sharing wisdom, correction, and even reproof, but we are not supposed to tear each down through criticism.

Still, not ready to give up, I decided to check out the dictionary regarding terms.

> Criticism - the expression of disapproval of someone or something based on perceived faults or mistakes.
>
> Critical - expressing adverse or disapproving comments or judgments.

That defines what I am guilty of but provides little justification for my behavior. Most of us know we should not base anything on "perceived faults," and "express judgments," though that rarely stops me.

As I was getting nowhere with this search, I decided to change my tactics. I started entering words like "gifts and fruit," hoping to find something along the lines of criticism of others. Instead, these came up:

> Now concerning spiritual gifts, brothers, I do not want you to be uninformed. 1 Corinthians 12:1 (a)
>
> But the fruit of the Spirit is love, joy, peace, patience, kindness, goodness, faithfulness, gentleness, self-control; against such things there is no law. Galatians 5:22-23

I am beginning to get the picture. God does not want me to be ignorant, uninformed regarding His will, gifts, and fruit. However, He also will not allow me to blame Him for my flesh. If I read these verses again conviction should settle in regarding how I speak to and about others.

Words that are building up others, give grace to those that listen, and are not based on perceived faults or based on judgment are approved, whereas criticism and being critical are not even in the Book of all Books.

If I listen to what I say to and about others, my words should resemble the list Paul presents as evidence of the Spirit's presence in my life. Maybe there really is no gift of criticism and I need to repent of how I speak. Maybe I am not alone in this process, but who am I to judge.

## Questions to Ponder or Discuss:

1. How easily do I see the faults in others? Am I quick to point those out?

2. What would those that know us the best say about us regarding a critical spirit?

3. What is the bulk of our speech – life-giving or critical life-draining?

4. Is there ever a time to offer positive criticism to one another? If so, how and when?

Discussion Starters

# A Case of Mistaken Identity

Riding to church early Sunday morning with one of my two favorite son-in-laws, we began to discuss the current political environment. As this season of the election cycle rolls around (pick one, anyone), I wish I lived on a desert island.

Every two years we are inundated with promises that will not be kept, lies that are boldly proclaimed, and relentless assurances that if we don't act now, all will be lost. "This is the most important election of my lifetime," rings in my ears since the first one I participated in in the early 1970's.

While much has been lost from my perspective, and every election is important and has consequences, the Kingdom of God is still intact, and still my primary focus. What triggered this post was something Jeffrey shared on our drive together.

While remembering the exact words is not an overall strength I possess, the gist of it is that we are fighting the wrong enemy. Our foe is a liar, deceiver, and loves to sow strife, discord, and division. What better way to succeed than to divide and conquer.

Our foe is not those that disagree with us over our choice for a political office. Yes, we may strongly disagree with choices made, and policies put forward that most likely won't be implemented perfectly anyway, but our enemy is not that person.

The Scriptures are clear:

- And the great dragon was thrown down, that ancient serpent, who is called the devil and Satan, the deceiver of the whole world—he was thrown down to the earth, and his angels were thrown down with him. Revelation 12:9

- For we do not wrestle against flesh and blood, but against the rulers, against the authorities, against the cosmic powers over this present darkness, against the spiritual forces of evil in the heavenly places. Ephesians 6:12

- For though we walk in the flesh, we are not waging war according to the flesh. For the weapons of our warfare are not of the flesh but have divine power to destroy strongholds. 2 Corinthians 10:3-4

- Be sober-minded; be watchful. Your adversary the devil prowls around like a roaring lion, seeking someone to devour. 1 Peter 5:8

There are of course more verses, but these are sufficient for this discussion. We are all engaged in a war and we have an enemy and that foe is the devil. This enemy is a liar, deceiver, hates us, and is actively seeking to devour us. Perhaps some of those running for office are in his service. Maybe those that you support are not.

Like many other issues in the Church, good people can disagree over them and still be Christians. This must extend to political discussions as well. Our enemy is not those running for office or those that favor a particular candidate. In fact, every one of those verses shared above was written while the writers lived under crazed, demonically inspired if not possessed, despot rulers. Those writers were not allowed to vote.

Our enemy is clear from Scripture and he is not a Democrat, Republican, Libertarian, or of any other political party, but he is of the sowing strife, discourse, hatred, division, and destruction party. We are told to be on guard for a reason. We were given armor and weapons to battle this foe, and he is not a running for office this year, for he already is the prince of this world:

> And you were dead in the trespasses and sins in which you once walked, following the course of this world, following the prince of the power of the air, the spirit that is now at work in the sons of disobedience... Ephesians 2:1-2

Please vote while we still have this freedom. Please share your views and convictions passionately. Please be persuasive in your appeals. But in all of this, please remember who we are really fighting and Whose Kingdom really matters.

## Questions to Ponder or Discuss:

1. What did Paul mean when he said that we do not war against flesh and blood in Ephesians 6:12?

2. If the devil is already defeated by Calvary, why do we still need to be aware of him and his deceptions?

3. How does the enemy of our souls use division to destroy?

4. Should a Christian even be involved in political issues? Why or why not?

For Our Consideration

# Be Given to Hospitality

Being devoted to one another and sharing with God's people will lead us to learn how to practice hospitality.

> Love must be sincere. Hate what is evil; cling to what is good. Be devoted to one another in brotherly love; honor one another above yourselves. Never be lacking in zeal, but keep your spiritual fervor, serving the Lord. Be joyful in hope, patient in affliction, faithful in prayer. Share with God's people who are in need. Practice hospitality. Romans 12:9-13

> Above all, love each other deeply, because love covers over a multitude of sins. Offer hospitality to one another without grumbling. Each one should use whatever gift he has received to serve others, faithfully administering God's grace in its various forms. 1 Peter 4:8-10

If you have invited people over to your home, you know that it takes practice. Getting by that uncomfortable feeling at the start, trying to figure out what to feed them, what will we do all night? It really does take practice! But as the old saying goes, "practice makes perfect." Perfect in the Bible usually means maturity. As you step out in faith to show yourself hospitable, I guarantee - you will mature!

One sure way to grow is to attempt to have relationships within the Body of Christ. People who just attend a church and never become related to anyone can easily drift away. We all need friends. We all need people who will be there during the bad times and during the good times. We need each other.

The writer of Ecclesiastes said it well, "though one may be overpowered, two can defend themselves. A cord of three strands is not quickly broken" (Ecc. 4.12). Our love for our Lord is only as strong as our love for one another.

If you attend the church that I speak at for any length of time you will hear me say that, "the world will know we are His disciples by our love for one another." It's how we get along with each other that will make a difference, not our preaching, tracts, T-shirts or bumper stickers. But whether we really can and do love each other!

Having people in our homes produces lasting fruit. Our children can have additional role models that reinforce what we teach them. They won't feel like we're the only ones, or maybe you're not the strictest parents in the world after all. Interaction with others broadens our little world.

We must learn to accept each other with all our faults. Relationships build character. Think of how boring life would be if we were alike. The differences are what make life interesting. If two were exactly alike, one would not be needed. By interacting with each other, we are given many opportunities to extend grace and mercy. To give each other some room to be different. To give each other the grace we want everyone to give us! It's only after we get past the surface relationships that we can truly start to grow together. The only way I have ever found to get past the surface is to spend time together.

The church life is more than what we do on Sunday morning; it includes what happens during the week. I would challenge you to step out and show yourself friendly to others. Take that first step and invite someone to your home. Practice hospitality. It will get easier and

## For Our Consideration

better as you practice. Try it for one year. If you don't agree with me after that time that you and your family have grown, I will take you and your family out to lunch at the restaurant of your choice!

When times get tough, it's the relationships that will see you through. I've never met a lonely, depressed person who was given to hospitality. I've met many who were not! It's hard to be down in the dumps when you are trying to figure out how to bless others.

Show yourself friendly and you will have friends! Use the gifts God has given to you by blessing others. Catch the vision for relationships and step out and take a chance on meeting someone new this week!

## Questions to Ponder or Discuss:

1. Think about the last time you invited someone over to your home. How did it go? Was it enjoyable or a chore? What would you change?

2. Why is hospitality such a big deal to God?

3. Why do we need friends and how do you define the term?

4. Describe your best relationship and why you chose it to consider.

Discussion Starters

# Death to Self?

The very first message I taught at Hope Family Fellowship was centered on embracing the cross as a disciple of Jesus. Since that first Sunday in 1993 until today, the concept of death to self through cross embracing is always close to the forefront of my mind and messages. But, what does it mean?

Jesus stated that to be His disciple we must take up our cross and follow Him. (Matthew 16:24 and Luke 9:23.) In fact, the Luke passage includes the word, "daily," implying a repeated decision. Okay, but what does it mean in my world?

The purpose of the cross in Jesus day was to produce a painful death to its bearer. The cross was intended to inflict pain, suffering, humiliation, and ultimately death to the one carrying it. The cross was final and total in its purpose.

When Jesus turned to those that desired to follow Him and told them to grab a cross, they at least had some idea of what a cross looked like, and what it meant to those that carried it.

We tend to think in terms of the top of a church building or perhaps a necklace. We have turned one of the most brutal forms of execution known to man into a decoration. Got it, we probably don't have the same insight as the followers of Jesus' did about the cross, but what does it mean to me?

Jesus presented a radically different call to those that heard Him than what they expected. Those who lived under Roman oppression were looking for their Messiah to ride in on a white horse and kick out the army that occupied their homeland. Jesus made His triumphant entry into the city on a donkey and ended up being the Sacrificial Lamb.

Jesus also told them to submit to the conquerors and to serve them. Jesus told them that their earthly life was not as important as their eternal one. Jesus told them that the Kingdom He represented was of a different sort, one that was entered by a cross.

I have read the Gospels and know all that Jeff...what does it have to do with taking up my cross daily?

Jesus, many times, explained the Kingdom in parables and stories. The meanings were sometimes hidden and required additional explanation and other times were crystal clear.

Finding a pearl of great price is easy to understand, the sower and the seed took some more explaining to grasp what Jesus was after. What about taking up our cross? Is that an easy to understand image or does it take some additional explanation to discover its hidden meaning? Jeff, you had better tell me soon or I will quit reading!

What does it look like to take up your cross daily (finally!)? The answer is, that it depends. (Arrghh!)

Okay, don't get so touchy. Let me explain. In every situation involving another person, there are at least four wills involved. There is my will, God's will, someone else's will and our ancient foe's wicked desires. God has a will and a plan that should be our first concern. The other person involved has feelings, a will, emotions, and needs that we are commanded to consider above our own. We, of course, have feelings, desires, will, and choices, and we must never forget that we have an enemy that wants to destroy us.

To understand what it means to take up my cross, I must filter every decision through a grid. By that, I mean that we must consider the will of our Father in heaven as revealed in His Word. What does

God say about it? If He has spoken regarding His will, then that is that, end of the story. If He has not spoken directly about it, which is the vast amount of cases, then we go to step two.

What does the Scripture mean when it tells me to "esteem others as better than myself" and "not to look out for my interest but others?" What do those verses mean when it says about "not placing stumbling blocks in front of others," and "I will never eat meat again if it bothers my brother?" What does the Scripture state regarding about "strong and weak brothers," "limiting my freedoms for others," and need I go on to discussing, "love one another?"

We are not alone and our actions must be tempered specifically about everyone else to fulfill the Royal Law - love your neighbor as yourself.

In addition to these considerations, we must never forget that we live in occupied territory controlled by the prince of the power of the air. We live as strangers and aliens among a hostile people. Our foe has a will and it is not pretty towards us - "kill, steal and destroy" does not imply being nice or playing fair. I must live in a way as to not give my adversary any ground or opportunity to advance his kingdom in my life or realm of influence.

So, what does it mean to take up my cross and embrace it? In a nutshell, it means to be willing to lay down my will and desires for God first and then everyone else next. Our life is not our own, we were bought with a price! We proclaim that Jesus is Lord, and so He is. His will must become our will and His Word must be our love and law. We are not to embrace our self, love our self, or improve our self, we are to take up a death-to-self cross.

A good phrase to adopt is something like this - "my life is not my own." When my schedule is interrupted by others, when my plans are changed, when my life is interfered with, I must remember that I belong to Another. My life is not my own. I have taken up my cross, will continue to embrace it, and will live a life of death to self. My will is not as important as God's will and my needs are to be subservient to everyone else's. Ouch. That sure flies in the face of taking care of number one theology that is popular in our day. Exactly.

Nowhere in the Scripture are we commanded to pamper our self, look out for our self and to think about our self before everyone else. In fact, we are commanded the exact opposite. Multiple places in the Book we are told to die to our self, love everyone with a self-sacrificial love, and to look outward not inward.

What does it mean to take up our cross and follow Jesus daily? In the simplest terms, it means to lay down my will for His, and to esteem everyone else as more important than myself thus learning to walk in the footsteps of Jesus.

I must begin in my home laying down my life for my family, becoming a servant to all and then work outward to everyone else I meet.

Are you kidding me? If I did what you talk about, everyone would take advantage of me! Hmmm...Maybe that is what we are here for anyway to give everyone else an advantage over our self. After all, the purpose of the cross is to humble and kill my flesh, not to fulfill its self-centered desires.

What else is a cross for if not to produce to death to self? We can wear a cross as a decoration, even decorate our buildings with it, but until we begin to embrace the one that kills our fleshly desires, we really are not walking as disciples...at least according to Jesus.

## Questions to Ponder or Discuss:

1. What do you think the original hearers of Jesus thought when He told them to take up their cross and follow Him?

2. With all the emphasis on self-help, will the death-to-self message of Jesus really fly in our day? Why or why not?

3. How could dying to our self and esteeming others as better than us help in our homes? Work? School? Church?

4. Is there an area of your life that you simply will not lay down upon the cross? Why?

For Our Consideration

# Grace vs. Works

Oh great, another discussion about a topic that people always fight about. Nope, not this time. We are saved by grace and called to work. We are not saved by works, but by the gift of God through the act of Christ. We live in grace and are left here on planet earth to work. Anything argued beyond those concepts and I will have to leave the discussion.

What I want to write about is how we use the word grace. While having a discussion with someone recently about the completion of their Master's program, they said, "Well, it was just God's grace." I wonder about that sentence. I know God's grace empowers and enables us, but where does human effort come into the equation? Did God's grace write all the papers, listen to the lectures, and take pages of notes? Did God's grace take the tests, stay up late and study, and fulfill the requirements for graduation? Didn't my friend have to show up, write, and produce something?

What about parenting? Many parents will say if their children turn out well as adults, "Well, it was just God's grace." Was it? So, God's grace was not with the parents who children rebel?

Was it God's grace that sat on the bed until two in the morning listening to a confused teenager? Did God's grace drive the van, coach the teams, and change the diapers? Where was God's grace when Adam sinned?

Parenting is a time intensive activity. It seems like some children will just be okay and others take a great deal more time. How does God's grace fit into parenting? Do we have to do something, should be doing something, or just leave it up to God's grace?

Now, before you label me as a heretic or someone that does not appreciate God's grace, I do, I really do. I love God's glorious grace and relish the fact that He pours it out in abundance. How could we live without God's grace? However, I wonder about the human aspect of our lives in relationship to God's grace.

Where does working hard come in regarding our jobs? How about studying? Dying to self? Battling our flesh daily? Training our children? Is it really all God's grace that does these things or is human effort involved?

If I want to run a mile without dying, can I just rely on God's grace and take off sprinting, or do I need to train a bit first? How about dieting? Memorizing Scripture? Developing any skill in any area? Don't these take human effort as well as God's enabling grace?

If a parent ignores their child, they may grow up well by God's grace, but it seems that the parents that train and invest in them, consistently do better. If I want to grow proficient in any skill or activity, I can just trust in God's grace, or I can invest the time and energy to learn and practice.

I am not discounting God's grace in any fashion, just the statement, "Oh, it was God's grace," Yes, it was God's grace. It also was an effort on your part to walk in that grace. It was hard work, diligence, endurance, faithfulness, and an investment of time. Why do we have the fruits of the Spirit mentioned in Galatians if all we need is God's grace?

Why do I need patience, kindness, faithfulness, gentleness, and self-control, if God's grace does it all? I'm just asking, not trying to pick a fight here.

Why are so many aspects of God type love an action if grace does everything? Endures all things, believes all things, and never gives

## For Our Consideration

up, sure seem like human effort and choices to me. We are told in many places in Scripture to put off, put on, lay aside, and take up. If, "Oh well, it's all by God's grace," is true, why so many commandments that seem to imply choice?

Perhaps what really matters is choosing wisely under the influence and empowered by God's grace. Yes, God's grace is poured out in abundance on each of us, and for that, I am eternally grateful. I am also told to work hard, and I guess I need His grace to obey that command as well.

## Questions to Ponder or Discuss:

1. What is your take on the grace vs. works issue?

2. Does it really matter what we do if everything is simply a product of God's grace? Explain.

3. Are we simply given the fruit of the Spirit or do we develop them over time? Explain.

4. Do our choices matter or is all under grace and whatever will be will be? Explain.

Discussion Starters

# Heart Battles

Our heart pumps blood throughout our physical bodies in a marvelous way. Flowing freely in our human bodies, the blood is essential to our survival. When the Scripture uses the word heart, in most places it is referring not to the physical pump, but to our thoughts, intentions, and place of our emotions.

> The heart is deceitful above all things, and desperately sick; who can understand it? Jeremiah 17:9

I do not believe the prophet is referring to my physical heart here, but something deeper.

> And I will give them one heart, and a new spirit I will put within them. I will remove the heart of stone from their flesh and give them a heart of flesh, Ezekiel 11:19

In this verse, we are promised a new heart, one that is tender and not hard like a rock. Salvation brings this promise to reality. After we are born again, our dead, hard heart is replaced with one that is tender towards the Lord.

Our hearts can grow cold, however, due to sin and unbelief:

> Take care, brothers, lest there be in any of you an evil, unbelieving heart, leading you to fall away from the living God. Hebrews 3:10

## For Our Consideration

In addition, we can lose something through trials, heartaches, and sickness if we are not careful.

> So we do not lose heart. Though our outer self is wasting away, our inner self is being renewed day by day. 2 Corinthians 4:16

Every day, moment by moment our hearts are working both physically, and in the sense described in these passages of Scripture. What direction are we heading in our hearts? Are we becoming tender or hard? Are we moving towards a firmer belief or growing colder in our faith? Are we losing part of our heart through the cares of this life, or are we being renewed? All excellent questions to ponder.

There is a battle raging for our hearts. I am not talking about clogged arteries, but a war to dull our hearts. The warfare is real and the goal is to wear out the saints. Part of the enemy's plan is to make us give up, give in, and simply grow lukewarm or cold. We must resist.

What can clog our spiritual hearts quicker than a greasy hamburger? Sin, worry, fear, ego, drifting, long-term trials, disappointments, dashed expectations, harsh words, unfaithful friends, a steady diet of the news, placing our hope in sports, politics, or people, and taking our eyes from the Lord, to name just a few. We need to guard our hearts or we lose something of real value.

Our hearts must remain tender to the Lord. We must take care lest we drift and find ourselves moving towards unbelief. Trials can strengthen us or ruin us, and it depends on our heart choices. A marketing guru friend of mine likes to state, "We are bombarded with 20,000 marketing messages every day." I think he is probably low in his estimate. Many of those messages we receive from TV, radio, the internet, billboards, books, magazines and our smartphones, are not

## Discussion Starters

directing us towards Christ, but away from Him. There is a battle for control of our heart.

We must guard our hearts and minds. We must renew them in the Word of God, through prayer and walk in fellowship with like-minded people. Our heart needs help to remain tender. Our natural heart needs exercise to keep it working well. Do we really believe that our spiritual heart will be fine if we just ignore it or live on spiritual junk food?

Our lives are busy and we have many voices screaming for attention. Our time is limited, and frankly, there are many things in this life that are discouraging. As I sat looking over an extensive prayer list recently, it was easy to become overwhelmed. So many real people with real pain that never seems to end. It is a temptation to lose heart, as Paul stated above, but we must not.

The battle is real and so will be the victory. Jeremiah cried about the deceitfulness of our hearts and the frustration of trying to figure it out. "Who can know it?" cries the prophet. Fortunately, we are not left there for the next verse (Jeremiah 17:10) gives the answer:

**"I the LORD search the heart and test the mind"**

As we draw near to the Lord He will show us our hearts. God will not only show us them, He will redeem them for His glory. God will pour in the healing necessary for us to endure. God will give us the strength to carry on. We will not lose heart because we know that God began a good work in us and He will complete it.

For Our Consideration

The battle for our hearts may rage daily, but we know Who wins. We may be knocked down, but we will get up and overcome through God's enabling grace. Do not give in or up saints, keep on walking, our hearts need the exercise.

## Questions to Ponder or Discuss:

1. When is the last time you had a heart checkup? Not the physical one, but opened your heart before the Lord.

2. Are there any heart blockers in your life? How do you deal with them? Explain.

3. As time rolls by is your heart becoming more tender or harder? Why?

4. How do you receive a tender heart or reverse a hard one? Explain.

Discussion Starters

# Who Ya Listening To?

From the time we are old enough to understand our native language, people were telling us to listen. Every parent tells their child to not run with scissors, play with knives, get too close to the fire, quit hitting your brother or sister, and no, we are not there yet.

As we age we enter our education years and there are instructors telling us what to read, how to write, and when it is okay to go to the restroom. We finally reach adulthood and then we will quit being told what to do. Right.

Almost everyone has heard the tale of the teen that was sick and tired of being told what to do so they ran off and joined the Marines. Let me know how that works out for you. "Did I tell you to bleed marine, stop it, immediately." The soldier yells "Sir, yes sir" as they continue to do pushups.

It seems that our lives are populated with people who are always going to tell us what to think, how to act, and when to do so. Since this is mostly true, we would be wise to learn to listen well.

The Bible is full of stories of real people who did listen to counsel, but not to the right counsel. It seems that humans have not changed much over the last few thousand years. Today, in our modern, forward, enlightened high-tech age, people still seek and even listen to counsel. Some of it is good, some not so much.

Reading through 1 Kings I noticed two examples of people who listened to counsel with dismal results. Consider these two passages:

> But he (Rehoboam) abandoned the counsel that the old men gave him and took counsel with the young men who had grown up with him and stood before him. 1 Kings 12:9
>
> So, the king (Jeroboam) took counsel and made two calves of gold. 1 Kings 12:28

Two kings in the same chapter who listened to counsel. Two disasters. The first one lost most of his kingdom and the second one became famous for idolatry. So, are you saying we should not listen to counsel? No, but we need to make sure the counsel we listen to is giving us godly wisdom and guidance.

Many people offer opinions, views, advice, and counsel that simply are wrong. How many people have counseled themselves out of a marriage, a job, their home, and church because they listened to the wrong people telling them the wrong thing to do?

We have an enemy and he is a liar. While I can't necessarily prove my theory, it seems to me that whenever someone is facing a crossroad or crisis, our foe assures that there is someone there to give wrong counsel.

- "Go ahead, get divorced, you will be so much happier."
- "You didn't marry the right person, but this one will be."
- "You deserve that money they cheated you out of; you really should fudge on the expense report."
- "I did it and it was the best thing I ever did."
- "Come on, everyone else is doing it."
- "Everyone will think you are goodie-two-shoes if you do or don't do that."

- "I know they said it, but they didn't really mean that."

You get the picture. Parents, pastors, prophets, and bosses are often ignored by people listening to the wrong counsel. The Scriptures teach that we are to get counsel, listen to older, wiser people. We are to seek out those more experienced and learn from them. We can avoid a great deal of pain and heartache if we would learn to humble ourselves and listen, at least listen to godly counsel.

There are those who would offer bad counsel and those who would offer the wise, godly kind. How do we know the difference? It really is not a guessing game as much as we think. Here are two ways to know: the Lord has placed people in our lives who are authorities and He has given us His Word.

Everyone is under some type of authority. We would be wise to learn how to listen to them. And, we know that the authorities over us have been given that authority by the Ultimate Authority and they will give an account for what they do with this delegated task. (See Romans 13:1 and Part Two of this book for further details on this all-important topic).

If the authority is telling us to do something that does not violate God's Word, then we better have a very good reason to ignore it. If the authority is telling us to do something that does violate God's revealed Word, then we must obey the Higher Authority. For the record, and simply as an example, these do not violate God's Word:

- Staying pure before marriage
- Staying married if possible (caveat - flee physical abuse for safety reasons)
- A curfew
- Cleaning your room and mowing the lawn

## For Our Consideration

- Turning off electronic items
- Keeping your promises
- Paying your taxes
- Working hard at your job

Anyway, you get the idea. There are many issues that we are given instruction about from those in authority, and we would be wise to listen. On the other hand, there are those who would give us wicked, ungodly, or uninformed counsel and we would be better served to not accept it.

If someone is telling us to violate God's Word, we don't have to pray, we need to ignore their counsel. God will not lead us to disobey His Word. If someone is leading us away from following the Lord, again, we know this is not good counsel.

The issues that are not clearly commanded or forbidden in Scripture get a bit harder to decide. Many of us old homeschoolers, for example, were advised not to do so by parents and school educators. Since the issue was not clearly defined in Scripture, we were free to seek the Lord and make the best possible decision we could make with the information we had.

The same is true with whether to have and watch TV, go to movies, date or not date, how many children to have, and the list could go on for pages. While there are many people passionate about these views, the Scripture is vague enough on them to have many interpretations. There are of course principles to follow and then there is also the leading of the Holy Spirit.

Here is the bottom line in my opinion. We have God's Word. We have those God has placed in authority over us. We have older, wiser people in our lives. We would be wise to listen to godly counsel. We will be fools to violate God's Word and listen to the wicked voices.

So, who are you listening to, and why? Where is their counsel leading you?

## Questions to Ponder or Discuss:

1. The people that "have your ear," are they leading you to Christ or some other direction?

2. Is being willing to listen to others a heart issue? Explain.

3. How do you determine if counsel is good or bad?

4. Does God speak to us through authority? Explain.

For Our Consideration

# Have We Lost Something?

I love reading old sermons and booklets. Sometimes it is tempting to just stand up on Sunday morning and read the words of these wise saints from long ago. After reading Calvin, Spurgeon, Pink and many others from bygone eras, it crosses my mind that I really have little to share.

Before you write me concerned about my psyche, I fully realize that God uses various people in multiple ways to speak to their generation, so no fears; I am not suffering from some inferiority complex. However, I do wonder if we have lost something over the centuries in the depth of what we share.

This morning while reading a J. C. Ryle's (1816-1900) excerpt from a sermon entitled, *What it costs to be a Christian*, I came across these thoughts:

> "There must be no separate truce with any special sin that he loves."

> "He and his sin must quarrel if he and God are to be friends."

Just soak in those two sentences for a while. How many times have we made a special truce with our favorite sin? We are willing to expose, repent of, and even confess to others some of our sins, but we hold back on that one sin we really enjoy. We proclaim that we want to be totally free, yet in our hearts, we know we are still stroking that one sin we cling to. We have made a special truce with it. We boldly shout, "Death to all of my sin," yet we have made a backroom deal with that one no one knows about.

We will not be completely free until we declare war on every sin. Making a secret agreement with our self will not do. We really are only fooling an audience of one. In fact, we really are not even fooling our self. We know, and we know that God knows, what really is going on behind the veil of our words. We have made a truce with a foe we should be battling. Defeat is guaranteed when we shake hands with our sin instead of crucifying it.

How about the second quote? It seems that we are destined to fight with someone or something. Ryle states it clearly, yet powerfully. If we refuse to fight with our sin, we will fight against God. Our friendship with God cannot grow if we harbor a friendship with our sin. We must choose for we cannot serve two masters. Friendship with the world means hostility to God, so says James, and it seems we really cannot be friends with sin and God at the same time either. I pray we choose wisely.

In the same short message, Ryle adds this jewel while discussing the cost of discipleship:

> "In attending to these things, (guarding one's behavior) he may come far short of perfection; but there is none of them that he can safely neglect."

Another excellent thought to ponder. Just because we will not achieve perfection does not mean we gain a license to neglect or fail. I wonder how many modern believers understand this, beginning with me. It seems that we sometimes act like since we cannot achieve perfection, we might as well not even try to live a holy, pure, godly life.

Can we safely neglect the disciplines of Christianity because we are not perfect and live under grace? I do not believe Ryle would say so, nor many other older, wiser saints. Grace is not an excuse to sin but includes the empowerment for holy living. When we confuse these two points, we are close to abusing the best gift we ever received.

Let me stop today with this thought - In our busy world, we still must allow time for contemplation. I am not sure if there is a smartphone app for this yet, but there probably will be soon. "Download this free app to think deeply in less time than you ever imagined." (For all you entrepreneur types out there, that is a gold mine waiting to be developed.)

We know we should spend more time thinking, praying, contemplating before the Lord, but we want an easier way to do so. To paraphrase Ryle, we may come short of perfection but we cannot safely ignore or neglect these matters for long.

Discussion Starters

## Questions to Ponder or Discuss:

1. Is there any sin that we have made a special truce with?

2. Is there anything in your life that you refuse to let go of? Any area where Jesus is not Lord?

3. Can we safely neglect discipline? Explain.

4. What are the major time stealers in your life and what can you do about them?

For Our Consideration

# Holiness, Sin and other Offensive Words

Let's revisit what was shared in the last article from another angle. "There must be no separate truce with any special sin that he loves." Now, there is a sentence. No, I did not write it, but I can't seem to get it out of my brain after reading it. J. C. Ryle (1816-1900) wrote this in a sermon entitled, Holiness.

> "In attending to these things, he may come far short of perfection; but there is none of them that he can safely neglect."

What "things" is Ryle writing about?

> "The believer must be like a soldier, daily standing his guard like he is on enemy ground. He must take heed to his behavior every hour of the day, in every company, and in every place. He must be careful over his time, his tongue, his temper, his thoughts, his imagination, his motives, his conduct in every relation of life. He must be diligent about his prayers, his Bible-reading, and his use of Sunday."

Wow. Not a typical message you hear today. Even mentioning the word holiness from the pulpit stirs up controversy in some circles. Pictures of hair buns and dreary faces immediately surface, but should they?

## Discussion Starters

Didn't Peter tell us to be holy like God is holy? (1 Peter 1:15-16) And, isn't the third Person of the Trinity called the Holy Spirit? Why the reaction to the call to holiness?

If holiness causes a stir when taught, what about dealing with sin? There is a teaching circulating through the social network world that grace is supreme. Grace covers everything. Grace means you cannot sin any longer. Grace, grace, grace, all you need is grace. Christians are under grace, so what we do really does not matter.

For the record, I am very grateful for God's glorious grace. Every aspect of it - saving grace, healing grace, preserving grace, empowering grace, and any other aspect of grace you want to accent. I am not a believer in excusing grace, however, but amazing grace. Grace is not a license to sin. Grace is not a cover for sin. Grace is not a reason to sin. Grace is a gift to us to assist us in our walk with the Lord.

The blood of Jesus cleanses us from all sin. The cross deals with sin. Sin is confessed and repented of by the believer and forgiveness is received. This "grace is a license" teaching is not a new teaching but an old one already dealt with in the pages of the New Testament.

> What shall we say then? Are we to continue in sin that grace may abound? By no means! How can we who died to sin still live in it? Romans 6:1-2

> What then? Are we to sin because we are not under law but under grace? By no means! Romans 6:15

> Live as people who are free, not using your freedom as a cover-up for evil, but living as servants of God. 1 Peter 2:16

For Our Consideration

Believers sin, at least John the beloved says so in 1 John. When we sin, we go to our Great High Priest Jesus, confess our sin, and receive forgiveness. We do not, nor should not ever just glibly laugh off our sin as unimportant or not really a big deal. After all, I am under grace so why bother, or so goes the currently popular teaching.

The wages of sin are death and the wages are always paid. Whenever a believer sins death is unleashed. My sin is forgiven but the consequences of my sinful choices will almost always follow. Yes, there are times that God does not allow those consequences, but that is His realm, not mine.

If I lie, steal, lust, cheat, or kill, consequences will follow each of those choices.

- If I lie to my wife, she will eventually find out and her trust of me will weaken.
- If I steal from my job, eventually I will be found out, and lose credibility.
- If I lust after someone or something, while no one may know it, I do, and God does, and my heart has a hard place formed on it that will not soften up until I repent.
- If I cheat on my taxes, eventually the IRS may find it and I could go to jail or at least end up on the nightly news bringing shame to my Lord and to my family.
- If I kill someone, I will be found out and end up in prison or on death row.

# Discussion Starters

I may be under grace, as some folks teach regarding each of these sins, but while living under that grace, I still may violate trust, weaken credibility, become calloused, end up in debt, or in prison.

Wouldn't it be better to not use grace as a cover-up for evil but as empowerment to walk in holiness? As Ryle so aptly stated, "There must be no special truce," and, "He and his sin must quarrel," if we are to walk under and in grace. A proper understanding of grace should lead to holiness, and not sensuality, carnality, excuses for my flesh, or sinful indulgences.

## Questions to Ponder or Discuss:

1. Why does the word holiness seem to stir up such disagreements?

2. What is the difference between being diligent and being a legalist?

3. Can I be forgiven of my sin yet still suffer for it? Explain.

4. Explain how grace should lead to holiness and not to gratifying our flesh?

# What about Them?

There are many ways to skin a cat-- okay, not sure why they wanted to skin the thing in the first place, but I think the old saying has something to do with there being multiple ways to go about doing it. I'm sure the skinned cat does not really care, but that is not really the point.

As far as I know, every believer sins. Some will debate that sentence, but just concede it to me for the sake of this discussion so we can move along. Good people make mistakes, fail, fall short, leave out what they should do and do incorrectly what they do end up doing. Lovers of Jesus lose their tempers, give into lust, allow hurts and unforgiveness to dwell in their mind, give way too much grace to themselves and way too little to everyone else. In short, only Jesus is perfect and everyone else is in some state of imperfection.

So, what do we do about that? How do we walk with those other sinners, or if you prefer, imperfect, not completed, work-in-process, mistake prone saints? Over the last thirty-five years or so of serving as a pastor I can safely say that there are at least two types of people. There are many different shades, but again for the sake of moving along, let's stay simple. There are those that are more black and white oriented, and those that lean towards being grayer in focus. The first group tends to like very straight lines and clear boundaries and second prefer a bit more curved with flexible interpretations. Both tend to think the other is mostly wrong.

For me, I seem to bounce between the two. On some points, I am strong and mostly inflexible and on others, I want softness and bending. Am I confused? Probably, but that is not really the point of this either. While I have been on an extended vacation I have been chewing on this verse:

> And the Lord's servant must not be quarrelsome but kind to everyone, able to teach, patiently enduring evil, correcting his opponents with gentleness. God may perhaps grant them repentance leading to a knowledge of the truth, and they may come to their senses and escape from the snare of the devil, after being captured by him to do his will. 2 Timothy 2:24

Paul wrote to his young spiritual son Timothy, just before Paul was going to be executed. Paul knew his time of departure was at hand, and I imagine that if I knew my death was near, I would write what was most important. I would want those that read my last words to know that these principles are what I want to be remembered after my death.

Paul encourages Timothy to be kind, teach well, and patiently endure evil. I assume Paul meant the evil in others based on the rest of the verse. Timothy would spend the rest of his life surrounded by imperfect people. Sinful people. How did Paul tell him to deal with them? Kindly, patiently endure evil, offering correction with gentleness. Timothy would correct and teach, but God is the one that grants repentance leading to truth and freedom.

I need to learn this. My job is to not be quarrelsome, but kind to everyone. Everyone? Yes, everyone. I need to learn to teach as best and I can with the God-given resources provided. I need to learn how to be patient with others with their sin and evil. Yes, correction of others is part of the process, but with gentleness. If I do my part well,

## For Our Consideration

God may perhaps grant them repentance and freedom from the trap they live in.

Wow, I have a lot of growing to do. Some of the frustration between the two types of people enters in with the definition of undefined words.

The Bible is frustrating at times to me for that very reason. Why didn't God define, with precision the actions He wanted us to take? For example:

- What does not be quarrelsome mean? Where does debating and clarifying fit in? How do I correct someone without seeming to be argumentative?
- What does be kind mean? How kind is kind, and who determines that anyway?
- What does patiently enduring evil mean? How long? What evil? All manner of evil, or just some of it? How long is patient enough?
- Who are the opponents and how gentle is gentle? What does correcting mean?
- Why does it say, God "may grant" instead of "will grant" repentance? And, what does leading to the knowledge of the truth mean?

I could go on to how did they become ensnared in the first place? What role did the devil play? So, the devil does have a will, and how do we know what that will is? Just a glimpse into my thought process, but enough is enough.

As I chew over and over on this passage, it becomes clear to me that there are many ways to define the words used. There are multiple shades of meaning, and more importantly, further applications in personal relationships than I have thought of before.

This much I know with certainty. I am a servant of the Lord. The rest of Paul's charge is being learned and lived out in varying degrees. How kind am I really? How argumentative do I remain? How patient am I with other's sins and shortcomings? Am I always gentle? Am I as concerned with people being delivered from the snare of the devil as I am with being right in my opinions and views?

The bottom line is I need to prayerfully consider this verse's fulfillment in others more, while continuing to ask the Lord to be gentle with me, and perhaps grant me repentance in the places where I fall so short. As someone stated years ago, "We all have areas we need to grow in, and they are called blind spots for a reason - we don't see them."

## Questions to Ponder or Discuss:

1. Why do you think God created different personalities types while knowing all the issues that would cause?

2. Why do you think God left so many gray type areas undefined?

3. Ask someone that knows you and that you trust if you are argumentative? What do you think they would say?

4. How do we know if we have any blind spots and what can we do about them?

For Our Consideration

# Christian Sensuality

I don't get it. Why is it that Christian men and women feel the need to be sensual, seductive, half dressed, and look like they want to jump into bed with anyone and everyone? From Facebook to Pinterest, Twitter to Instagram, Christians pose in slinky clothes, fashion model like poses, and everyone applauds them. Why?

Why is it that if someone (male or female) shows cleavage, thigh, rippled abs, skin tight clothes highlighting their private parts, everyone uses words like, beautiful, lovely, gorgeous, stud, hot, etc. instead of words like, shameful, seductive, provocative, sensual, and stumbling material? Where has our discernment gone? Have we forgotten how to blush?

In the effort to avoid the dreaded word, "legalism," have we swung so far over to license? Don't we have a responsibility to present our temples (bodies) in a holy, modest way? Is Hollywood setting the standard of modesty instead of the Church? Why do we have to go sensual and bare our bodies to be considered attractive and lovely?

The Scripture states clearly that beauty should come from within, not from highlighting our bodies:

> Do not let your adorning be external—the braiding of hair and the putting on of gold jewelry, or the clothing you wear—but let your adorning be the hidden person of the heart with the imperishable beauty of a gentle and quiet spirit, which in God's sight is very precious. For this is how the holy women who hoped in God used to adorn themselves, by submitting to their own husbands. 1 Peter 3:3-5

Why shouldn't our clothes point to our faces instead of other parts of the body? With the proliferation of porn, the destruction of marriage through sexual immorality, and addictions running rampant, why isn't the Church rebelling against these trends? I ask again, have we lost our discernment?

Solomon warned his sons, and us, to avoid the harlot or sensual, seductive, woman (or man). Consider this passage for just a moment:

> And behold, the woman meets him, dressed as a prostitute, wily of heart. Proverbs 7:10

There are many aspects to consider here, but one clear one is that the woman was dressed in such a way as to communicate that she was available for hire. Our clothing matters and speaks to reveal our intentions. Shouldn't we, as ambassadors for Christ, living epistles known and read by all men, consider what we are saying with what we are wearing?

There is another disturbing trend arising over the last decade or so. Young couples court or date, attempt to remain sexually pure and then marry. Almost as soon as saying "I do," the husband begins to demand that his wife change. He asks her to be more seductive, show more skin, and be sexier. Get tattooed, pierced, show cleavage, shorten the dresses or shorts and act more sensual. As if to show off his trophy, the man demands that his wife moves towards sensuality. Instead of protecting and cherishing his bride, the husband instills in her the seeds of destruction that will bloom sooner than later.

In addition, for some reason, some guys now think that porn is okay. Bring the porn into the bedroom and let's play porn stars. Get

## For Our Consideration

kinky, weird, stretch the boundaries of propriety and demean the girl for not readily being willing to throw off moral restraint. The guy begins to mock and ridicule the standards that were initially attractive to him. We wonder why young married couples struggle to stay together long enough to turn into older couples in our day.

### Have we lost our discernment?

If we keep looking at the world for our acceptable standards we are in deep trouble. The Scripture should be our standard of behavior and thinking patterns. If we continue to imitate the nations around us, we are not going to be an effective light to them. If we look like, act like, think like, and respond just like the world, we will not be successful in changing it.

Sensuality arises from the heart. When we are posing, dressing, and wanting others to look at us, what are we really thinking at that moment? Are we bringing glory to God with how we look and act or are we somewhere else? What is our motive for our behavior? I believe we need a serious heart change if we ever expect to make a real difference in our world.

Paul challenged his readers with this thought:

> But among you there must not be even a hint of sexual immorality, or of any kind of impurity, or of greed, because these are improper for God's holy people. Ephesians 5:3 (NIV)

When we are exposing, highlighting, or drawing attention to the private parts of our bodies, are we really obeying this verse? When we are demanding that our spouses show more, highlight their bodies, be sexier, hot, or whatever the latest word is, are we pushing the boundaries of proper behavior? Have we lost our discernment? Have we forgotten how to blush?

Finally, I know the comments, arguments, justifications, and responses that could be sent to me, for I have heard them all before. "The guys have the problem. (True) They need to quit looking with lust. (True) I'm free in Christ. (True, with restraints based in love) What do you want me to wear, a bag or something? (No, just consider others as more important than yourself in how you dress) You are trying to put me in bondage and you are a legalist," (Both untrue, legalism has to do with attempting to gain approval with God, and I am not even anywhere near that, I am simply asking you to think about what you are doing and why) and the list could go on.

My appeal is simply for us to ask the Lord if we have compromised or adapted to the culture around us in how we present our bodies to each other either in person or online. Are we walking in moral purity, really valuing others to not place a stumbling block in their way? Is there a "hint" of impurity, sensuality or immorality in how we look, act, speak, and conduct ourselves? Have we lost some of our discernment? I am just asking the questions, you are the one that must answer them between you and the Lord.

For Our Consideration

## Questions to Ponder or Discuss:

1. Does this discussion bother you? Why or why not?

2. How would you define discernment?

3. How would you define legalism?

4. How would you define the word hint that Paul used?

Discussion Starters

# It Ain't Judging If You Are Sinning

The buzz phrase in our day is, "Don't judge," but is that a Biblical concept? Are we never to judge? Are there still rights and wrongs in our day or is that period over? Is this the season of grace and we can do whatever we want and everyone else just needs to not be bothered with it?

Here is one of the key verses many use for not judging - Jesus said:

> Judge not, that you be not judged. For with the judgment you pronounce you will be judged, and with the measure you use it will be measured to you. Matthew 7:1-2

But Jesus also said:

> Do not judge by appearances, but judge with right judgment. John 7:24

Hmmm... The context of course rules in how we interpret and apply all passages, but bear with me...
Paul said:

> Do you suppose, O man—you who judge those who practice such things and yet do them yourself—that you will escape the judgment of God? Romans 2:3

For Our Consideration

And Paul also said:

> For though absent in body, I am present in spirit; and as if present, I have already pronounced judgment on the one who did such a thing. 1 Corinthians 5:3

> For what have I to do with judging outsiders? Is it not those inside the church whom you are to judge? 1 Corinthians 5:12

Hmmm... Context still rules, but there seems to be a whole lot of judging going on here.

James said:

> There is only one lawgiver and judge, he who is able to save and to destroy. But who are you to judge your neighbor? James 4:12

Reading Romans 14-15 will reveal an extensive discussion regarding judging one another. Are the writers of the NT confused, or am I? My theology does not allow for the Scripture to be in error, so that narrows down the options from my perspective.

Perhaps my real problem with the whole, "Don't judge me" thing is that often (please don't overlook that word before you judge me, often does not mean always) someone who is stating this phrase is pursuing some sort of sinful behavior. Immorality, drunkenness, cursing, carousing, sensuality, pornography, and a host of other

## Discussion Starters

behaviors have all been granted impunity under the "Don't judge me" sentence. But should they be given it?

Because I am a new creation in Christ, under the New Covenant, saved by grace, a temple of the Holy Spirit, and many other wonderful truths, am I now free to sin at will? What about the warnings sprinkled throughout the New Testament about sinning, rebuking and confronting one another, crucifying my flesh, dying to sensuality, resisting deception and the devil, not imitating evil, and a host of other commands and prohibitions? Do they not apply nowadays?

While some will not agree with me, here is my take on judging. Judging implies making definitive statements about the unknown motives of someone's heart, thoughts in their head, and reasons behind their actions. This territory is for God and the person alone, and for me to state what they are, puts me into the place of a mind reader - not a good place to be.

In addition, we are not to pass judgment on others regarding debatable or disputable matters (Romans 14:1). Should Christians own a TV? Are movies acceptable to watch? Should a believer listen to a certain type of music, ride a motorcycle, eat at a casino, etc. These (and a multitude of other behaviors and choices) are subject to personal preference and are not directly addressed in Scripture.

Regarding disputable matters, I personally believe that we need to examine our own motives and make sure whatever we do is pleasing to the Lord, is not imitating or promoting the devil's kingdom, and is not purposefully causing someone to stumble or trip over our words or actions. We are free in Christ, but we do not live alone. All things are indeed lawful, but not all things are profitable. Our actions and freedoms affect many others and therefore we must take that into consideration before we act.

For Our Consideration

Sinful behavior, on the other hand, is not debatable. Sin is to be repented of, never accepted, rationalized or grown accustomed to. Arguing about personal rights and freedoms is the wrong discussion in my opinion. Sinful behavior is sinful behavior regardless of the feelings, emotions, or arguments attached. Murder, rebellion, immorality, adultery, theft, drunkenness, abusing parents, gossip, slander, gluttony, or anything else sinful are still sinful according to God's standard revealed in His Word.

Stating that sin is wrong and therefore needs to be repented of, is not judging, it is agreeing with God and His Word. There are still absolutes in the Absolute Book even in a world dominated by situational ethics and relativism.

We are to grow up as we walk with Christ for the Scripture states:

> And it is my prayer that your love may abound more and more, with knowledge and all discernment, Philippians 1:9

> But solid food is for the mature, for those who have their powers of discernment trained by constant practice to distinguish good from evil. Hebrews 5:14

Learning what the Scriptures state, not what we want them to say, and aligning our lives with them, should be our goal. Learning how to grow in love, knowledge of Christ, and growing in discernment is a sign of maturity. Discernment grows as we renew our minds with God's Word and learn to think more Biblically. We are not to adapt our thinking and behavior to the culture around us, but we are to embrace the Scriptures as our standard of truth.

The bottom line to me is that I should never justify the sin in my life but repent of it as it is exposed. If someone points out my sin, they are not judging me, they are loving me.

## Questions to Ponder or Discuss:

1. What do you believe the Scriptures teach about judging others? Why?

2. How to we determine what debatable matters are?

3. How do we learn to walk in love towards those that hold differing views on debatable matters?

4. What does the Word of God say about sin?

For Our Consideration

# Is Education Evil?

In 1973 when I became a believer in Jesus, advanced Biblical education was viewed with a sneer. The Holy Spirit was moving freely, and going to seminary was referred to as a doorway to quenching. It seems that forty years have not changed much of that view.

Seminaries are still referred to as cemeteries and those who have pursued advanced degrees are considered tainted and somehow nearly spiritually dead. I understand where some of the views originate, and there are seminaries that seem to produce more agnostics and atheists rather than strong believers. However, is that an indictment of higher education or is it the theology being taught?

I have multiple advanced degrees and my faith has not been ruined. In fact, it has been strengthened. Being blessed to read widely, write extensively and to sit under some of the greatest instructors in God's Kingdom, has not hurt me. Nor do I believe has the Spirit been quenched.

For those who remain skeptical, let me challenge some of the prejudice against education by considering the authors of the Scripture. What would our Bible look like today if it was written by uneducated men? We know a great many of the authors that God used, and even the ones who are unknown could probably read and write, though contrary to the norm of their day. Those who dictated their words due to not being able to read or write used trained, educated men to write them down and not fellow illiterates.

Here's a quick rundown on some of the men God used in Scripture to give us His Holy Word. Think about how many books each one

Discussion Starters

wrote and imagine what the Bible would be like without these educated authors:

- Moses - he was educated at the school of Egypt and trained as a royal student.
- Ezra - a first rate scribe, trained in the Law of God
- Solomon - gifted by God with wisdom and wrote books to be studied
- Daniel - chosen because of his education by a foreign king to receive even more education
- Many (though not all) of the prophets were highly educated
- Luke - a physician
- Paul - a highly educated Pharisee

While we are not to glory in our flesh or become arrogant over our minds, God uses trained ones. Yes, God can and does use those who have not trained academically, but does that mean we should avoid education?

Some of the greatest minds in Church history were highly educated.

- Augustine
- Luther
- Calvin
- Newton
- Schaeffer
- C. S. Lewis

Paul told his spiritual son Timothy to study to show himself approved (2 Timothy 2:15) so he could rightly handle God's Word.

## For Our Consideration

Why is it harmful for those of us that desire to learn to do so? Not everyone needs to become a scholar, but we should be thankful that some have done so.

Throughout the pages of Scripture, you will encounter well educated, gifted men and women. These diligent people preserved the Bible, built beautiful items for God's temple, wrote, preached, served, and made a difference in their world. Their studies and training did not hinder them but opened broader doors of service for them.

Studying and advanced education will not hurt us if we remain true to God's holy Word. If we reject the Bible as our standard of truth then the issue is not too much education but ignorance. God has given us His Word to train us, renew our minds, and to reveal His will and purposes for us. If we reject the Bible, we are unwise and all the education in the world will not help us.

God's Word has been preserved and translated into every language by some of the best-educated people who ever lived on earth. Where would our English (or any other language) Bibles be if not for educated people? Being smart, trained, educated and gifted is not wrong. The people that God has gifted are a blessing, not someone to mock and make fun of due to their education. Would you go to an uneducated doctor for your health issues? Aren't you glad that he or she studied advanced topics and became skilled?

The issue is not a seminary, but becoming the best-trained tool, we can for use by the Master. I am grateful for the education I have received. I am thankful for wise instructors who love the Lord. God has gifted many people with a strong intellect and I am very thankful that we can learn from them. Solomon asked for wisdom and God was pleased. I pray we would not choose ignorance because of a false prejudice.

Discussion Starters

## Questions to Ponder or Discuss:

1. How do we guard our hearts and mind against error?

2. Should every young person attend college? Why or why not?

3. Does the Scripture approve or disapprove of education? Explain.

4. What advantages and pitfalls await those that attend education outlets?

For Our Consideration

# Three Essentials

I spent a bit of time recently engaging someone on social media. Most of us probably have the major outlets that open opportunities beyond our own circles. This person took offense at my message from 1 John 2:1-2 which states that the believers can and will sin.

Normally, I would just pass on this type discussion because it always ends ugly. This time, however, I went ahead and responded to the comment challenging my understanding of the Gospel. Like most of these conversations, it ended with me being labeled as Biblically ignorant, not born again, trapped in a false understanding of grace, using the wrong translations, etc.

After multiple attempts to address the actual Scriptures instead of their talking points, the opponent, ended with the traditional, "I'm going to wipe my feet as I leave you in your rejection of the truth," comment. I thanked them and encouraged them to make sure they had a large mat for all the feet wiping they were going to do.

This experience led me to think about this quote from J. C. Ryle:

> It was one of the last sayings of a famous divine that there were three things which were essential to healthy Christian teaching—doctrine, experience, and practice. He said that if doctrine alone were brought forward to a people there was a danger lest they should turn out Antinomians; that if experience alone were brought forward to a people there was a danger lest they should turn out enthusiasts and sentimentalists; and that if practice alone were brought forward, there was a danger that they would turn out legalists.

## Discussion Starters

Our lives should be a healthy mixture of the three points mentioned – doctrine, experience, and practice. It seems like the Holy Spirit sometimes may emphasize one of these more than the other, but we certainly need all three to mature properly.

If we are called to teach regularly, shouldn't we include all three of these aspects into our messages? When I teach homiletics, my challenge to those listening is to make sure you can answer the "so what?" question in each message. When you are finished sharing what you believe the Lord gave to you, what difference does it make to your listeners?

By including doctrine, experience, and practice in every message, we will certainly raise the potential to answer that critical question. Our doctrine precedes our actions, which are often refined by our experiences. We learn from our success and failures and we install habits or practices into our daily lives as a result.

If we regularly ignore any of these three in our messages, we will drift towards lawlessness, legalism, or emotionalism, as Ryle shared. By including all three, we will increase the potential that everyone that listens to us is challenged, encouraged, and given practical tools to walk out their daily lives for the glory of God. While there are more goals than this in teaching, there certainly should not be less.

For Our Consideration

## Questions to Ponder or Discuss:

1. How do you respond when someone disagrees with you?

2. Do you see value in understanding doctrine? Why or why not?

3. What role should our personal experiences play in developing our spiritual life?

4. How do our actual lives reflect what we really believe?

# Living for what Matters

Reading a book about a family that has been called to leave their home and move to a third world nation, reminded me about our daily choices. Life is often hectic and confusing regarding priorities. Most of us would agree with the traditional view (and order) of what we should value:

- God
- Family
- Job/Ministry

I wonder what our schedules would reveal. Do we really give God the most time and attention? How about our family, do they come in second over other pressing matters? As men, or as the provider for the home, do we really place the source of our income as lower? How many of us pastor types give more attention to ministry than to either God or our family? Not accusing here, I am just asking questions. I also realize that there are times that these three will be mixed up and in a state of flex. Life is like that.

The family in the book was upper middle-class folks living in a great neighborhood. God calls them to sell everything and move to the other side of the globe. During the yearlong process of selling off everything, a revelation hits. All the stuff* they possessed, was just that, stuff. The amount of time and energy that went into buying it seemed like such a waste as they sold it. (*Stuff is a technical term meaning, bits, and pieces, things, possessions, or whatever else I want it to mean in this article.)

For Our Consideration

Garage/estate sales will provide a reality check like little else. The items we just had to have or our life would be ruined, are now being sold for a quarter. Tools, books, pictures, toys, gadgets, and just about anything else can be purchased at these sales for pennies. Makes you think, doesn't it?

The important items in our lives are not composed of our stuff, but our relationships. We have a relationship with our Heavenly Father, our Lord Jesus, and the Holy Spirit. Our spouse, children, and grandchildren are people that we know and love. Even at our job or ministry, most times it is very relationship-centric. We work with people, interact with them, sell to them, buy from them, and in general, are never very far away from someone.

Stuff, on the other hand, is just that, impersonal, maybe pretty, comfy, high-tech, shiny and nice, but still just something we use and eventually dispose of stuff.

What should we be investing our time and energy into then? I think the order above is correct. We must do whatever we can to reorder our lives to have time to spend with our Heavenly Father. We must make time in our lives to read and enjoy His Word. We must seek to know Him, and grow in our love of Him. This is our first and primary goal for all else pales in comparison. Loving God is the great and first commandment and we demonstrate our love with time.

Our families should be next. If we are married, our spouse should be a top priority. If children come along, we must invest time and effort into developing a relationship. These primary relationships are going to last a lifetime. They deserve time and effort.

The same is true with our church families. We have the same Dad. We are brothers and sisters and we will spend all of eternity together. We must learn how to get along and to live in unity. Like most

## Discussion Starters

families, arguing and fussing will take place. We are family though, and we will work through it. We must, for those outside the Family are observing our behavior.

We must also do a good job working and serving, for the Scripture tells us to work as unto the Lord. Work is not our Lord, and it is a lower priority than the others are, but we still must work. We are made in the image of God and God is not lazy. He calls each of us to work to further the Kingdom of His Beloved Son. We work to serve and work to eat. We do not worship work or destroy the higher relationships for the sake of work. Work is a means to an end and not the end. Relationships are the end.

For the record, I am not opposed to stuff. I like stuff. Nice stuff is, well, nice, but it still is just stuff. We all know that stuff is all going to burn. Even if we die before the end of the earth, we know that all the stuff we accumulate will eventually end up in a garage or estate sale and someone else will buy our stuff for pennies.

So, what we should we live for then? What should we invest in with our time and money? What should be the priority? Well, not stuff, but God and people would by my answer. What would you say?

For Our Consideration

## Questions to Ponder or Discuss:

1. Is God opposed to the accumulation of stuff? Explain.

2. Do you agree or disagree with the order listed at the start of this article? Why?

3. What is your view regarding the importance of relationships?

4. Why do you think Jesus picked money to contrast two masters in Matthew 6:24? Explain.

# Suffering and Faith

I was speaking with a couple of young men in my office and the topic of suffering came up. Really, it was more a conversation surrounding why God allows such things in His creation. The philosophers love to discuss this subject and often issue a forced choice set of presuppositions that goes something like this.

> God is either not all-powerful or He is not all-loving (good) for He cannot be both. If God were all-powerful, He would stop or remove all evil (suffering). If He were all- loving (good), He would not allow suffering (evil). Since there is suffering (evil) in the world, He is either not all-powerful or not all-loving (good).

On the surface, this "logic" seems sound for why would a supreme, all-knowing, all-powerful, all-loving God allow malignant cancer in His universe. If God is God, then He could simply banish it, forbid it, or remove it; He did none of these.

God chose to allow humans free will and with that choice, came the consequences of their choices. God did not make us robots and He does not make us love Him. It is a choice. God could have done anything He wanted but He did not choose to follow the "logic" of the philosophers. God chose otherwise.

The point of this writing is not to definitively answer the charge of the philosophers but to answer another question connected to it. For those who are interested, and are not daunted by a large book, Randy

## For Our Consideration

Alcorn has written an excellent response to these guys entitled, *"If God is Good: Faith in the Midst of Suffering and Evil."*

Where my thoughts went because of my discussion with these young men is to the concept of faith. "Without faith, it is impossible to please God," states Hebrews 11:6. Faith is an interesting concept and a wonderful topic of study. With faith, we can please God, quench the fiery darts of the enemy and move mountains. Without it, we cannot please the One that we should desire to please the most.

Hebrews 11:1 clearly tells us what faith is - "Now faith is the assurance of things hoped for, the conviction of things not seen." I love the word hope - "the earnest expectation of good." Whatever may befall me, I have hope. God is good and He will turn whatever happens into something good. At least according to His plan and purposes, which most times are way beyond my understanding, but I know it will be good because I have faith.

There are many things I cannot see with my eyes, but I am convinced that they are real. I can't see air, electricity, the earth's rotation, and atoms, yet I know they exist. I have not seen God, yet I know He exists. I have faith, and faith sustains me, even in times of suffering and evil. When everything crashes around me, I have faith. When the enemy attacks with a full onslaught, I have faith. When people disappoint, friends betray, health fails, and all manner of evil abounds, I have faith.

This is not blind optimism, for those that know me well know that is not exactly a strong suit of mine. I tend to be somewhat pessimistic, okay, Eeyore and Puddleglum are my heroes, but I will save that story for another time. Faith is different from being optimistic. I know everything will work out for the best according to God's plan because I know God. I know God's Word and it is true, therefore I am not blindly hoping things will work out, I know they will even if I suffer and die.

To be transparent, faith is not always my initial response. My emotions are not totally under the Lordship of Christ, I just have not matured to the place where I immediately rejoice when suffering and trials hit.

I know what the Scriptures state regarding such things but my mind often interferes with my faith. For me, faith is a process. After the initial reaction, I calm down and remember, call to mind as the bible states, and I come to a place of rest. God is faithful. God is just. God is love. God is all-powerful. God is all-wise. God is all-knowing. God is all-powerful. God is. Since these are true, and I know that He loves me, I can move to a position of faith.

While living on planet earth we will have trials and hardships, suffering and pain, longing and loss. We will also have a measure of joy and pleasure, but all of it is prep work for eternity. We are citizens of another country. We serve another King. We are bound for another city, a heavenly one. In this, I have great faith.

By the way, there are multiple presuppositions in the philosopher's forced choices above and we must learn how to recognize them when we encounter them so we are not swayed by them. Just because someone presents us with a forced choice, that does not mean we should take one of them. Their choices may be completely wrong, to begin with, and thus invalid. In this case, these learned folks are adamantly implying many conclusions that they cannot possibly know.

For Our Consideration

## Questions to Ponder or Discuss:

1. Why do think God allows suffering?

2. What does faith mean to you?

3. Why does God value faith so much?

4. Is there a difference between faith and optimism?

Discussion Starters

# The First Sin?

> But godliness with contentment is great gain, for we brought nothing into the world, and we cannot take anything out of the world. But if we have food and clothing, with these we will be content. 1 Timothy 6:7-8

Many theologians argue over what the first sin was committed in God's universe. Was it Eve eating the fruit or Adam standing there not stopping her? Or was it Satan, formerly Lucifer being filled up with pride and losing his high position as the angel most likely in charge of worship? While we do not really know all the timing issues, and there are excellent arguments on all sides, I would like to explore another possibility.

Discontentment must rank up there high on the early sins in the universe. Lucifer was not content with his place and wanted God's, and Adam and Eve wanted more knowledge than God had allowed them to have, thus they ignored God's commandment.

At the root of most sinful choices is discontentment. Greed - I am not content with what I have so I must have more. Lust - I am not satisfied with my spouse, singleness, or how my needs are being met so I must have more. Envy, anger, being absorbed with self, disobedience, and just about any sin can be tied directly or indirectly to discontentment.

Think about those children of Israel wandering around in the desert...what was at the root of their problems - complaining about God's miraculous provision. The Scripture says that their shoes did not wear out and neither did their clothes. (Deuteronomy 8:4) This

## For Our Consideration

multitude awoke each day and had angel food cake...ok, manna, but it was still food from heaven. Here is one scary verse:

> And the people spoke against God and against Moses, "Why have you brought us up out of Egypt to die in the wilderness? For there is no food and no water, and we loathe this worthless food." Numbers 21:5

"Loathe this worthless food???" Miracles were witnessed every day. Supernatural food and water were received and the visible presence of God displayed in either a cloud or pillar of fire, yet discontentment reigned. How easy it is to slip into complaining instead of being thankful and what a dramatic difference it makes when we do so.

I understand that there are complicated issues associated with many marriage problems for example, but once we begin to entertain discontentment, they are greatly compounded. If we begin to think about our lot in life from a non-Biblical viewpoint, we will quickly begin to be dissatisfied. Once we move from thankfulness to complaining we are heading down the wrong path and destruction is on its way.

Statements like, "Why can't you be like..." or "I wish I had done..." or "If only I had..." typically end up on the wrong side of contentment. Comparing our spouse to an illusion in the media or to someone else's spouse will lead to not fully appreciating the gift God gave us. If we are married, we took vows and promised to love the other person until death. Given the rampant divorce rate among born-again Christians, something is amiss.

What usually happens is we do not take our thoughts captive to the obedience of Christ and we begin to enter discontentment. Once we walk down this path the only way back is to quit complaining and begin to give thanks to our God. Sure, things will still be messy, but complaining never helps anything and giving thanks to God always does.

"Godliness with contentment is great gain," Paul stated. What is discontentment then except the doorway to great loss and further ungodliness? Paul furthered stated that there is a secret that each of us must learn –

> Not that I am speaking of being in need, for I have learned in whatever situation I am to be content. I know how to be brought low, and I know how to abound. In any and every circumstance, I have learned the secret of facing plenty and hunger, abundance and need. I can do all things through him who strengthens me. Philippians 4:11-13

Giving thanks instead of complaining is a choice. Being content is a learned behavior that is based on our view of God, His sovereignty, and the Scripture. What comes out of our mouth is always birthed in our brain and what is in our brain needs to be filtered through the Word of God. We can do all things through Christ who strengthens us! We can even put away complaining and start being thankful. Today, right now, immediately, quickly...

I have not settled the debate as to the first sin in God's creation, but I know what is typically behind my sins, discontentment. How about yours?

For Our Consideration

## Questions to Ponder or Discuss:

1. What do you think was the first sin?

2. Why is it so easy to be discontent?

3. How does being discontent destroy a marriage?

4. Why is giving thanks a remedy for discontentment?

Discussion Starters

# What is Forgiveness?

Forgiveness is a gift from our Heavenly Father. We forgive others because we are forgiven. Jesus told many stories about forgiveness. One of Jesus' key men was Peter. We know from the Bible that Peter struggled with both anger and unforgiveness. When Jesus was being arrested in the garden on the night He was betrayed, Peter is the one that swung the sword at a man's head. He missed, and only cut off an ear, but the intent was clear.

Peter also had a problem with forgiveness. In Matthew 18, Jesus tells His followers how to confront sin and to gain restoration. After Peter heard these words, he asks Jesus a question. "Lord, how often will my brother sin against me, and I forgive him? As many as seven times?" Peter thought he was being generous with the unheard number of seven times. Jesus' answer was as shocking then as now - "I do not say to you seven times, seventy times seven."

To further illustrated His point, Jesus tells the story of the unforgiving servant. While the details are important, what really should shock us is the punch line to the story. "So also, My heavenly Father will do to every one of you, if you do not forgive your brother from your heart." What will Jesus' Father do? Turn everyone over to the torturers until they pay every penny of their debt if they refuse to forgive!

To forgive means we release, let go of, and set people free from the debt they owe us. Jesus did this for us freely, and we must do so for others.

Are there benefits to forgiving others? If avoiding torture is not enough, then how about being Christ-like? Jesus forgave, and so must we. In addition, we receive grace when we forgive others. The Golden Rule states "Do unto others as you would have them do unto you." I want forgiveness when I mess up, so I must give it first.

Forgiveness leads to freedom and unforgiveness leads to bitterness. Have you ever been around someone that is angry and bitter? Did you wonder how they became so? Somewhere in their past, they would not forgive. As they nursed that hurt or deed that was done against them, it grew. Each time they pulled it out and went over it in their mind it grew and became worse. As the years went by the deed became huge. Eventually, bitterness consumes the one who refuses to forgive. After being consumed by unforgiveness, our words change. So, do our actions. We began to be hard, cynical, critical, and just unpleasant to be around. We do not have to become bitter but we will if we refuse to forgive others as we have been forgiven.

How can parents teach their children to forgive others? Children catch what we are, and not only what we tell them. We must model forgiveness to our children if they are to learn how to forgive. We must learn how to say we are sorry first if we hope to instruct our children in how to do it.

Children listen to everything. When mom and dad are being unkind or unforgiving, the children know it. What do the little ones around us hear coming out of our mouths as parents? As we talk on the phone to someone, what do the children hear? If we walk around grousing all day about someone that hurt us, what do we think our children will do when they are offended? If we wonder how we sound then listen to our children playing. Observe what they are saying and then realize where they first heard it. Ouch.

Parents need to be around to observe their children's behavior and hear their words if they are going to able to offer correction. As we hear

## Discussion Starters

our children speak of wounds, anger, bitterness, unforgiveness, we must take them back to how much we have been forgiven by Jesus. We did not deserve it, and neither does the one that hurt you, but we must forgive. We are forgiven and we must forgive. There is no substitution for talking and modeling with our children. We cannot, must not delegate this away to someone else.

People often say, "You can forgive but never forget." Is this true? God does not have amnesia and neither do we. God promises to forget our sin but it is a willful choice He makes. We must do the same. In most of our lives, there is pain, offenses, and deeds done by those that wrong us. We can choose to forgive people, but we will not soon forget what happened.

Forgiveness is not a one time choice, but every time choice. When someone has abused us, hurt us, abandoned us, or betrayed us, our brain records the event just like a cut or bruise in our bodies. We will heal, but deep wounds leave scars. We can forget many of the details, but most of us will not forget that we suffered pain.

What we must guard against is becoming bitter over the wounds. Scars take time to heal and forgiveness does not remove the pain.

But, what does forgiveness in practice look like? Forgiveness is a choice of our will. A battered spouse can forgive her attacker but the bruises will remain for quite some time. A willful choice is made to forgive because we know we are also guilty of many sins. We can and should flee an abusive situation but we must not make it worse by becoming bitter over it. Bitterness is never an appropriate response. Forgiveness always is.

For Our Consideration

Jesus died for us, loved us, and forgave us before we asked or even knew we needed it. We must do the same to those that hurt and offend us. Freely we have received, freely we give. I am not denying the pain endured, we just do not need to go through it repeatedly by embracing it. Forgiveness leads to freedom, and not forgiving, well, that leads to more pain.

## Questions to Ponder or Discuss:

1. Why is forgiveness such a big deal to God?

2. Does God really mean that He will do to us as we do unto others? Explain.

3. Does God really mean He won't forgive us if we won't forgive those that have sinned against us? Explain.

4. Is there anyone that you need to forgive? Will you do so?

Discussion Starters

# If - A Huge Word

Some of us struggle with forgiveness and restoration for ourselves and in extending it towards others as freely as God seems to give it. God freely forgives/restores us:

> If we confess our sins He is faithful and just to forgive us our sins and to cleanse us from all unrighteousness. 1 John 1:9

The word "if" starts the sentence in our English translation and is critical to the discussion. Jesus died to provide forgiveness for sins, but our personal application begins with "if we confess…" The movement for cheap grace and "sloppy agape" is not new. Paul, the champion of grace, was dealing with this issue in Romans 6:1-2 when he stated:

> What shall we say then? Are we to continue in sin that grace may abound? By no means! How can we who died to sin still live in it?

Repentance, forgiveness, and restoration are tied together. Repentance is the turning away from sinful actions and lifestyle and turning towards a godly one. Repent and be baptized, repent for the Kingdom of God is hand, repent and confess, repent or perish, and dozens of other such references sprinkle the New Testament. Confession and repentance is a choice and a requirement to receive both forgiveness and restoration.

While I do not pretend to understand everything here, this verse in Hebrews certainly means something:

> For if we go on sinning deliberately after receiving the knowledge of the truth, there no longer remains a sacrifice for sins, but a fearful expectation of judgment, and a fury of fire that will consume the adversaries. Hebrews 10:26-27

There are those that seem to think that they can live in sin without any consequences. Lying, immorality, cheating, stealing, rebellion to authority, gossip, and a host of other sins, and they simply say, "I am under grace." This is a scary place to be in my opinion, and I am certainly not referring to these folks when I speak of freely restoring fallen brothers and sisters.

Peter has some choice words for those who practice and teach what is false in 2 Peter 2. I will not quote the whole chapter, but certainly could. Consider these thoughts though:

> 2:2 – And many will follow their sensuality, and because of them the way of truth will be blasphemed. (What we practice speaks of what we believe.)

> 2:12-14 – But these, like irrational animals, creatures of instinct, born to be caught and destroyed, blaspheming about matters of which they are ignorant, will also be destroyed in their destruction, suffering wrong as the wage for their wrongdoing. They count it pleasure to revel in the daytime. They are blots and blemishes, reveling in their deceptions, while they feast with you. They have eyes full of adultery, insatiable for sin. They entice unsteady souls. They have

hearts trained in greed. Accursed children! (They were present in the Church.)

2:18-19 – For, speaking loud boasts of folly, they entice by sensual passions of the flesh those who are barely escaping from those who live in error. They promise them freedom, but they themselves are slaves of corruption. For whatever overcomes a person, to that he is enslaved.

Peter goes on and says that it would have been better for them not to be born! Harsh words, or perhaps not.

Giving into sensuality, boasting, adultery, immorality, pride, and all manner of corruption, and justifying the behavior by saying that I am under grace is clearly false teaching and insulting to the sacrifice of Jesus. The people Peter was referring to were part of the church for they attended the love feasts and are referred to as children, which is a family term. Yet, they lived as false teachers and presented a false picture of freedom in Christ.

Jesus died because of my sin, and to free me from its power, not so I could keep on living in it under the claim that I live in grace. I am free in Christ, but not to sin; I am free to walk in purity, holiness, love of others, and submission to authority, death to myself, and a host of other such freedoms. Nowhere in Scripture will you find that we are now free to live in sin because of the blood of Jesus Christ. That is a perversion of the grace of God poured out for us by the sacrifice of our Lord.

John the beloved apostle of love states it clearly:

> He is the propitiation for our sins, and not for ours only but also for the sins of the whole world. And by this we know that

## For Our Consideration

> we have come to know him, if we keep his commandments. Whoever says "I know him" but does not keep his commandments is a liar, and the truth is not in him. 1 John 2:2-4

The next time someone living in overt, unrepentant sin tells me they are under grace, I guess I will just tell them they are a liar like John the apostle of love says, and go from there...BTW – if you are reading this and living in blatant, unrepentant sin, the Word of God is clear -confess and repent, and you will find cleansing, forgiveness, and restoration.

## Questions to Ponder or Discuss:

1. Does God really mean the word "if" in the verses quoted?

2. Why does God forgive us our sins yet often does not remove the consequences of those choices?

3. Is it possible for a Christian to really bring shame to the name of Christ? Why or why not?

4. Why is repentance mentioned so often in the New Testament and why does it matter if we are under grace?

Discussion Starters

# How Should a Christian "Dress"?

The Bible is very specific on how a Christian should dress. I am not writing about how we clothe our bodies, but how we clothe our inner man.

> All of you, clothe yourselves with humility toward one another, because, "God opposes the proud but gives grace to the humble. 1 Peter 5:5 (All verses are NIV)

> Therefore, as God's chosen people, holy and dearly loved, clothe yourselves with compassion, kindness, humility, gentleness and patience. Bear with each other and forgive whatever grievances you may have against one another. Forgive as the Lord forgave you. And over all these virtues put on (clothe) love, which binds them all together in perfect unity. Colossians 3:12-14

> You were taught, with regard to your former way of life, to put off (unclothe) your old self, which is being corrupted by its deceitful desires; to be made new in the attitude of your minds; and to put on (clothe) the new self, created to be like God in true righteousness and holiness. Ephesians 4:22-24

> Put on (clothe) the full armor of God... Ephesians 6:11

For Our Consideration

We have a free will. We can decide how we want to dress. We will decide what type of "clothing" our inner man wears. Will we be clothed with humility, kindness, compassion, gentleness, patience, and love, or something else? What will people "see" when they spend time with us? What will people remember from spending time with us? What "fragrance" will people remember when our time with them is through?

> But thanks be to God, who always leads us in triumphal procession in Christ and through us spreads everywhere the fragrance of the knowledge of Him. For we are to God the aroma of Christ among those who are being saved and those who are perishing. To the one we are the smell of death; to the other, the fragrance of life. 2 Corinthians 2:14-16

People remember what we look like, "smell like," and sound like. Our lives should reflect Christ. Our words and actions should create a hunger and thirst for Christ in those we meet. We need the grace of God to help us obey Him and to do His will. Our desire must always be to be pleasing to our Lord in everything we say and do.

As we pray and seek the Lord about how to get "dressed" each day, ask Him to help you pick out the right clothes. For example, the garment of praise, the belt of truth, and the overcoat of love. Try picking one area that you lack the most, and focus on that one for a week. If compassion is lacking, ask God to help you put on (clothe) a heart of compassion towards someone that day. Ask God to bring someone into your life that you could show compassion to today.

I have learned that most of the time God provides the opportunities to demonstrate these qualities within the walls of our own homes. Ask God to open your eyes to see how to get "dressed" properly at home first. God has placed within your sphere of influence everyone needed to help you mature in your dressing habits. You can choose what you wear each day, pick wisely!

## Questions to Ponder or Discuss:

1. Why do you think the apostles in this article use clothing as an illustration in their writing?

2. Does it really matter how we treat others? Why or why not?

3. What does Paul mean when he states we are a fragrance?

4. How do we gain more compassion, humility, etc.?

For Our Consideration

# I'm Balanced, but I am not so Sure about You!

Have you ever noticed how often we think we are right about something, only to find out later we are dead wrong? We all tend to think we are right about almost everything, for who willingly clings to a false opinion or view? Our opinions are not opinions, but facts. If everyone would just see it my way, we could all get along just fine. Many of us believe, whether we are aware of it or not, that we are balanced and everyone else is either right or left of us. We, our thoughts and opinions, become the defining definition of what is balanced, and therefore correct.

If everyone thought and acted just like me, then wouldn't life be just peachy. Instead of embracing the differences in marriage and relationships, we become frustrated because not everyone is like us and we fuss and argue about the differences. If they would just change, (think and act as I do) everything would be fine.

What is true today was also true in Jesus' day. The story is told of how denominations really started, though this cannot be verified and perhaps involves some stretching of the facts.

Some friends brought a blind man to Jesus to be healed. Jesus asked him "Do you believe that I am able to do this?" After the man answered yes, Jesus then gave them the formula to get blind eyes healed, "According to your faith will it be done to you," Jesus said. Then Jesus touched his eyes and they were opened. All those watching the miracle then "knew" how this eye healing stuff works. You say the formula and place your hands on his eyes. Thus, "The

## Discussion Starters

laying on of hands to heal blind people by the formula ministry" was birthed.

Sometime later, other people brought another blind man to Jesus. Jesus gave them the formula of spitting on this man's eyes and placing His hands on him and the man's eyes were opened. Those who watched now knew the correct formula to open blind eyes. Thus, "The spitting in the eyes of blind people so they can be healed society" was birthed.

Still later, a third blind man was brought to Jesus by another set of folks. Those watching saw the "Spitting on the ground and making mud to heal eyes club" being birthed.

From this day on the three camps were at odds with each other. Camp A would say, "The only proper way to heal blind eyes is by repeating the specific words of our Lord and placing your hands on the blind person's eyes." "No, no, no," says camp B, "The only spiritual way to heal blind eyes is by spitting in their eyes, any other way is of the devil." Camp C was shouting by this time, "You must spit on the ground, what kind of insensitive person would spit in the eyes of a poor blind person?" And, the fighting has been going on for two thousand years…

Ridiculous, you say, that does not happen today, you mutter, but all of us spend time in camps. It may not be how to heal blind eyes, but what about these camps: Worship styles, TV/entertainment standards, dating/courtship, types of education for our children, how we dress, speak, use our spare time, how we minister, evangelize, how many children we may or may not have, where we go for vacation, how we spend our money, what type of house we live in, hair length, whether we like sports or not, how we pray, which translation is correct, preaching styles, and the list could go on forever.

## For Our Consideration

Estimates regarding how many denominations there are that share space on the planet range between 3,000-42,000 depending on the source. Wouldn't it be logical that each would probably believe that they are balanced and the preferred one or they would not be in it?

Inherent in holding strong opinions is that we believe we are right in holding them or we would not keep on holding them. If we believe we are right, then it is just the next step in assuming that anyone that does not hold our view must be wrong, or at least not as informed as we are.

But, I am right in my opinions and everyone else is entitled to it, we joke, but when will we stop exceeding what is written in the Scripture and start obeying it instead? There are countless areas that we overstep our limits regarding each other in which we have no business doing so. God is very creative and is not limited to our opinions of how someone else's life should be lived. We are commanded to love one another and leave the perfecting of one another to God.

If you have matured in some fashion and others around you have not, perhaps God is not working in this area in their life. Maybe God has placed a higher priority with them on other issues. Maybe, you needed that growth sooner than they did. The truth is we don't know and it really is not our business. I am not referring to sin issues. If sin is involved, we have clear instructions on how to deal with the sin. I am referring to the thousands of non-sinful choices that we make as individuals following Christ.

When we can move to appreciating the differences in each other instead of criticizing them, we will be maturing in Christ. Jesus could heal in many ways, and one was not right and the others wrong. Jesus could love a wide variety of people from all walks of life, they did not all have to be the same. The only requirement He gave was to follow Him as Lord and to learn to love one another. We would all benefit by memorizing the following Scripture:

> Who are you to judge someone else's servant? To his own Master he stands or falls. And he will stand, for the Lord is able to make him stand. Romans 14:4 (NIV)

Let us quit knocking the legs out from under each other by criticizing and putting each other down. Instead, let us help one another stand firm in the grace of our Lord Jesus until the day He returns or we go home!

Holding strong views and convictions is not the problem, believing that everyone else is wrong who does not agree with us is. After all, there is more than one way to heal a blind man!

## Questions to Ponder or Discuss:

1. How many strong opinions do we hold and how many do others hold that disagree with us?

2. If we are right in our views doesn't that make everyone else wrong that disagrees with us? Why or why not?

3. Why is it wrong to judge others? Is there ever a time when it is right to judge?

4. Why does God allow Christians to disagree over so many issues?

# Family

"A man ought to live so that everybody knows he is a Christian… and most of all, his family ought to know." Dwight L. Moody

# Generational Ripples

"Beloved, let us not grow weary in well doing," was written long ago by a man that knew Love Himself. An obvious question should be, "why not?" It is tiring to do well. It is often frustrating to "do unto others" and not do "to" others. Why should I turn the other cheek simply to be slapped on it? The way of Jesus is sometimes hard.

One aspect to consider is that each time we obey the above commands from Jesus we open the door to miracles. Really? That seems like an overstatement. What is a miracle anyway? A working definition for me is the supernatural breaking into the natural. Of course, the parting of the Red Sea, healing disease and raising the dead are miracles, but to obey? Doing well and not growing weary? Treating people, the way they should be treated, and not as they treated us? Miracles?

Each of our lives are made up of daily, minute by minute decisions. We decide how we will spend our time, where we will go, what we will wear, how we will speak, and how we will respond to others. We have a choice to not return evil for evil, to repay wicked behavior with kindness or to endure quietly the unkindness of people. We are not victims. We may be victimized by someone, but we are not victims. We have a choice of what we do with what has been done to us.

One way to help us answer my opening questions is to use a familiar picture. Almost everyone has thrown a stone into a pond or watched a drop of water fall into a container and noticed the ripple effect. The object lands in the water and creates a splash. From the initial entry point, ripples go out in all directions. Depending on the

## For Our Consideration

size of the body of water receiving the rock or object thrown into it, the ripples can go for a long distance or double back quickly.

I would suggest that every action we take causes ripples. What we say and how we say it causes a ripple. How we respond or how we do not, does the same. An act of kindness creates a ripple and so does anger. How far and wide the ripples expand depend on the circumstances and those involved.

Some of us are still living with the ripple effect of another's actions or words decades earlier. Others have just begun to feel the wave. What we say and do will make a splash. We will not be able to control the ripples or bring them back once released.

While there are negative ripples like anger, hatred, abuse, neglect, and such, there are also positive ones. When we do an act of kindness. When we hold back a harsh word and speak life and love instead. When we go out of our way to be gracious, patient, tender, comforting, and generous. When we act like Jesus instead of ourselves, we unleash ripples.

The waves released by walking in obedience to our Lord can and will produce lasting fruit. The problem we face is lack of information. We cannot see the result of our actions or words, but there is One Who does. God knows the outcome of every word, action, inaction and even intention. God knows and completely understands the entire ripple effect and that is amazing.

What we do today will affect someone generations from now. What we say to our spouse, child, friend or a stranger will create a ripple. An act of kindness can impact someone hundreds of years into the future in ways we cannot even begin to comprehend.

The other side is also true. An act of hatred, harsh words, crippling mental games, abuse or neglect can hinder someone for decades and even alter how they interact with their children and grandchildren. How many adults do we know that are still trying to live up to their parent's expectations? How many are still living in fear, doubt, worry or dealing with regrets from what they may have endured while children?

How many times have we heard that we are just like our parents? Many of us have said, "I am becoming just like my mother or father." That may be a good thing, or not, but it is almost always true in some fashion. Each of us is a product of all of those that went before us. Our lives are not lived in a vacuum but in conjunction with history. Billions of decisions were made by millions of people and every one of them matter.

No matter how far back you trace your ancestry you will find that there are people that have a direct influence on who you are today. Decisions made by distant relatives determined your physical attributes, your location on the globe, and many of your inherited tendencies. We are all a product of other's ripples.

Many argue over whether there are accidents or if everything is already planned. The answer is we don't know. Perhaps. God only knows. What does seem clear is that we seem to have a choice in many matters. We decide to speak or to be quiet. We decide to go somewhere or not to go. We decide to entertain bitterness, anger, and hate, or we choose to go another direction with our personal pain.

Maybe it is all foreordained and we don't know it. Maybe we really don't have any say and all is already predetermined and we are simply walking it out. Maybe. Life and the Scriptures seem to state something else. We have a choice and are given commands to follow or not to follow.

For Our Consideration

## Questions to Ponder or Discuss:

1. Do I agree or disagree with the long-lasting impact of my life as discussed in this article?

2. Am I living out ripples from my parents? If you are aware of them, how?

3. Is it possible to change the ripples that I am sending out daily? How?

4. What does "God being in control" mean to me?

# Generational Faith Impartation

For a couple of years, I enjoyed a roundtable discussion with some excellent brothers in the Lord. This live radio show included a guest in addition to our regular panel. Recently we had the privilege of talking to a man that has dedicated his life to serving families through the Awana program.

For over forty years this man and his bride have been deeply involved in trying to help families engraft Scripture into their hearts and minds through the Awana ministry. The Awana program is an internationally known ministry that features many innovative ideas for accomplishing this task.

What struck me during this conversation was a statement that this dear saint made. He quoted a study conducted by the group to see how many of their young people are staying in the faith after graduation. Many church-wide studies point to a dismal failure, but not theirs. If a child will stay in the program, and their parents are involved with them, they are experiencing a 90% success rate. Here is the actual quote from the Awana website:

> "For years leaders have recognized that kids who do the best in Awana programs have help at home. A recent Awana® alumni study shows not only that, but also over 90 percent of those Awana kids still attend church at least once a week as adults!"

## For Our Consideration

Awana, for the first time, is now offering their program for homeschool families because they see the direct correlation between parental involvement and the successful transference of faith from one generation to the next.

My Ph.D. dissertation was entitled, "*A Biblical Analysis of the Roles of the Family and the Church Regarding Faith Impartation.*" One must have a long title when writing these things. My hypothesis was that the more the parents are involved the better chance you will have to be successful in imparting faith generationally. The Awana study seems to confirm this.

Part of my research included studies by Brian D. Ray, Ph.D. Dr. Ray has interviewed over nine thousand home educated children that are now adults living on their own. His conclusions were like what the Awana study found. While many in the traditional church are losing 70-90% of their young people in the first year of college, this group was retaining their parent's faith system in over 90% of the cases. Hmmm.

Many years ago, I was having a discussion along these lines with a Christian school administrator. This man had dedicated his life to helping students and as we chatted, he said something very insightful. While the direct quote eludes me, it went along the lines of - it really does not matter what method of education someone chooses for their children, what matters is parental involvement. Are we seeing a pattern here?

I know there are families that are messed up and there are children that do not have their parents intact. However, for those that do, parental involvement seems to be critical to faith impartation. Christian marriages are falling apart and the next generation pays a huge price tag when they do. Perhaps that is why the enemy of our soul works so hard to destroy the basic family structure. If parental involvement is a key to faith transference it is not a huge jump to state the other side - parental neglect impedes it.

Even our world system seems to understand the principle. "Parents, the anti-drug," and "Do you know where your children are right now" campaigns have flooded the TV airwaves paid for by our tax dollars. Why? Homework is given by teachers and students are encouraged to enlist their parents to help them. Why? In extreme school cases, parents are even brought into the classroom to help the teacher. Why?

Maybe what the Awana group, Dr. Ray, and even our humanistic society realize is that God was correct all along. The family unit is the best possible place to reach the children. The family structure, when intact, presents the highest and best opportunity to shape the future generation. God put it this way:

> Love the LORD your God with all your heart and with all your soul and with all your strength. These commandments that I give you today are to be upon your hearts. Impress them on your children. Talk about them when you sit at home and when you walk along the road, when you lie down and when you get up. Tie them as symbols on your hands and bind them on your foreheads. Write them on the doorframes of your houses and on your gates. Deuteronomy 6:5-9

As parents, we have a wonderful opportunity to shape the next generation. Will we seize it or will we squander it away? As a father of adult children, I can testify to the fact that the time of direct influence we have is fleeting. The children grow up quickly and soon just come over occasionally to visit with their own children in tow. We can still

## For Our Consideration

influence but not like when they were living in our home. We must seize the time we still have, to make a difference.

Whatever you choose to do with your time I pray that your family will take large amounts of it. Invest wisely for you can only spend the time once. God will redeem and He will forgive but God does not recreate time for us. I pray that we will invest in the things that matter the most.

If your home is already broken and you are a single parent the job remains the same. Invest whatever time you have left with your children to help them deal with the pain and heartache they endure. Divorce is not the unpardonable sin but the consequences of it impact the children in deep ways. The children need the parent's time even more after the trauma of divorce, not less. God will give you grace and strength to walk through these days.

Draw near to Him and He promises to draw near to you. God loves you and your children. Spend time with them and make sure they know that as well.

## Questions to Ponder or Discuss:

1. Why is it important for parents to help teach their children?

2. Why do you think the statistics are so poor on faith impartation to the next generation?

3. Why do you think the devil seems to hate marriage so much?

4. What changes could be considered in your life to help strengthen your marriage, family and other relationships?

For Our Consideration

# Choose Your Friends Wisely

> He who walks with the wise grows wise, but a companion of fools suffers harm. Proverbs 13:20

If you are concerned about whom your children run with, you have probably been accused of being overprotective. Well, we are protective, but are we overprotective? Are we supposed to be under protective? It seems to me that one of our jobs is to ensure that our children (or our spouses or we!) do not have fools for companions.

There is a real enemy who hates you and your family. His mission is to destroy you any way he can, through any means possible. One of the oldest tricks in the book is to add a fool to your family. A fool is not a simpleton or someone with a low IQ, but someone who says there is no God, or does not honor God with his or her lifestyle. The Devil will try to lead you astray through the company you keep or allow the members of your household to keep.

Paul said in I Cor. 15:33 "Do not be misled: Bad company corrupts good morals or character." There is a price to pay for allowing a "fool" into your family's life. We must be careful whom we allow our children to associate with. Our children are so impressionable. We need to know who is making the impression, and what that impression is!

Should you allow your child to spend the night with someone? How long should I allow my child out of my sight without checking on him? We should be constantly watching for bad attitudes? If I see an attitude problem, should I find out where it came from? These questions and hundreds more should go through your mind as a parent. God will hold us responsible for the influences we allow into our children's lives from TV, books, electronic devices, or friends.

The friends we should encourage our children to be with are those who will challenge them to walk with the Lord. Friends, who will pull them up to a higher calling, not drag them down into mediocrity. Our children need good role models, godly role models who reinforce what we are teaching them at home, not "friends" who tell them "your parents are so weird," or "your parents are so strict," etc.

Choosing whom you interact with on a regular basis can be one of the most important decisions you ever make! A wise man will hang around with wise men and will become still wiser. A fool will hang around with fools, and sink even further.

I've often said, "the big difference between a child who avoids trouble and the child who ends up in trouble, is one word, supervision."

When we make a commitment to be actively involved in the lives of our children, we are on our way to success. We must know whom our children are with and the results of being with them. For example:

- What type of influence are they?
- Do they encourage my children to respect me, or reject my authority?
- Do they encourage them to walk with the Lord, or to try the "forbidden fruit"?
- When I do allow my children to spend the night, how's their attitude when the return?
- Does it require hours of "deprogramming"
- Did they watch movies and do activities that I would not have approved of if it was in my home?

For Our Consideration

    All of this may seem like too much bother, but the stakes are incredibly high! Our children are at risk. We are given the task to see to it that they choose wisely, and make good friends. Bad company will corrupt good morals. It rarely works the other way around!

    Proverbs 27:23 - "Know well the condition of your flocks." I believe this applies to our families. We need to be involved enough to see the dangers and hide our families and ourselves. We need to see the influences in our children's lives and help them make the correct decision. If we pay the price now and help them make good decisions when they are young, we will save ourselves (and them!) much grief when they are older.

    Proverbs 29:15 - "A child left to himself will bring shame to his mother." We do not have to do much to fail as parents. Just leave our children alone. We must help them choose correctly until they are able to choose on their own.

    Let's see to it that our children do not walk with fools, but with the wise. Then they will be wise when they grow up and can train their children to be wise after them.

## Questions to Ponder or Discuss:

1. Are we too busy to be involved in the details of our children's lives? Does that make us too busy?

2. Does God really mean that we can become a fool by the people we choose to hang around with? Does this apply to our children?

3. On the other hand, can we really gain wisdom by choosing friends that are wise? Why or why not?

4. How do you define supervision and why does it even matter?

For Our Consideration

# Is God in a Hurry?

If I had a complaint against the Bible and I don't, but if I did, it would be because of all the gaps. Have you ever noticed how long there is between some verses? For example, in Gen. 16:16 Abraham is 86 years old and in the next verse, he is 99 -a 13-year span that we know nothing about. What about Joseph, who was in prison for many, many years but his time there, is covered in just a few verses? Judges and Kings fly by covering centuries of time, yet we are often given just a glimpse. Entire lives are sometimes given in a verse or two.

What we forget (at least I do) sometimes is that the Bible is full of real people with real lives. Sometimes we are given detail into their lives and other times not. Even those we think we know a great deal about, we really don't. Moses' life spans 120 years and we only see snippets of it. Abraham, David, even Jesus we are given just a glimpse. Just the highlights. What I wonder about is all the time we don't know about. What were they doing?

The Bible is full of many heroes. Great leaders, mighty men of war, women who saved entire nations, shepherd boys that killed giants. Wonderful preachers speaking to huge crowds and mighty evangelists. Then there is everyone else. The normal folks. Millions of them. What were they doing during their time? The Bible is populated with multitudes of unknowns, at least to us.

One of my favorite Bible characters is Philip. We read a bit about him in Acts 6-8. He served as a deacon waiting on tables during the potlucks. When persecution began at the hands of Saul, Philip leaves and heads down to Samaria. He faithfully shares his faith and a mini revival breaks out. God says to leave so he heads towards Gaza. He shares his faith with a guy riding along in a chariot and then disappears from the narrative for many, many years. We do not hear about him again until chapter 21 where he hosts Luke and Paul, and it is stated, that he had four grown daughters who prophesied. I would love to know Philip's parenting methods. What did Phil do for all those years? What type of husband was he? How did he spend his days?

In the Scriptures, we are only given a glimpse of the lives people lived. We often see the mountain top experiences of our heroes and rarely the day to day routines. I know they had them. Moses in the desert, Abraham too, even Noah building the Ark for about a century. Every day, they got up, went about their business and then went to bed. So, routine. So mundane. So, like us.

The truth for most of us is that our life is lived between the mountain top experiences. I like the mountains but one cannot live upon the peaks for there is little air, no vegetation, and almost no life. We live in the valley. We work, live and die in real life. The same is true with our calling to make disciples.

Our discipleship takes place where we live day by day. We are called to make disciples and the vast majority of the time this will take place in the mundane, the valley, the every day. We may visit the mountains, we may breathe heavenly air for a minute or ten, but our lives are lived out in the ordinary.

God did not and cannot make a mistake and He has placed right around us those that we can impact. We are to invest in the lives of those closest to us. We begin discipleship at home. If we hope to have a generational impact it starts here. All of us, if the Lord tarries, are going to die. What will be remembered and by whom? What will those who know us the best say about us when we leave this earth? It should matter to us. It greatly matters to those around us.

For Our Consideration

Studies show that few in the nursing homes regret not working more or spending more money on entertainment. The primary regret is that they missed the opportunity to invest in their family. Will we? Most of us live ordinary lives with an extraordinary calling - to invest in the lives of those around us. Will we take up the command to make disciples beginning with those at hand? If we will, we will have fruit that lasts for generations.

Want to know where to begin discipleship at home? It's not hard. Try reading together as a family, turn off the TV, computer and smart phones and pick up a book, okay, use an eBook or Kindle, but read together and then just have some face-to-face time discussing what you read. Bring what the Lord has shown you into the discussion and you will make a lasting impact.

Learn to live your day to day life in the presence of the Lord. Our Christianity should make a difference in how we live our lives. Our family should be the first and primary ones impacted by our walk with the Lord. If they are not, then perhaps we need to reevaluate what we are doing and why.

God is not in a hurry. If you are reading this, then you still have time to change. Start today. Spend whatever time you have left on this planet to live for God's glory, beginning at home. Perhaps that is what Philip did, and his kids turned out well.

## Questions to Ponder or Discuss:

1. Why do you think the Bible was written the way it was?

2. What do you think the life of the typical Bible character was really like?

3. How can God use the ordinary to do the extraordinary?

4. What does it mean to live your life totally for the Lord where you live?

For Our Consideration

# Family Forgiveness

Forgiveness of sins is one primary reason Jesus came to save the descendants of Adam. Another reason was so the children of God could learn to walk in forgiveness towards one another. We freely forgive because we are freely forgiven. This is especially true in our homes for the potential for unforgiveness is huge. Consider Jesus' answer and the example presented to His disciples after they asked Him to teach them how to pray.

> Give us this day our daily bread, and forgive us our debts, as we also have forgiven our debtors. And lead us not into temptation, but deliver us from evil. For if you forgive others their trespasses, your heavenly Father will also forgive you, but if you do not forgive others their trespasses, neither will your Father forgive your trespasses. Matthew 6:11-15

As Jesus explained to His disciples how to pray, these words must have been as shocking to them as they should be to us. "Forgive us our debts as we also have forgiven our debtors," and "If you forgive your heavenly Father will also forgive, but if you do not forgive others…neither will your Father forgive your trespasses." This is an amazing, often overlooked promise from the Lord Jesus Christ. How we forgive others has a direct relationship to how we are forgiven.

In Matthew 18:20-22 Peter was discussing how many times to forgive his brother and was feeling generous when he suggested the unheard-of amount of seven times. Jesus must have shaken him to the core when He explained that number needed to be greatly multiplied. In fact, in the rest of chapter 18, Jesus tells His shocked disciples a story about two men that were debtors. The first one owed a king an amount of money that was staggering and yet the king felt compassion and released the man from the debt. This recently released, forgiven man finds a man that owes him just a few coins and he begins to choke him and soon sends him off to jail, despite his pleas for mercy. The king is told what happened and severely disciplines this ungrateful wretch. While we may agree with the moral of the story, the punchline is just that, a punch. In verse 35 Jesus ties it all together with this sentence – "So also my heavenly Father will do to every one of you if you do not forgive your brother from your heart." Ouch. Jesus is the One that said it, and it is a promise.

In our daily interaction within our homes, conflict will arise. Feelings will be hurt, good intentions will be misunderstood and counted as something less than that, discipline will be misapplied, words will be stated harsher than they should have been, in short, wounds and offenses are bound to happen. What we do with them will have a tremendous impact on the spirit of our home.

If we are the offending party, we must seek forgiveness from the one we hurt. As parents, it is a very healthy action to ask for forgiveness from our children if we have overstepped, overstated, or overreacted. The Scripture states that fathers need to be careful not to provoke their children to anger (Ephesians 6:4) and we can do so by failing to ask for forgiveness from our children when we are in error. Pride is wrong regardless of our position and walking in humility is always the right response.

The same response of asking for forgiveness is true in husband-wife relationships, children to parents and child to child. Children will need

## For Our Consideration

to be trained to think and act this way, and a helpful method to get this into the spirit of a home is for the parents to model it.

When this asking and receiving of forgiveness takes place, a home will navigate the difficult relational waters that naturally occur with people sharing the same space. When forgiveness is not taught or modeled, anger, resentment, and bitterness can take root. Hurts, wounds, and sins that are not confessed and cleansed by walking through forgiveness, fester and can turn into a mess relationally. The Scripture states it this way:

> See to it that no one fails to obtain the grace of God; that no "root of bitterness" springs up and causes trouble, and by it many become defiled; Hebrews 12:15

This verse states that we have a responsibility to make sure that we do not allow this bitter root to take up residence in our homes or us. If we fail here, this verse promises that trouble and defilement will follow. One sure way to avoid this root causing damage to our homes is to practice the giving and receiving of forgiveness quickly.

We did nothing to earn the forgiveness of our Lord Jesus Christ. We did not have to perform in a certain way, we did not have keep our noses clean for a set amount of time, or any other such condition that we sometimes place on others. We received forgiveness when we asked for it, and so should those that hurt us.

Technically, we received forgiveness before we asked for it, even before we knew we were guilty and dead in our sins and trespasses, therefore we should forgive others quickly, and that includes those under our roof. Jesus even forgave those that crucified Him (and they certainly did not ask for forgiveness) and presented a pattern to follow.

We do not need to debate the point of timing regarding when to forgive however, we simply need to give as we have received.

> Put on then, as God's chosen ones, holy and beloved, compassionate hearts, kindness, humility, meekness, and patience, bearing with one another and, if one has a complaint against another, forgiving each other; as the Lord has forgiven you, so you also must forgive. Colossians 3:12-13

Relationship difficulties are common and will happen in every family. How will we deal with them? I would suggest we begin by rereading what Jesus told His disciples.

## Questions to Ponder or Discuss:

1. If God has forgiven us must we forgive others? Why or why not?

2. Why does forgiveness matter in the family circle?

3. Why is bitterness so devastating to relationships?

4. Do we have to forgive everyone for everything? Why or why not?

For Our Consideration

# The Second Biggest Decision

A young man requested that I write something about what is important for him when considering a prospective bride. I thought perhaps you might find it interesting as well.

Next to salvation, choosing your life partner is the biggest decision you will make this side of eternity. This choice is not like buying a car or bringing home a new puppy but will have a direct influence on you every day for the rest of your life. Choose wisely.

Biblically speaking marriage is supposed to be a lifelong commitment between a man and a woman. In our day, divorce runs rampant, but that does not change the standard held out in Scripture. A man can trade in his car and give his puppy away, but his spouse is non-returnable in God's eyes. Even with the exceptions given in Scripture, the preferred goal is one spouse for life. My often-used saying is, "It is far better to be happily married for forty years then to be miserably married for fifty!" If it takes ten years to find the right woman, it is better to wait.

There are many verses directly related to marriage and I would strongly encourage any young man to review them often as he enters the time of seeking his bride. I will not develop them here but a partial listing includes...

- Malachi 2:13-16
- 1Corinthians 7
- Ephesians 5:22-33
- 1 Peter 3:1-7

and of course, dozens of others scattered throughout the book of Proverbs. A life partner will have a direct impact on your ability to serve the Lord and therefore must be chosen carefully.

While most young men are attracted to the outside of the prospective bride, and that is good and normal, the inside is far more important. Beyond physical attractiveness, many traits should be considered. I am assuming that you are a strong believer and desire to please the Lord in your life. If you are not, then you have no business looking for a spouse now anyway!

I am not going to develop the timing issue for when to consider taking a spouse but I would strongly encourage you to work with your parents as to this critical decision. There are two primary questions regarding marriage: when and who.

A few questions to discuss, and have good answers for, include:

- Am I able to take on the responsibility of a wife and family both spiritually and financially?
- Are my parents in agreement that this is the right time?
- Is my walk with God consistent enough?
- Am I attempting to get away from a problem via marriage?

While no one is ever completely ready for marriage, when we get the release from the Lord and the authorities in our life regarding timing, we begin the exciting process of prayerfully seeking our prospective mate!

Here are three key points to consider when looking for a potential spouse:

1. Does the young lady love the Lord with a heart to serve Him? Marriage is hard work sometimes and our relationship with the Lord

is our anchor to steady the ship during the storms. If her love for God is not strong, her love for you will also not be. There will be a direct correlation between her love for her Lord and her love for her husband. If the Lord is not first in her life she will not have the necessary foundation upon which to build.

2. Does the young lady love the Word of God? Given the changeable nature of our society and our emotions, we must build upon something that does not shift like the sand. The Scripture must be a priority and our basis for our belief system. Considering a young lady that has little or no Scriptural understanding is not wise. God's will and ways must be first and not human emotions and intellect.

3. How does the young lady get along with and treat her family? After you say, "I do," you are family! If she is cold, angry, selfish and rebellious now, how do you think she will be shortly after you are married? If she has an attitude problem towards her authorities before marriage, do you think that will change when you step into the position of being her authority? If she is self-absorbed now will that change after marriage? From a more positive point of view, if the young lady is a servant now, that will most likely grow. If she is kind and generous now, those attributes will also continue. If she can lovingly submit to her parents today, that is usually a good indication that she will honor and respect you after you marry.

There is nothing magic that takes place during a wedding ceremony. What a person is before they say, "I do," will simply be more clearly revealed after the wedding celebration takes place. Most people are on their best behavior during the courtship process and this can lead to some artificial representations. It is best to observe from a distance before jumping into a relationship. How a young lady treats her family, friends, and authorities can be observed and is usually a pretty good reflection of how she will soon treat you. Again, choose wisely.

The three points above are by no means the full picture, but if these three are not there, I would very quickly walk away! In addition to loving the Lord, the Word of God, and personal observation of her interaction with those around her, there are multiple other factors to prayerfully consider. For example, her maturity level, emotional stability or moodiness, common interests and dreams, vision for the future, family planning goals, the handling of money, and communication skills all should be considered regarding compatibility.

A good rule of thumb is that if everyone around you is questioning the relationship, so should you! The old saying is that "love is blind." I pray that you will not be.

Marriage is wonderful, a mystical picture of Christ and the Church, and God is the One Who came up with the idea. Adam and Eve were the first married couple and all of history will end with a wedding feast! Jesus performed His first miracle at a wedding and God has specific commands for those that will marry. A young man takes a bride and this decision will affect him for the rest of his days. It is an exciting time and marriage is a gift from God. I pray that each young man will seek the Lord regarding this choice and that many godly generations will come forth as a result.

For Our Consideration

## Questions to Ponder or Discuss:

1. Why is marriage considered the second biggest decision someone will make in their life?

2. Why is it important for the young lady to love the Lord and the Scriptures?

3. Why is it important to observe a young lady with her family if possible?

4. What would you list as the most important traits to be considered in a marriage partner?

# The Second Biggest Decision - Ladies' Version

Next to salvation, choosing your life partner is the biggest decision you will make this side of eternity. When your prince charming comes around, how will you recognize him? What if he is not on a white horse but in a junkier car? When he asks for your hand, should you give it? Choose wisely.

Biblically speaking marriage is supposed to be a lifelong commitment between a man and a woman. In our day, divorce runs rampant, and many forces are attempting to redefine the family, but that does not change the standard held out in Scripture. Once the rose-colored glasses are removed and real life settles in, the man you marry is non-returnable in God's eyes. Even with the exceptions given in Scripture, the preferred goal is one spouse for life. My often-used saying is,

> "It is far better to be happily married for forty years then to be miserably married for fifty!"

If it takes ten years for the right man to come along, it is better to wait. Being single and serving the Lord, is better than being married and miserable. I have spent the last 35 years of my life testing this sentence in the counseling office. It is true. Your life partner will have a direct impact on your ability to serve the Lord and your personal well-being, and therefore must be chosen carefully.

## For Our Consideration

Most couples that marry begin their relationship by initially being attracted by appearance. For the record, that is normal and acceptable. Who wants to marry someone they cannot stand to look at? As those of us know that have a few years on our bodies now, looks come and go. What is possible to look like at 20 is near impossible at 40 or 50. Weight comes, hair leaves, and lines deepen. Young Prince Charming will turn into Old King George sooner than later. We all age, so basing our relationship simply on looks is foolish.

Beyond physical attractiveness, many traits should be considered. I am assuming that you are a strong believer and desire to please the Lord in your life. If you are not, then you have no business looking for a spouse now anyway! Your relationship to the Lord must be primary in your life for when hard times come; it is what will help carry you through them.

This is not about how to get a husband or the best method to use, but what to look for in a prospective one, so I will not develop that topic. I also am not going to develop the timing issue regarding ages and such. God has given you parents and pastors that can help you in this arena. If possible, stay under your father's protection and ask your family about the prospective spouse. Often, your brother(s), if you have one, can provide insight into how a guy thinks and what his motives are in any given situation. Be humble and listen to those that God has put in your life and you will rejoice later if you do.

Perhaps a few questions might be in order as to your motives for considering marriage:

- Am I ready for the commitment?
- Are my parents in agreement, not just giving in to me, but are they supportive of this relationship?

# Family

- Is my walk with God consistent enough?
- Am I a servant or selfish?
- Is this the right time?
- Am I attempting to run away from home by this relationship?
- Do I like my prospective mate or are there many things I intend to change in him after he says, "I do?"

While no one is ever completely ready for marriage, when we get the release from the Lord and the authorities in our life regarding timing, we begin the exciting process of prayerfully waiting for our prospective mate! While the young man chooses his bride, the young ladies are given the task of waiting, patiently until chosen.

Shortly after birth, and often while they wait, many young ladies make extensive lists on what to look for in their future groom. Praying specifically about this is good, so I would not want to dampen that list, but I would suggest that these three things that I told my daughters be included.

1. Does the young man love the Lord with a heart to serve Him? Marriage is hard work sometimes and our relationship with the Lord is our anchor to steady the ship during the storms. If his love for God and His Word is not strong, his love for you will also not be as strong as it could be. There will be a direct correlation between his love for the Lord and his love for his wife. If the Lord is not first in his life, he will not have the necessary foundation upon which to build. Firm foundations provide something good to build upon, what do weak ones do?

2. Is the young man teachable? A know-it-all, arrogant young man typically grows into a know-it-all, arrogant older man. God is opposed to the proud but gives grace to the humble, the Bible teaches, and who

does not need or want more grace? Being young and inexperienced is not a fault, being proud and unteachable is. If no one can speak into the life of a young man before marriage, what do you think the chances of your being heard by him are after marriage? How quickly does the young man repent and admit that he was in error about something? How does he line up under the authorities in his life? How does he treat his parents and siblings?

All give insight into how he will treat you later. Many daughters love their fathers and often wish their future husbands could be like their dad. If they are teachable when young, the father will be able to speak into his life to help him grow. If he will not listen to anyone about anything, what chance is there of that happening? God is and will be gracious, but the road may be difficult should you have to watch God discipline and break a proud husband.

3. Is the young man kind? Proverbs 19:22 in the NASB translation, states, "What is desired in a man is kindness." If you marry a kind young man, you will be most likely end up being married to a kind older man later. If you marry a self-centered, selfish, harsh young man, you most likely will spend a great deal of time in counseling and crying. How does this man interact with his family, peers, those of the opposite sex? How does he treat those less fortunate? Is he generous? A harsh man does not make a loving husband, and overlooking this fault will lead to a lifetime of pain. If a young man is not nice and kind to you during the period of pursuing you when he is on his best behavior, what do you think he will act like after he has caught you?

There is nothing magic that takes place during a wedding ceremony. What a person is before they say, "I do," will simply be more clearly revealed after the wedding celebration takes place. Most people are on their best behavior during the courtship process and this can lead to some artificial representations. It is best to observe from a distance before jumping into a relationship. How a young man treats his family, friends, and authorities can be observed and is usually a pretty good reflection of how he will soon treat you.

Again, choose wisely. Marriage is a pressure-filled experience. If children follow, the pressures increase. It is best to make sure that what is squeezed out of your man by pressure include a love for the Lord, teachableness, and being kind!

The three points above are by no means the full picture, but if these three were not there, I would very quickly walk away, or better yet, never begin the relationship! In addition to loving the Lord, being kind and teachable, there are multiple other factors to prayerfully consider. For example, his maturity level, emotional stability or moodiness, common interests and dreams, vision for the future, family planning goals, the handling of money, and communication skills all should be considered regarding compatibility. A wife in the Biblical sense helps complete the man. She is given to him to help him in his life to accomplish what God desires. If you do not like what God has called him to do or become, why would you want to partner with him for life?

A good rule of thumb is that if everyone around you is questioning the relationship, so should you! The old saying is that "love is blind." I pray that you will not be. Listen to those that are more objective and love you; they just might see something that you do not.

Marriage is wonderful; a mystical picture of Christ and the Church, and God is the One that came up with the idea. Adam and Eve were the first married couple and all of history will end with a wedding feast! Jesus performed His first miracle at a wedding and God has specific commands for those that will marry.

For Our Consideration

A young lady becomes a bride and this decision will affect her for the rest of her days. It is an exciting time and marriage is a gift from God. I pray that each young lady will seek the Lord regarding this choice and that many godly generations will come forth as a result.

## Questions to Ponder or Discuss:

1. Why is marriage considered the second biggest decision someone will make in their life?

2. Why is it important for the young man to love the Lord and the Scriptures?

3. Why is it important to observe a young man with his family if possible?

4. What would you list as the most important traits to be considered in a marriage partner?

# A Challenge to My Fellow Grandparents

> Grandchildren are the crown of the aged, and the glory of children is their fathers. Proverbs 17:6

As I was sitting in the hospital room holding our fifth granddaughter, the revelation hit me that I was no longer a young man. I know it should have dawned on me sooner, but I was too busy to dwell on such things. Having turned sixty-one recently (and eight additional grandchildren later,) my thoughts yet again turn to those who will follow in my steps when I leave this earth for my reward. What am I leaving them? How will I be remembered?

When our first granddaughter arrived, there was an instant bonding between us, at least from my point of view. I held her in my arms and delight filled my heart as I gazed at that little girl. I marveled and rejoiced that I had lived to see this day. At age 42, it was quite a jolt to be a grandfather, but it was a delightful shock!

When Lydia arrived, my wife and I needed to evaluate our roles as grandparents. We were not her parents, yet there seemed to be something we were supposed to be doing beyond what the bumper stickers proclaimed about grandchildren (Spoiling them and sending them home, or spending their inheritance.) There certainly was a strong generational connection, but we were not sure what our responsibilities were.

Those of us, who have given our lives for the raising of our children, can find it somewhat confusing as to our new roles as grandparents.

For Our Consideration

As parents, we exercised almost complete control over our children until they were adults. Eating, sleeping, education, clothing and just about every other decision was made on behalf of the child, or at least in concert with them. As our children grew, we were very involved right up until they left our home. Now, here is a newborn baby and the temptation is to resume our former roles. However, this must be resisted! These little ones are not ours but belong to other parents who are just beginning the task we have completed. So, what are we supposed to do as grandparents?

Here are a few lessons we have learned on this grandparent journey over the last nineteen years.

First, pray often for the new parents. They need wisdom and insight on how to adjust to the new family member and they will need an abundance of guidance as the child grows.

Second, be available to assist in babysitting, house cleaning, cooking, and any practical matter needed. Like so many, it would have been wonderful to have a night out now and again when our children were young. We simply did not have that option. Now we can provide that for our grown children and they have all told us that it is such a blessing!

Third, always remember to turn the heart of the child back to the parents. These precious gifts are not yours but belong to their parents. Our job as grandparents is to reinforce what the parents want, not to contradict or undermine.

Sometimes this can be challenging because by the time we become grandparents we certainly have learned a few things from our experiences. We observe the mistakes of youth, and the temptation is to jump in and give an unsolicited opinion. A proverb I coined years ago goes like this:

## Woe to the man who gives his opinion when it is not being asked, it will be reckoned unto him as a curse!"

If we develop a trusting relationship with our children as they age, our opinions will be asked for and valued when they are older and in need of our assistance. However, giving our opinion to our adult children before it is asked for, will result in being labeled as a meddler and can damage your relationship for years.

One key point is that we must never undermine the parents to the grandchildren even if we disagree with the parents. If we observe harmful or dangerous behavior, then we must appeal to the parents discreetly, but never turn the hearts of the children away from their parents.

We must reinforce what the parents are doing, not undercut it. Remember what you wish your parents had done when you had your children still at home...then try to be that person! When a grandchild asks us for anything, if the parents are around, we always send them back to the parents, thus keeping the lines of authority clear. Grandparents that sneak behind the parents' backs are teaching rebellion and disrespect for authority, so we must be careful what we teach by our actions and attitudes!

As grandparents, we are modeling to another generation (whether we realize it or not) what it looks like to walk with God. Self-focused grandparents are missing a great opportunity to invest in the future.

Our culture glorifies self-gratification and unfortunately, many godly people have bought into this lifestyle without considering the outcome of this choice. The thought goes something like this, "I have lived my whole life raising my children, now I'm going to enjoy life and take care of me!" This lifestyle is evidenced by multitudes of grandparents moving to the coasts or deserts instead of staying by their families. From my perspective, this is a waste of experience and a loss to the next generation. Someone said years ago that very few people in nursing homes regret not spending more time at the office or on vacation, but almost all regret the time lost with their families. We never get to spend time twice so we must choose wisely the first time!

Even if you feel you have nothing to offer because your life has been full of mistakes, you have your love and experience to offer. One of the best ways to gain knowledge is by learning from other people's mistakes and then trying to avoid repeating them. How beneficial it would be for the older generation to pass on to the younger one the wisdom that was learned from all those mistakes! Do not waste them by keeping them all to yourself! Experiences should be passed on to those that follow us, both good and bad, for each possess a lesson or insight.

As grandparents, our goal should be to be godly examples that love and serve the next generation. We need to avoid violating the parents' authority and instead reinforce it to their children. We are not called to spoil grandchildren, but to help in the training process of them. We are blessed to enjoy this gift from God and take our responsibilities seriously, and not simply live to gratify our flesh. Another generation is at stake and we must give ourselves selflessly to assist in capturing it for Christ!

I appeal to the grandparents (and future ones) that may be reading this to consider their involvement with the next generation. Is warmer weather worth missing this opportunity? Playing golf and having abundant free time is great, but what about investing in your grandchildren or great grandchildren? What about taking time to share your story with them?

I love the ocean and taking walks enjoying breath-taking views, but I would rather not ever see them again, than miss my grandchildren's lives! I can visit the ocean but moving away from my family is not an option. I would rather shovel ten feet of snow than miss the fellowship and joy of my children and grandchildren. Wouldn't you? Your family needs you more than the RV Park or your Bunko partners.

What could you do to help? How about offering to teach the child or children one day a week for the frazzled mom? Perhaps babysitting to allow the parents a night out for pleasure or even some necessary shopping time?

Please consider writing out your personal testimony for the next generation, sharing some of your success stories or failures, focusing on what you learned from them. We all have so much to offer—may we not waste our knowledge!

Please prayerfully consider where and how you live out the rest of your days. It is not too late to reengage in the battle, for the next generation is at stake!

For Our Consideration

## Questions to Ponder or Discuss:

1. Do you believe that God calls His children to a life of service? Why or why not?

2. Are there areas in which you wish your parents acted differently? What can you do differently?

3. Do you agree that much is lost from generation to generation when grandparents move away? Why or why not?

4. If grandparents can undermine the authority of parents, how can they support it? Explain.

# Marriage

"We judge ourselves by our intentions. We judge our spouses by their actions. No wonder we think we're better!"

Anne Moodie

For Our Consideration

# Living Words, Killing Words

The Bible is the only Book I know that says about itself:

> For the Word of God is living and active, sharper than any two-edged sword, piercing to the division of soul and spirit, of joints and of marrow, and discerning the thoughts and intentions of the heart. Hebrews 4:12

Contained with the pages of the Scriptures, are living words. Words that can change our lives, and our marriages. Consider these verses for just a moment through the lens of our marriages.

> When words are many, transgression is not lacking, but whoever restrains his lips is prudent. Proverbs 10:19
>
> There is one whose rash words are like sword thrusts, but the tongue of the wise brings healing. Proverbs 12:18
>
> The wisest of women builds her house, but folly with her own hands tears it down. Proverbs 14:1
>
> Gracious words are like a honeycomb, sweetness to the soul and health to the body. Proverbs 16:24
>
> Death and life are in the power of the tongue, and those who love it will eat its fruit Proverbs 18:21
>
> A word fitly spoken is like apples of gold in a setting of silver. Proverbs 25:11

In the world of preachers, a sermon on controlling our tongues and words is always a sure way to bring conviction, and fill the altar with repentant sinners. Who among us does not struggle with what we say? Some struggle with rash words and others tend to be more gracious, but almost everyone sins with their words. If you do not believe me, just ask James:

> For every kind of beast and bird, of reptile and sea creature, can be tamed and has been tamed by mankind, but no human being can tame the tongue. It is a restless evil, full of deadly poison. With it we bless our Lord and Father, and with it we curse people who are made in the likeness of God.
> James 3:7-9

What effect do our words have in our marriages? Life or death? Gracious or harsh? Choice or nasty tasting? Are we building up our spouse or ripping them to shreds with our words? Are we enjoying the fruit of our words? Excellent questions to consider.

If our marriage is not what we wished for. Not what we expected. Not what we hoped for. Perhaps a good place to start is listening. What would we find, better stated, hear, if someone followed us around for a week and recorded everything we said to our spouse?

I have observed that many times we will say something to our spouse that we would never say to someone else. A tone is used, volume in increased, harshness is added that we would not use with most people. Why do we do that?

Some might say, "I have no control, they make me so mad and I can't stop." Really? Ever have the phone ring during one of those times and answer it? Do we change, or do we continue with the same tone with whoever is on the phone?

Or, if someone offered you one million dollars to stop your anger right now, would you? Could you? What if Jesus appeared physically, right in the middle of the dispute, would we change how we speak? I wonder.

Another option to get a glimpse into how we really speak is to listen to our children. What do we hear coming out of our children's mouths when they are playing with their toys or sibling? Most children will play mommy and daddy with dolls or stuffed animals. It might be instructive to listen to how the little mommy's and daddy's talk to one another. Remember where the children heard that from in the first place. Ouch.

It is interesting to me that the very one we love so much is often the recipient of the worst of our verbal behavior. Why do we drop our guard instead of raising it even higher? Why do we care more about what a relative stranger thinks of us than our life partner by covenant? Why would we be embarrassed if someone walked into the middle of an argument with our spouse but we are not embarrassed by how we are speaking while in it? I wonder.

I am sure there are multiple reasons why we treat our spouses differently than others. Perhaps we are more comfortable and therefore drop the social restraints required with others. Maybe we know that our spouse must stay with us and will not reject us so we can just be our self with them. (Of course, that thought raises some issues about pretense, but we will have to address that issue some other time.) Maybe we just do not realize how harmful our words really are, or can be.

If we are not content or happy with the condition of our marriage, then I would suggest trying to change how we speak about, and to our spouse. If life and death are really in our words, if we can build up, or tear down, if our words can be like a sword thrust, or bring healing, if our tongue really is a beast to tame, then we need to evaluate what we are saying and why.

Perhaps it would be wise to go on a word fast and abstain from speaking. Maybe it would be good to only speak positive words for a day and see what happens. Make a choice to spend an entire day in avoiding saying anything harsh, negative, or critical regarding your spouse.

How about not saying anything if it does not build up our spouse. I wonder what would happen. I have a suspicion that the atmosphere would change some in our homes and we may just like it so much we suspend the trial period and make it a way of life. What could it hurt to try?

## Questions to Ponder or Discuss:

1. Does God really care how we speak? Explain.

2. Why is there life and death in our words? Explain.

3. What can we do to help get control over the words of our mouth? Explain.

4. Why do you think we often treat our spouse or children differently than others? Should we?

For Our Consideration

# Does Your Marriage Have a Prayer?

I am not referring to survival, though that may very well be at stake; I am referring to focus. Have we stepped back from our marriages and asked why God wanted us to do this in the first place? Why did God come up with the idea of two people getting together and spending the rest of their days trying to figure out how to live as one? What was He thinking? Was He bored and needed some entertainment?

If we remember the Garden of Eden account in Genesis, we can get a glimpse into what God was thinking. After all, it was God who told Adam, "that it was not good for him to be alone." God is the One who said, "I will make a helper suitable for Adam." God's idea, therefore it is logical that He must have a plan and reasons for this activity that we know as marriage.

I do not pretend to know all of God's reasons but here are some for our consideration. First, Adam was incomplete without Eve. I don't mean that being single means you are less of a person than someone who is married, I simply am saying that being married will help you to grow and change in ways that being single will not or cannot.

When we are single, we have a greater say over many areas of our life. Our time, habits, preferences, goals, can all be developed without the opinion or possible impact on anyone else. This is not true when we are married. We no longer are alone and our actions affect more than ourselves. Paul the apostle put it this way:

> I want you to be free from anxieties. The unmarried man is anxious about the things of the Lord, how to please the Lord. But the married man is anxious about worldly things, how to please his wife, and his interests are divided. And the unmarried or betrothed woman is anxious about the things of the Lord, how to be holy in body and spirit. But the married woman is anxious about worldly things, how to please her husband. I say this for your own benefit, not to lay any restraint upon you, but to promote good order and to secure your undivided devotion to the Lord. 1 Corinthians 7:32-35

When we are single, we can maintain a more, "undivided devotion" to the Lord than after we are married. Adam would become someone different with Eve than without Eve.

I have a friend whose first wife died after they were married for 20+ years. I knew this man well in the context of his first marriage. I now know him in the context of his second marriage, and while he is the same man, he is different. Being married to his second wife has brought out different characteristics than being married to his first wife. Adam with Eve would be different from Adam without Eve. The same is true with each one of us.

In addition to our personalities developing in conjunction with someone, another reason for marriage is partnership and the maximizing of impact. Consider this passage:

> Again, if two lie together, they keep warm, but how can one keep warm alone? And though a man might prevail against one who is alone, two will withstand him—a threefold cord is not quickly broken. Ecclesiastes 4:11-12

## For Our Consideration

Two heads are better than one. Two viewpoints often provide insights that would be missed by only one. No two people think exactly the same way and that is a good thing.

In marriage, a husband and wife will often view the same situation from completely different angles. If they can grow to the place where they respect and value each other's viewpoint, instead of always trying to talk the other one into their own, they will have more wisdom, and probably make better decisions.

God usually draws two people together that are very different in temperament, skill sets, and personality. Why? Does He really have some warped sense of humor or is this part of His plan to help both people develop, grow and mature?

If two people are exactly alike, one is not necessary. Since most people will marry someone that is vastly different from them, the growth opportunities abound. Of course, we must get past the obstacle of our pride in thinking we are always correct, but that is possible. Take it from someone who is proud, it can be done. Not only can we humble ourselves and learn from our spouses, we must if we want to become all that God desires for us.

Another reason for marriage, and this one is both resisted and often overlooked, is the power in prayer that can take place in the union. God states in His word this powerful truth:

> Again I say to you, if two of you agree on earth about anything they ask, it will be done for them by my Father in heaven.
> Matthew 18:19

What an amazing coincidence that marriage involves two people. A husband and wife that will learn to pray together will have great strength and intimacy. The opposite is also true. Almost any Christian married couple will readily agree that they should pray together but how many do? Other than a quick bedtime prayer with the children or a short blessing over the meal, how many couples pray together? How many should? What would happen if we did?

While I do not know the answer to all those questions I do know this much. Our marriages would be better off if we learned how to pray together. I also know that our enemy hates praying couples and he will do whatever he can to thwart it. Why? What does he know that we do not seem to? Why is it so hard for a couple to pray together on any regular basis? Should it be? Why would most of agree that we need to pray together but studies show that most of us don't?

Again, those questions need to be answered and the sooner the better. They need to be answered in our marriages and today would not be too soon. Our marriages are under attack at a record rate - do they have a prayer? If not, why not? Now, that is a question to consider, isn't it?

For Our Consideration

## Questions to Ponder or Discuss:

1. Why do you think God came up with the idea of marriage?

2. With the shifting value system of our culture, why is it important for Christians to maintain the Biblical value of marriage?

3. Why is it that opposites often attract and marry each other?

4. Why does the enemy of our souls hate marriage so much?

# God is Pro-Marriage

Sometimes we forget that God is love and He is the one that came up with the whole love idea, not the sin, sick world we live in that has perverted everything. God is the Creator of us, all of us, including our emotions, romantic feelings, physical desires, and our brains. Human love was His idea from the beginning, and the Bible is a love story from beginning to end!

In the very middle of the Bible is the Song of Songs, a love story, a human love story. There are of course Messianic implications about Jesus, but the book is primarily dealing with love between a man and a woman.

Human love is normal, desirable and part of God's plan. Remember God is the One who said, "It is not good for man to be alone!" Man was not alone, he had God, yet God said man needed something more.

I know some of you have been burned, suffered in bad relationships, and are a bit skittish about this topic, but that does not change the pattern or God's original intent. Fallen man, with the aid of our foe, has often attempted to distort and pervert what God has created, and love is no different. If you need help, get it and get it quickly! However, let's not throw out everything because some have messed it up. Here is a good principle to live by:

**The correction to abuse is not disuse but proper use.**

God's plan includes men and women falling in human love (then choosing to walk in God-graced love), getting married, having children and passing along their faith to them! This is good; in fact,

## For Our Consideration

God said it was very good after He created male and female. (See Genesis 2)

Most young people should find someone to marry, produce children and change our world through the power of a godly family - that is good and God's typical method from the beginning of time. Christians should be pro-family, pro-life, and pro-marriage between a man and woman because God is!

I recently spoke on Psalm 45 during a Sunday message. This Psalm is a love song that presents a picture of a king and his bride. The king is a real Prince Charming and is described in the first five verses. The bride is pictured just as one would expect for a wedding. Her attendants are there and she is dressed to the max with expectations abounding.

During this message, I said that just about every little girl, beginning at a very young age, begins to dream about her wedding. While little boys are making animal noises and throwing dirt around, many little girls are having their dolls get married.

To verify this, I circulated around our church after the service popping into the various groups of young ladies standing around chatting. I asked each group, "Did you all do what I talked about today and pretend to have your dolls get married?" Their replies were humorous to me and each was repeated several times depending on the group I invaded.

- "I didn't have my dolls get married but my stuffed animals."
- "I used my brother's little cars"
- "I didn't have dolls, but used marbles." Marbles?

Planes, toys, rocks, marbles, stuffed animals, and yes, even dolls all marched down an imaginary aisle and took vows before some sort of preacher. Interesting. Perhaps God placed this in these little girl's hearts after all.

My own grandchildren performed a "marriage ceremony" for their dogs when they were going to go into the puppy business because after all, they couldn't very well make puppies and not be married!

The point to all of this is that God is the one that made us the way He did and it is not weird but godly. God is pro-marriage and pro-family and so should we be! God is the One that chose to be called our Father. Jesus is referred to as our brother, we who are born again are called a family and we are headed to a wedding feast described in Revelation 19. God is pro-family.

Part of the mystery of marriage between a man and a woman is what God was after by joining them together in the first place. Paul, in Ephesians 5:32, says that marriage is a profound mystery and refers to Christ and the Church, and your guess is as good as mine is as to what all Paul meant. In addition to presenting a mysterious picture, God also expects marriage to reproduce.

Some couples can have multiple children and some cannot. Some will adopt and others will choose not to have children, but God still expects marriage to reproduce. Even if physical children do not result from a marriage, God expects all of us to have spiritual ones. That is called discipleship.

For those that do adopt or procreate children, the Word of God addresses what God is after in Malachi 2. Many see only tithing in Malachi, but read what God states here:

> And this second thing you do. You cover the LORD's altar with tears, with weeping and groaning because he no longer regards the offering or accepts it with favor from your hand.

> But you say, "Why does he not?" Because the LORD was witness between you and the wife of your youth, to whom you have been faithless, though she is your companion and your wife by covenant. Did he not make them one, with a portion of the Spirit in their union? And what was the one God seeking? Godly offspring. So, guard yourselves in your spirit, and let none of you be faithless to the wife of your youth. "For the man who does not love his wife but divorces her, says the LORD, the God of Israel, covers his garment with violence, says the LORD of hosts. So, guard yourselves in your spirit, and do not be faithless."

What was God seeking by the marriage union? Godly offspring. God expects us to reproduce and He has designed marriage to be an integral part of the spiritual, generational implementation process. God hates divorce (not the divorcee by the way) partially because of what happens to the next generation. God is pro-family and pro-marriage and so should we be.

The next time you walk by a little girl playing with two of something like cars or marbles, slow down a bit and listen...you might just drop in on a wedding, and I bet God smiles every time.

## Questions to Ponder or Discuss:

1. Is marriage the norm or exception for most Christians? Why?

2. Why does Paul say marriage is a picture of Christ and the Church?

3. Why is godly offspring a seemingly big deal to God?

4. Are you pro-marriage? Why or why not?

For Our Consideration

# Intense Fellowship

Every couple fusses and argues now and again. I once served on an elder board where a man said that he and his wife never had an argument in all the years they were married. Really, come on, sixty years and no fights? What he meant is that he and his wife did not scream and yell, etc. Okay, I buy that. My marriage of over forty-two years has not been that way. We fuss, and engage in what I call "intense fellowship."

We are both strong people with strong opinions and we state them strongly. In other words, a recipe for arguing and hurting each other's feelings. When we were first married, it was rough. I mean real rough.

My bride and I both came from dysfunctional families and we never learned how to disagree agreeably. We did learn, however, how to fight, yell, and break stuff and storm out of a room. Nice. By God's grace, we survived, and have learned how to walk in something that is critical if a marriage is going to make it long term - forgiveness.

Forgiveness of sins is the primary reason Jesus came to save the descendants of Adam. Another reason was so the children of God could learn to walk in forgiveness towards one another. We freely forgive, because we are freely forgiven. This is especially true in our homes, for the potential for unforgiveness is huge.

Forgiveness has been addressed in a previous article in reference to the family at large, but I want to repeat some of it here regarding marriage.

Consider Jesus' answer, and the example presented to His disciples after they asked Him to teach them how to pray.

> Give us this day our daily bread, and forgive us our debts, as we also have forgiven our debtors. And lead us not into temptation, but deliver us from evil. For if you forgive others their trespasses, your heavenly Father will also forgive you, but if you do not forgive others their trespasses, neither will your Father forgive your trespasses. Matthew 6:11-15

As Jesus explained to His disciples how to pray, these words must have been as shocking to them as they should be to us. "Forgive us our debts as we also have forgiven our debtors," and "If you forgive your heavenly Father will also forgive, but if you do not forgive others…neither will your Father forgive your trespasses." This is an amazing, often overlooked promise from the Lord Jesus Christ. How we forgive others has a direct relationship to how we are forgiven.

In Matthew 18:20-22 Peter asked how many times he should forgive his brother and was feeling generous when he suggested the unheard-of amount of seven times. Jesus must have shaken him to the core when He explained that number needed to be greatly multiplied.

In fact, in the rest of chapter 18, Jesus tells His shocked disciples a story about two men that were debtors. The first one owed a king an amount of money that was staggering, and yet the king felt compassion and released the man from the debt. This recently released, forgiven man, finds a friend that owes him just a few coins and he begins to choke him, and soon sends him off to jail, despite his pleas for mercy. The king is told what happened and severely disciplines this ungrateful wretch.

While we may agree with the moral of the story, the punchline is just that, a punch. In verse 35 Jesus ties it all together with this sentence – "So also my heavenly Father will do to every one of you if you do not forgive your brother from your heart." Ouch. Jesus is the One that said it, and it is a promise.

In our daily interaction within our homes, conflict will arise. Feelings will be hurt, good intentions will be misunderstood and counted as something less than that, discipline will be misapplied, words will be stated harsher than they should have been, in short, wounds and offenses are bound to happen. What we do with them will have a tremendous impact on the spirit of our home.

If we are the offending party, we must seek forgiveness from the one we hurt. As parents, it is a healthy action to ask for forgiveness from our children if we have overstepped, overstated, or overreacted. The Scripture states that fathers need to be careful not to provoke their children to anger (Ephesians 6:4) and we can do so by failing to ask for forgiveness from our children when we are in error. Pride is wrong regardless of our position, and walking in humility is always the right response.

The same response of asking for forgiveness is true in husband wife relationships, children to parents, and child to child. Children will need to be trained to think and act this way, and a helpful method to get this into the spirit of a home is for the parents to model it.

When this asking and receiving of forgiveness takes place, a home will navigate the difficult relational waters that naturally occur with people sharing the same space. When forgiveness is not taught or modeled, anger, resentment, and bitterness can take root. Hurts, wounds, and sins that are not confessed and cleansed by walking through forgiveness, fester and can turn into a mess relationally. The Scripture states it this way:

> See to it that no one fails to obtain the grace of God; that no "root of bitterness" springs up and causes trouble, and by it many become defiled; Hebrews 12:15

This verse states that we have a responsibility to make sure that we do not allow this bitter root to take up residence in our homes or in us. If we fail here, this verse promises that trouble and defilement will follow. One sure way to avoid this root causing damage to our homes is to practice the giving and receiving of forgiveness quickly.

We did nothing to earn the forgiveness of our Lord Jesus Christ. We did not have to perform in a certain way, we did not have keep our noses clean for a set amount of time, or any other such condition that we sometimes place on others. We received forgiveness when we asked for it, and so should those that hurt us.

Technically, we received forgiveness before we asked for it, even before we knew we were guilty and dead in our sins and trespasses, therefore we should forgive others quickly, and that includes those under our roof. Jesus even forgave those that crucified Him (and they certainly did not ask for forgiveness) and presented a pattern to follow. Here is Paul's command to us:

> Put on then, as God's chosen ones, holy and beloved, compassionate hearts, kindness, humility, meekness, and patience, bearing with one another and, if one has a complaint against another, forgiving each other; as the Lord has forgiven you, so you also must forgive. Colossians 3:12-13

For Our Consideration

Relationship difficulties are common and will happen in every family. How will we deal with them? I would suggest we begin by rereading what Jesus told His disciples.

## Questions to Ponder or Discuss:

1. Do we really believe what Jesus said about forgiveness? Why or why not?

2. What is the difference between being hurt and offended, or is there one?

3. Is there someone in your life that you struggle forgiving?

4. Does forgiving mean the same thing as forgetting what was done to us? Explain.

## Why Should I Stay?

Over the last forty years or so, I have heard this question from both men and women as they sat in my office crying. "My spouse doesn't love me anymore so what's the point." Just as frequently I hear, "I don't love them anymore," from the spouse that wants to leave. While not always true, most of the time when I hear this phrase it means that someone else has entered the picture.

The spouse that does not love anymore has moved their affection on to someone else. A co-worker, which by the way is where the highest percentage of immorality takes place, a fellow-hobby enthusiast, a friend's spouse, or even a fellow laborer in the church. I am not questioning the feelings of this type of love, just the definition, and decisions behind it. Most people really do believe they fall in and out of love and have little control over it.

The process of falling out of love starts quickly and often shortly after the honeymoon. Reality takes the place of fantasy and real life can be difficult. The many irritants that were overlooked during the pre-marital days now become like splinters under our emotional skin. The man, who is typically in conquer mode before the wedding, has his prize and quits trying to win her. The woman, who was mysterious and playful, often loses her mystique and sense of humor chasing toddlers around all day. If we add arguments, money problems, hormones, in-law pressures, and unrecognized demonic temptations to the dashed expectations, a moral failure is not far away.

Enter the new love. The male co-worker, who is kind, sensitive, always clean-shaven, smells nice, knows how to listen without being critical, and has your genuine interests first and foremost in his mind. The female that you spend a great deal of time with at work or church that has perfect hair, skin, smell, and figure. Her smile and laughter, the way she makes you feel like a real man, just is overpowering. You simply cannot help yourself; you have fallen in love with someone else.

Time out. Take a breath, step away from the immorality ledge, and think. Resist the devil and he will flee from you. Submit to his lies and he will destroy you and your family. With the divorce rate running rampant in our churches, which decision is winning? The statistics are well known so I won't bother to repeat them. Godly men and women are falling in droves to a lie and illusion.

If we could think clearly about what we are about to do we would most likely stop. The illusion of perfection in the temptation is just that, an illusion. Mr. Wonderful really does not look like that all time. When he is not at work, he doesn't shave and his clothes are wrinkled. His breath is bad and if he were married to you, he wouldn't listen to you as he now does. If he knows you are married and is still pursuing and flirting with you, he does not have your best interest at heart and he is really a jerk. If he was willing to act this way with you, what makes you think he won't with the next pretty face?

Ms. Wonderful is just as fake. Do you really think she rolls out of bed looking like that? How long does it take her to reconstruct herself? Do you think she never has emotional mood swings or hormonal imbalances? What will she become if she submits to your play for her? Depressed, guilt laden, and insecure most likely. What about her spouse and children, they come with the pretty package. After you run off with her do you really think she will never criticize you or complain like that wife you already have back home? In the words of the famous segment on a prime-time sports show, "Come on man." What are you thinking?

If we would stop and learn to resist the initial temptation, we would fare far better. Our enemy loves to wreak havoc in the family and generational destruction takes place when a home falls apart. Why just settle for taking down a single person when you can influence multiple generations though one foolish act? Our enemy is shrewd and we are often easy prey for him.

We need to take our thoughts captive to Christ and His Word. We need to learn how to discern the enemy's tactics and resist them. The truth is you will not be happier with someone else. The reality is that if you leave your current spouse for an illusion you will end up disillusioned. I understand that there are instances of abuse and for those cases, you need to seek professional help and flee to safety. What I am addressing here is the plethora of godly men and women that are chucking away their marriages and families for a huge lie.

Why should you stay? God hates divorce. God wants godly offspring and marriage provides the best possible opportunity for this to take place. Don't just take my word for it, read this:

> Another thing you do: You flood the LORD's altar with tears. You weep and wail because he no longer pays attention to your offerings or accepts them with pleasure from your hands. You ask, "Why?" It is because the LORD is acting as the witness between you and the wife of your youth, because you have broken faith with her, though she is your partner, the wife of your marriage covenant. Has not the LORD made them one? In flesh and spirit they are his. And why one? Because he was seeking godly offspring. So, guard yourself in

## For Our Consideration

> your spirit, and do not break faith with the wife of your youth. "I hate divorce," says the LORD God of Israel, "and I hate a man's covering himself with violence as well as with his garment," says the LORD Almighty. So, guard yourself in your spirit, and do not break faith. Malachi 2:13-16

Besides the destruction caused through immorality, the result of choosing it will not satisfy you. Grief, guilt, emotional heaviness, financial burdens, and yes, even more relationship difficulties always follow. If children are involved then you end up giving up your rights to lead them and end up sharing with people that you most likely will not agree with on critical topics.

Ex-spouses remarry and children end up like a ping-pong ball bouncing between houses and mixed families. As the children become teenagers, they often pit the parents against one another to get what they want. Threats of moving in with dad or mom almost always work in getting their self-centered wishes fulfilled. A house divided will not stand and as the old song goes, "The children are the broken pieces when a home falls apart."

Feelings come and go and we must not be ruled by them but make them come under the authority of our Lord Jesus. We can learn to love our spouse and we must resist the allure of another. Proverbs 7:27 states accurately that the immorality road ends up in death. We would be wise to choose another path to walk on while we still can.

1 Corinthians 13 gives us the signposts to follow and if we take that road, we will end up in life, not death. Read this love chapter every day and ask the Lord to give you the grace to do it and see what happens to your falling in and out of love. Love is a choice and not primarily a feeling.

A quick note to those that have fallen in the past before I close. Failing does not make us a failure. If you can correct the mistake and save the marriage, do so. Get help and get it now. If everyone has moved on to new marriages then ask for forgiveness and rest in God's grace. There are no second-class citizens in God's Kingdom, just dearly loved children. We learn from our mistakes and share with others the lessons we gained hoping that they won't have to be repeated. Jesus died for sinners like you and I and we rest in that promise from our Father.

Go ahead and fall in love with your spouse again...better yet, don't ever fall out of love in the first place.

## Questions to Ponder or Discuss:

1. Why you think so many Christian marriages are ending up in divorce court?

2. Why is sexual immorality one of the few sins we are told to run from?

3. Does the enemy of our souls really hate marriage? Why or why not?

4. If Biblical love is not primarily an emotion then what is it? Explain.

For Our Consideration

# How's Your Prayer Life Guys?

C. S. Lewis is said to have wondered if God was a sadist. Looking at those that God calls into paid ministry, we at least know He has a sense of humor. Turning our eyes, a bit closer to home, many couples struggle relationally and then we blame God. "My wife doesn't understand me," the man complains. "My husband is about as sensitive as a rock." the wife moans. In our quiet moments, we reflect on whether God really knew what He was doing when He made us male and female.

"Does this dress make me look too fat," asks the wife to her husband. Most men that have been married for any length of time recognize this as a potential no-win question. Whatever the answer the outcome will most likely not be what is expected or desired. Anything short of "you are perfect dear just the way you are" will most likely end in a mess. Even with this tried and true answer, accusations of dishonesty will most likely follow.

The scientific community has finally figured out what God designed from the beginning - men and women are different. We look different, think differently and while we share a common language, we speak it differently. After four decades of counseling, I have learned to speak a little bit of "woman." I am not proficient and it will most likely never be as easy to me as my native tongue, but I am beginning to grasp some of the basic underlying concepts.

This is not a new revelation for many have tried to explain the dilemma. *Men are from Mars, Women are from Venus* was a popular book (selling over 7 million copies) for quite some time. Others have attempted to address the differences in word pictures such as, "men are waffles and women are spaghetti."

Whatever the attempt, the differences remain and they are not new. The Apostle Peter shares one of the most difficult passages for men in all the Scripture in 1 Peter 3:7:

> "Likewise, husbands, live with your wives in an understanding way, showing honor to the woman as the weaker vessel, since they are heirs with you of the grace of life, so that your prayers may not be hindered."

The "likewise" is there to connect the verse to the previous section which also begins with a likewise to connect it to the paragraph dealing with submission to authority. Peter ended verse six with "do not fear anything that is frightening," and walking in submission to an imperfect husband is about as frightening as it gets for a woman of God. However, God places the responsibility on the husband to live with his wife in an understanding way, and this should scare us men to our core.

Why should we be afraid of this verse? The last sentence explains the answer - "so that your prayers are not hindered." How I treat my wife, has a direct impact on how effective my prayers are. Hindered is defined as, being cut off, to impede, to interrupt, to place an obstacle in the way, okay, you get the idea, if I am not treating my wife well, my prayer life will be damaged.

The "understanding way" part is what usually gives us fits. Some translations use "according to knowledge" and that is fine. The point is that we as men must figure out how to live with our wives in a way that is pleasing to the Lord or we don't have a prayer...and I mean literally!

So, what does it mean to live with your wife in an understanding way? Great question and the answer is, it depends. What will show honor to you wife? What will edify her? What will encourage her? What will meet her needs now? What will bring her joy and peace in the situation? What will demonstrate your love to her as if Jesus loved her? Wow, that is a mouthful.

What I just wrote is a challenge, yet it is Biblical. Even a casual reading of Ephesians 5:25 - "Husbands love your wives, as Christ loved the church and gave himself up for her," should provoke us to think. How did Christ love the Church? What did He give up for Her? Most of us know that to follow Christ we should take up our cross daily, but sometimes we forget that cross carrying begins at home. It is sometimes easier to love those across the pew or ocean than to die to our self for those under our roof.

Ken Nair in his challenging book entitled, *Discovering the Mind of a Woman* asks a haunting question. I will paraphrase but Nair asks if after being married to you for however long you have been married is your wife better off or not? Everyone brings issues and problems into marriage for there are no perfect people, but how are we doing?

What does this mean? Let's say your wife is a mess emotionally. Did she start out that way or become that way under your care? If she started out that way, is she better or worse after living with you? If she became that way after being married to you, how is your prayer life? Are your prayers being hindered? If your wife is getting worse after being married to you for five, ten or twenty-five years, what does that say to your leadership and understanding skills? Wow, is that harsh! Is it? Or, is it perhaps what Peter is attempting to address?

I am neither a medical doctor, nor a physiologist, or psychologist, and I understand that there can be physical, mental and emotional disorders that affect a person's emotional stability. I am a pastor and there is a spiritual dimension that must not be overlooked if these others areas are clean, and this is what Peter is referring to. We as husbands have two very clear commands to obey regarding our wives; we are to live with them in an understanding way, and we are to love them in the same way Jesus treated the Church. If we are failing in either or both, our wives will be impacted adversely.

On the other hand, our wives are not simply victims that have no choice as to how they respond. They can and must bear up under bad leadership, but should they have to because of us? Shouldn't we be living in such a way as to help not hurt our brides? Shouldn't we be growing in our daily lives to reflect a more Christ-like attitude at home, where it counts the most? Shouldn't we make it our ambition to grow daily, to love our wives, and to walk in obedience to our Lord's commands?

The next time you are tempted to get angry with your wife, or when you simply do not understand what she is talking about, remember your prayer life. Your reaction will either help or hinder it. What will you choose?

For Our Consideration

## Questions to Ponder or Discuss:

1. Why did God make men and women different?

2. Honestly, how is our prayer life?

3. What message are we presenting to our children through our marriage? How about the lost?

4. Is our wife better or worse after living under our leadership? What would she say about this question?

# Different is Good

In the beginning, God created Adam and Eve. For the record, and to be politically incorrect, God did not create Adam and Steve or Amy and Eve. God, in His infinite wisdom, decided to create man and woman - different physically, emotionally, and mentally.

God decided to create man and woman to perfectly express Himself to His creation. It would take both to present a full picture of what it means to be made in His image. One is not better or worse, and one is not less important, both are needed, - differing roles, but of equivalent value and worth. God said that the husband and his wife are joint heirs in Christ.

> Likewise, husbands, live with your wives in an understanding way, showing honor to the woman as the weaker vessel, since they are heirs with you of the grace of life, so that your prayers may not be hindered. 1 Peter 3:7

My bride and I have been married for over forty-two years. I would be lying to say that every moment of every day has been filled with bliss. In fact, while the first year was a disaster, there have been many times when our marriage was a mess.

My wife would admit that she has issues and so do I. We were young, selfish, and hard-headed when we married. Today, we love each other with a deep, abiding love, but that did not simply happen overnight. If fact, there were many times when both of us would beg God for a way out. By God's grace, He did not answer those requests, at least in the way we expected.

We would not divorce because we did not allow for any back doors to our marriage. That does not mean that we didn't struggle, for we did. Since this is written from my point of view, I will leave my wife's struggles out of the discussion and share with you what I have learned over the years. I pray that you can glean some helpful truths here, men.

At some point in time in our marriage, while I can't remember the exact moment, it seems like we were married for about fifteen years or so, the above verse became real to me. God expected me to learn how to live with my wife in an understanding way. She is a daughter of the King and how I treated her had a direct impact on my relationship with that King, even all the way down to my prayers. Wow, I needed to have my mind renewed.

Up until that point, I had spent the bulk of my time attempting to conform my wife into my image. If she could just think like me, act like me, respond or not respond like me, our marriage would be so much better. If Leslie could just be Jeff, life would be grand.

But God did not have Jeff marry Jeff, He had me marry Leslie. Leslie is different from Jeff. She thinks, reacts, and processes everything differently from the way I do. At some point, I began to entertain the thought that perhaps God added Leslie to me not to torture me, but to help complete His work in me. Maybe, just maybe He knew what He was doing when He gave me someone so different than me.

I began to wonder what would happen if I listened to her just to hear what she had to say and not to correct her to the proper way of thinking - my way. What if the Sovereign God of the universe knew that I needed someone different than me to help me see issues from another perspective? What if my wife, in all her differences was a gift from God? A unique thought to me at that time!

Looking back now I am embarrassed that it took me so long to see this truth. I regret the years wasted in attempting to change my wife into my image instead of embracing the differences. God knew that two points of view are better. God knew that my vantage point needed to be tempered and softened. God knew, and He gave me a blessing that I resisted.

When I quit fighting the differences and began to embrace them, growth came both personally and in our marriage. My wife didn't need to be me. The perspective she brought to the discussions was different but necessary to make better decisions. What I once considered a threat was now being embraced as a gift.

For the record, I am not perfect when it comes to remembering these truths. There are still days when I fight the differences. I slip back into the old way of thinking and begin to argue with my bride about her thoughts. The competitive side of me wants to win her over to my point of view instead of listening to what she says. I do this to my own hurt for God provided someone who is different because He loves me. When I cut her off, it is only hurting my potential. Two really are better than one and both views provide a needed perspective.

The next time your wife begins to challenge your plan or way of thinking guys I would recommend that you remember the words of life from Peter. Learn to live with your wife in an understanding way. What truth is your wife bringing that you do not see? What point of view is she stating that you need to hear? What could be embraced from what she is sharing that would make the decision better?

I know it is hard sometimes to listen to your wife. I know it is difficult to learn to speak "woman," for the way many wives communicate is different than guys. We tend to want the facts, and nothing but the facts, which leads to a solution. Our wives tend to want to share all the details, emotions, and seemingly disconnected information thus clouding the issue from our point of view.

But what if God wants us to slow down, learn to listen, and embrace the input from our wife? What if the information our wife is trying to communicate to us is important? If God gave her to us, and He did, and if God gave us someone different than ourselves, and He did, then it would be wise to learn to listen. In fact, our wife is a hand-picked gift from God.

God has given us one of His daughters to share our earthly journey with, and He did so because He loves us. Let's quit fighting the differences and begin to embrace them and see what happens in our lives. Let's learn to listen to hear what is being said with an open mind free of trying to correct. Let's let our wives be the gift God intended and receive this gift joyfully. Let's enjoy the differences and quit fighting them!

## Questions to Ponder or Discuss:

1. Why did God make men and women so different in the way they think and in their emotions?

2. What does Peter mean by commanding men to live with their wives in an understanding way?

3. Would it help us or hurt us to listen to others and especially our spouse? Explain.

4. What does it mean to value our spouse as a joint-heir in Christ? Should that affect how we treat them?

For Our Consideration

# Marriage and Mind Reading

Marriage is a gift from God and mind reading is typically thought of as magic practice. What can these two possibly have in common? For starters, both involve two people. Marriage was given as a gift to Adam in the Garden of Eden to combat his loneliness and incompleteness. Mind reading is attempting to try to figure out what someone is thinking without going through the bother of verbal communication.

Married couples often practice mind reading with mixed results. It is true that as you live with someone for a long time you can know what he or she is thinking, sometimes. After over 42 years of marriage, my bride and I can complete each other's sentences and thoughts on occasion. There are still times, however when we guess wrong and here is where it gets dicey.

Mind reading is a guessing game based on assumptions and preconceived views. We all practice it with people and probably do not even think about it. We drive down the road and we know that that person that just cut us off was not thinking, or they were doing it on purpose. The woman that was short with us at the church service really does not like us, or so we think. Our spouse states something more harshly than we think they should and we know why. Or do we?

Most of us suffer from too many conclusions based on too little information syndrome. We make 100% conclusions on about 1% information. We mind read. However, are we accurate? Do we really know what is going on in the mind of someone else? Do we have all the facts? Rarely. Yet, we jump to conclusions, assign motives, and usually bad ones to boot, we are judge, jury, and prosecutor and we often hang someone based on circumstantial evidence. Okay, I know we do not really hang them, but we get angry, rejected, hurt, and sometimes retaliate before we even know the facts. Well, at least I do.

While it does not happen all the time, sometimes God gives us just a little more insight into why the person acted as they did. Maybe the person that was driving rudely had something hot spill in their lap and they were not thinking about you at all. Perhaps the woman on Sunday had just walked away from someone that shared a tragedy in their life and they were deep in thought. You just happen to come upon them while they were trying to process and their aloofness had nothing to do with you. Is it possible that we do not always have all information in our marriages as well?

In marriage, most of us are less guarded with our spouse than we are with others. We know they are stuck with us and therefore we are not as concerned with how we speak. Sometimes we do not put up the fences in the conversation that we would with an outsider. We may say something in an unguarded tone with our spouse that we would never use with someone else.

I know my wife loves me, she has promised never to leave me, and I know she will not. I do not have to impress her or make her think something of me because she knows me. As long as we have been married, she knows me very well, and she still loves me. A fact that I am both surprised at and very grateful for.

What I am learning to do is ask the next question. I do not always do well at it, but I am learning. When my wife is harsher than she should be there usually is a good reason for the behavior. Something has happened that I probably know nothing about. A phone call, email, steady stream of small people complaining, stressful day, or something else has happened to trigger her response. Maybe I did something to bother her, maybe not, but the reaction is there for a reason.

I must learn how not to react to the reaction but seek the cause of the reaction. So many times, we waste tremendous amounts of emotional energy arguing about the reaction. In my wise moments, and for the record, there are not near as many as I would wish, I do not react; instead, I ask the next question.

What's the next question? It depends. What I need, if I am going to respond properly, is to understand what is underneath the reaction. I can ask, "Why were you so harsh?" but that typically is unwise. A better question is, "Did something happen that hurt you today?" Or perhaps even better is to give her a hug, hold her, and just listen. She will share about her day, an event or something that happened that caused her to react. I can waste a bunch of our limited time together fussing about her behavior or I can listen and help to soothe the hurt.

It has taken decades of being married to come to a startling conclusion. My wife does not always need my solutions, she needs my understanding. One day my bride placed her hands on my cheeks and spoke in that tone. You know the one guys, the voice inflection that says, "I am going to speak slowly and use small words so you will get it" tone. She told me, "I don't need your three solutions to my problem when I am sharing with you; I need a hug and your acknowledgment of my pain." As a man, that was a strange sentence.

We men tend to think along the lines of solution. There's a problem, I have the answer. Just ask me, I would be glad to share my wisdom. In fact, I can come up with multiple solutions to just about any problem. My wife did not want my solutions, she wanted my understanding, and that conversation has helped me to learn to ask the next question.

I am not a mind reader, I am a husband that needs to learn how to listen to his wife. If I ask the right questions, she will reveal her mind to me. What she shares is so much clearer and accurate than what I guess with my mind reading skills. As hard as it is for me to understand, my wife, many times does not need my answers or mind reading skills, she just needs a hug.

## Questions to Ponder or Discuss:

1. Have you ever guessed at what was upsetting your spouse or someone close to you and been wrong? Care to share the details?

2. How often do you think we have all the information necessary to make an informed decision about what someone is thinking before speaking to them?

3. What do you think of the concept of not reacting to the reaction? Explain.

4. Have you tried to ask the next question? Did it help?

For Our Consideration

# Marriage: The Perfect Tool for Spiritual Growth

While earning two doctorate degrees, a foundational principle was hammered into my brain - look for presuppositions. Underneath every thought, vision, and action lies something that motivates and underpins. With every thought and action taken, each of us functions with many presumptions.

For example, I operate under the presupposition that you can read when I write this. In addition, there are assumptions regarding who will read it, how they will respond, and if they will catch the intended humor in the above sentence. We all bring many presuppositions to every thought and conversation, even if we are unaware of possessing them.

I have a presupposition regarding marriage. In fact, I have several. God is good, God had a plan, God knew what He was doing, and God had specific ideas in mind by creating the institution of marriage.

Here is one of my important presuppositions - Marriage is the perfect tool to help us mature in Christ. God knew exactly what it would take for each of His children to grow up. God decided that most people would marry, reproduce, and fulfill His commands regarding discipleship, evangelism, and even caretaking of His creation.

While beyond the point of this article, marriage is a supernatural picture of Christ and the Church (Ephesians 5:32), the primary evangelism/discipleship tool for reaching the next generation (Deuteronomy 6:4-9), and God placed humans on earth to take care of it (Genesis 2:15).

# Marriage

What is the point of this writing is that marriage provides an excellent tool for spiritual growth. In fact, I believe it is one of the primary tools God uses to develop the fruit of the Spirit in His children's lives. There is a gift of singleness, but most of God's people will marry. Therefore, my presupposition is that God had a plan for this joining.

Science, along with detailed, extensive and expensive studies, reveals that men and women are different. I could have saved them a great deal of time and energy by simply asking any five-year old, but that is not the point. Men and women think differently, speak a different language and often have entirely different value systems. Is that by design or was it an oversight by the Creator? We must answer that question.

Your answer will determine your behavior. If God didn't have a plan for the differences, then the goal becomes conforming our spouse into our image. We will spend our days and energy fighting the differences instead of embracing them. If God did create us differently, then there is another purpose for His decision to do so.

I would suggest that He did create us on purpose and fully intended for there to be major differences. We are created physically and emotionally different. Any married couple quickly learns these facts. We tend to enjoy the physical differences and fight the emotional ones.

While not pretending to know the fullness of God's wisdom or intent in His creation mindset, I would venture to state that He knew in advance what He was doing, and why. What we can know with certainty is that marriage provides some excellent spiritual growth potential!

For example, the fruit of the Spirit grows in the soil of marriage almost unlike anywhere else. Built right into our day by day relationship are the opportunities to walk in love, experience joy, seek peace, learn patience, demonstrate kindness, practice goodness, remain faithful, become gentle and walk in self-control. (See Galatians 5:22-23)

What better place to demonstrate agape love than in our marriage? 1 Corinthians 13 graces the walls of most homes, but do we put it into practice within those same walls? We can often quote it, but living it out is harder when it comes to our spouse. Yet, God placed that person right there in our lives to learn to do exactly that! We learn to walk in Biblical love through marriage.

Love is kind, patient, does not envy, boast, is not arrogant or rude, does not insist on its own way, is not irritable or resentful, bears all things, believes all things, hopes and endures all things. Love never fails and love is the greatest of what abides.

What else besides marriage provides us with such an easy opportunity to grow in Biblical love? Who is closer to us to learn on and to put the love actions into practice? All the love attributes are action words. They require an object and I would suggest that our spouse is the perfect first choice.

As we look at spiritual maturity throughout the Scriptures, we will find descriptions that include such things as death to self, servanthood, esteeming someone as better than our self, humility, long suffering, patience, and overcoming all manner of sin. These and more are accomplished by marriage. We learn to grow in self-control, we learn how to speak life not death with our tongue and we learn how to curb our anger. It is almost as if God knew (sarcastic humor) what was needed for spiritual maturity and came up with the perfect solution - the marriage covenant.

Marriage

I would encourage you to read the following verses with your spouse in mind and see if my presupposition regarding marriage is true.

- John 13:34-35 - we demonstrate the reality of Christ by our marriage.
- 1 John 4:20-21 - if our spouse is not our brother or sister in Christ I don't know who is.
- Matthew 22:36-39 - two greatest commandments - love God, demonstrate it by loving your neighbor, again, if our spouse doesn't qualify as our closest neighbor I don't know who does.
- Galatians 6:10 - is our spouse of the household of God? I think so.

We often attempt to implement these verses first towards those outside of our home. I would argue that unless we begin within the home we are missing what God intended. Frankly, it is easier to love the stranger or someone across the globe, than loving my spouse, but I wonder what God thinks about that?

If my desire is to grow spiritually, then beginning to look for opportunities within my marriage is the place to start. At least, that is my presupposition. What's yours?

For Our Consideration

## Questions to Ponder or Discuss:

1. Why do you think God created men and women so different?

2. Do you have any unbiblical presuppositions regarding your marriage partner? How do you know?

3. Do you agree or disagree that marriage is a perfect place to develop spiritual fruit? Explain.

4. Do you agree or disagree that marriage is the perfect place to learn how to walk in 1 Corinthians 13 love? Explain.

# Section Two

# Let's Go Deeper

In this section, I have provided some more in-depth type articles and research for those inclined to dig a bit deeper.

The Scriptures provide everything necessary to live a godly life and should be our primary study tool. This Book we love is living and active and able to clear up deception and lies.

The Word of God is truth and we must align our lives with what is presented and not the other way around. Many seem to search the Bible to justify behavior instead of seeking to understand what the will of God is and align our lives accordingly.

As you read through what follows I pray you will be challenged to study these thoughts for yourself within God's Word. Make sure that what is presented is true and accurate.

No matter who the author or speaker is or what you may think of them, be diligent in proving all things and hold fast to what is true and accurate. No one is perfect and therefore we must study to prove all things accurate with the Scriptures.

Now, please give grace to each author and speaker, including this one! No one is perfect except Jesus and we are not Him. All the rest of us are in varying degrees of being messed up!

If you find some points you can't agree with, put them aside and consider why you cannot accept the viewpoint offered. If it is Biblical, then stick to it. If it is cultural or based on man's tradition, then I would challenge you to accept the Scripture and not hold to the teachings of men.

May God richly bless you as you study His Word!

# Contents

| | |
|---|---|
| One Another | 246 |
| Family Discipleship Thoughts | 251 |
| Family Practical Discipleship Tools | 271 |
| A Bible Study on Authority | 288 |
| Parental Authority and Marriage | 308 |
| Called to War – A Spiritual Warfare Discussion | 318 |
| Spiritual Incrementalism – A Three Part Discussion | 332 |
| Fatherhood – A Seven Part Discussion | 351 |

For Our Consideration

# One Another

Here are a few verses that list the "one another" type passages. If you spend the time to read these and look them up in their context, I am sure you will be both blessed and challenged as I was by doing this spiritual exercise.

Read each passage and think about how you are doing in walking out the insights, commandments, and wisdom within them.

Romans 12:10 - Be devoted to one another in brotherly love. Honor one another above yourselves.

Romans 12:16 - Live in harmony with one another. Do not be proud, but be willing to associate with people of low position.

Romans 13:8 - Let no debt remain outstanding, except the continuing debt to love one another, for he who loves his fellow man has fulfilled the law.

Romans 14:13 - Therefore let us stop passing judgment on one another. Instead, make up your mind not to put any stumbling block or obstacle in your brother's way.

Romans 15:7 - Accept one another, then, just as Christ accepted you, in order to bring praise to God.

Romans 15:14 - I myself am convinced, my brothers, that you yourselves are full of goodness, complete in knowledge and competent to instruct one another.

Romans 16:16 - Greet one another with a holy kiss. All the churches of Christ send greetings.

1 Corinthians 1:10 - I appeal to you, brothers, in the name of our Lord Jesus Christ, that all of you agree with one another so that there may be no divisions among you and that you may be perfectly united in mind and thought.

Ephesians 4:2 - Be completely humble and gentle; be patient, bearing with one another in love.

Ephesians 4:32 - Be kind and compassionate to one another, forgiving each other, just as in Christ God forgave you.

Ephesians 5:19 - Speak to one another with psalms, hymns and spiritual songs. Sing and make music in your heart to the Lord,

Ephesians 5:21 - Submit to one another out of reverence for Christ.

Colossians 3:13 - Bear with each other and forgive whatever grievances you may have against one another. Forgive as the Lord forgave you.

Colossians 3:16 - Let the word of Christ dwell in you richly as you teach and admonish one another with all wisdom, and as you sing psalms, hymns and spiritual songs with gratitude in your hearts to God.

For Our Consideration

1 Thessalonians 5:11 - Therefore encourage one another and build each other up, just as in fact you are doing.

Titus 3:3 - At one time we too were foolish, disobedient, deceived and enslaved by all kinds of passions and pleasures. We lived in malice and envy, being hated and hating one another.

Hebrews 3:13 - But encourage one another daily, as long as it is called Today, so that none of you may be hardened by sin's deceitfulness.

Hebrews 10:24 - And let us consider how we may spur one another on toward love and good deeds.

Hebrews 10:25 - Let us not give up meeting together, as some are in the habit of doing, but let us encourage one another–and all the more as you see the Day approaching.

James 4:11 - Brothers, do not slander one another. Anyone who speaks against his brother or judges him speaks against the law and judges it. When you judge the law, you are not keeping it, but sitting in judgment on it.

1 Peter 1:22 - Now that you have purified yourselves by obeying the truth so that you have sincere love for your brothers, love one another deeply, from the heart.

1 Peter 3:8 - Finally, all of you, live in harmony with one another; be sympathetic, love as brothers, be compassionate and humble.

1 Peter 4:9 - Offer hospitality to one another without grumbling.

1 Peter 5:5 - Young men, in the same way be submissive to those who are older. All of you, clothe yourselves with humility toward one another,

1 Peter 5:14 - Greet one another with a kiss of love. Peace to all of you who are in Christ.

1 John 1:7 - But if we walk in the light, as he is in the light, we have fellowship with one another, and the blood of Jesus, his Son, purifies us from all sin.

1 John 3:11 - This is the message you heard from the beginning: We should love one another.

1 John 3:23 - And this is his command: to believe in the name of his Son, Jesus Christ, and to love one another as he commanded us.

1 John 4:7 - Dear friends, let us love one another, for love comes from God. Everyone who loves has been born of God and knows God.

1 John 4:11 - Dear friends, since God so loved us, we also ought to love one another.

For Our Consideration

1 John 4:12 - No one has ever seen God; but if we love one another, God lives in us and his love is made complete in us.

2 John 1:5 - And now, dear lady, I am not writing you a new command but one we have had from the beginning. I ask that we love one another.

    We live our lives in community. Salvation is the most personal decision we will ever make, and afterward, we live the rest of our lives with and around other people. We live with many "one anothers."
    What would happen to our marriages, families, churches, schools, workplaces and even roadways, if we put into practice some of the verses just listed? I pray each of us would try and let's just see if we can't change the world!

Let's Go Deeper

# Discipleship Thoughts

### Section I. The Problem
**Marriage**

Christian marriages are falling apart in record numbers. If you want one disturbing sentence consider this one - "Divorce rates among conservative Christians were significantly higher than for other faith groups and much higher than Atheists and Agnostics experience." This reality should bother us greatly. We who take the name of Christ are divorcing our spouses at a higher rate than those that deny or ignore Him.

Studies abound to reinforce these statistics and George Barna sent shudders through the Christian Church when he released his findings a few years ago. Many leaders were upset over the results and questioned Barna's methods, but the reality in the pew cannot be ignored.

Ask most any pastor where the bulk of his counseling time is spent and he will most likely answer that it is dealing with marriage and family issues.

**Barna report: Variation in divorce rates among Christian faith groups:**

> Denomination (in order of decreasing divorce rate) % who have been divorced:
> Non-denominational ** 34%
> Baptists 29%

For Our Consideration

| Mainline Protestants | 25% |
| Mormons | 24% |
| Catholics | 21% |
| Lutherans | 21% |

** Barna uses the term "non-denominational" to refer to Evangelical Christian congregations that are not affiliated with a specific denomination. The clear majority are fundamentalist in their theological beliefs.

The frightening truth of these studies is that many who claim to know Jesus are not demonstrating the reality of the life-changing grace received in the home. Logic would state that after we are born again, the reality of this miracle would begin to be evident first with those that know us the best. Reality is not matching this logical conclusion.

While we may argue over the minutia of the details of the studies, the reality is that there are many Christian homes that are living in something far less than "oneness" that Christ stated was the goal of marriage. Many otherwise godly couples are living in truces or living parallel lives that rarely intersect. These marriages are better for the children than divorce, but not much.

Perhaps it would be helpful for pastors to begin to keep a log of the counseling they perform, as well as an evaluation of the crises meetings they attend, and see how many are directly tied to the breakdown of the family. Generic studies can be helpful, but keeping track of how our time is really spent will prove more profitable. If you are like most pastors, it will not take long to realize that the bulk of the crises that demand your time and attention are family related.

Let's Go Deeper

### The Next Generation Is in Grave Danger

It is hard to forget the picture that popped up on the computer screen one morning while perusing some typical news outlets. Two pre-teens were dangling their younger sibling out of a window in a high-rise apartment building by his hands. The two in the window stood expressionless in the photo shortly before letting the child drop multiple stories to his death.

And how could anyone forget the tragedy of the Columbine massacre or the mall killings in Minnesota by yet another gun-wielding student? By just about any standard used, the young people in America are in serious trouble and have been since the late 1950's.

We are bombarded daily with statistics giving us far too many details including teen crime rates, teen pregnancy and abortion, the impact of divorce, drug and alcohol abuse (even in pre-high school age children), suicide, and unthinkable violence, each of which are taking an incredible toll on the next generation.

Since 1991, the United States government has been conducting anonymous surveys specifically attempting to categorize the risky behaviors of youth. While the statistics are interesting, it will not do to bore the reader with the plethora of dangerous and sometimes deadly behavior engaged in by our young people. The title of the study, – *Morbidity and Mortality Weekly Report*, and the fact that as taxpayers must fund such studies, should be sufficient to illustrate the point.

In 1993, William Bennett shared a staggering statistic: "Violent crimes have increased 400 percent since 1960, with the most active incubator of this violence centered in the 10 to 17-year-old age group." Of course, many have come to expect that from non-Christian,

## For Our Consideration

unchurched young people, but this must surely be different in the Evangelical Church.

The organized church spends tens of millions of dollars each year to reach Christian youths via youth ministry and Christian schools. A quick Google search will reveal hundreds, if not thousands of Christian youth organizations worldwide. A partial listing includes the following: Youth for Christ, Youth Specialties, Youth Unlimited, Youth Ministry Exchange, Legacy Youth Ministries, National Youth Ministries, Teen Life Ministries, ELCA Youth Ministries, GBOD Youth Ministries, PCUSA Youth Ministries, Teen Missions, AFLC Youth Ministries, Nazarene Youth Ministries, etc.

This list does not include Christian school ministries or curriculum producers exclusively devoted to reaching the young. In addition, just about all major denominations are deeply involved in youth and children's ministry in some fashion. With such massive expenditures of time, money, and staff devoted to reaching young people, the Evangelical Church should be excelling in their goal of reaching the next generation for Christ.

However, consider some of these disturbing statistics: George Barna, the well-known pollster that focuses primarily on the Christian marketplace mentioned earlier, recently released a study showing that only twenty percent of teenagers retain their faith after they reach adulthood. A twenty percent success rate translates into four out of five youths leaving their faith shortly after graduating from high school. In addition, Mr. Barna maintains that if current trends continue, in ten years, church attendance will be half the size it is today.

Dawson MacAlister, national youth ministry specialist, remarked that 90% of youth active in high school church programs drop out of church by the time they are sophomores in college.

Southern Baptists, known for devoting large sums of time and money to Sunday school programs and youth outreach, also are struggling. At a recent Southern Baptist Convention, data presented indicated that 70-88% of their youth left after their freshman year in college. In the same study, the Southern Baptist Council on Family Life reported an even more staggering statistic: 88% of children in evangelical homes leave church at the age of eighteen.

Scott Brown, the director of The National Center for Family Integrated Churches reveals some insightful statistics from Thomas Rainer. Dr. Rainer formerly served as a professor of evangelism at Southern Baptist Seminary. His survey was concerned with people's general understanding of the Gospel and the application to their personal life beyond the walls of the Church:

>Born before 1946 — 65%, Born between 1946 and 1964 — 35%, Born between 1965 and 1976 — 15%, Born between 1976 and 1994 — 4%.

The comprehension of the Gospel, and what it means to live like a Christian, based on this survey, seems to be in a free fall from the 1940's to the 1990's. A drop of 61% between 1946 and 1994 is staggering.

A four-year study conducted by Professors Webber, Dr. Mason, Dr. Singleton, and Rev. Dr. Hughes, demonstrated this current deficiency in reaching youths. The parents of the students sent their children to a Christian school, at least partially for spiritual reasons, yet the students considered the intrusion of the staff and administration as a violation of their freedom.

## For Our Consideration

They objected to the school that taught them what they should believe. "Our principal pretty much told us we had to believe in God and the Church," said one student attending a Christian school. "Kind of annoying because we all feel that we want to believe in what we want to," she continued. "I was kind of confused. I just thought we don't have to do that because you tell us to." Their parents often have similar attitudes and are no more involved in the churches than their children.

Based on this sampling of studies referenced, it should be clear that the next generation of the Church is struggling to follow in the previous one's footsteps or considering the last quote, perhaps not. Parents have a tremendous amount of influence over their children's behavior and whether their children accept or reject Christianity. But it is possible they do not understand what they wield. It should be readily apparent that the parents and the church are both struggling to capture the next generation for Christ, despite the significant cost and the time exerted.

The Evangelical Church appears to understand the dilemma to some degree and is seeking answers through prayer. With the advent of the Internet, we can perform easy searches and discover such headlines as these: "Methodist Youth Conference Calls for Prayer for Revival," "Sparking Revival in Tomorrow's Church Leaders," "Pray for Revival in Youth Ministries," and, finally, "The Call," which is a national group dedicated to praying specifically for revival among the Christian youth.

These websites calling for prayer point out that there is a cry for revival directed towards the youth from many within the Evangelical Church. Revival is typically defined as "an act or instance of reviving: the state of being revived." For something to be revived, there must have been something lost or diminished. What has been lost is the faith and observable Christian behavior that is supposed to be passed on from parent to child. According to the data quoted above, the Church and Christian parents are failing in large numbers to instill their belief system into the next generation. The churches, schools, and youth ministries understand the need and that is why they pray for revival. Frustrated with their lack of success they call out to God to stir up the hearts of their youth.

### Summary

The Church seems to be struggling with the breakup of the home and the devastating results that follow. Jesus stated over 2,000 years ago the reality that most pastors walk in every day, "A house divided against itself will not stand." (Mark 3:25) A dysfunctional home will not produce as effective fruit as a functional one for the Kingdom of God. Children that grow up in a Christian home and then reject their parent's faith overwhelmingly state that hypocrisy in the home was the primary reason. The thinking is logical and poignant -"If your Christianity did not make any meaningful difference in the way you lived, why should I adopt it?" If the Church hopes to stem the tide of 70-90% rejection of Christ by the next generation, serious changes need to be made.

What follow are some practical suggestions and plans on how to begin to reverse the current trends of destruction. If we continue to do the same things expecting different results we are doing a great disservice to those we lead.

Change is not easy and is often resisted, but we must change to win the next generation and to stem the tide of destruction sweeping the Church. We must begin to make disciples in obedience to our Lord's commands, and the best place to begin is in the Christian home.

For Our Consideration

## Section II: Some Solutions

What follows are multiple helps and ideas to assist pastors in reversing the tide of destruction that is sweeping the family and Church. Perhaps all of them cannot be adopted, but just because we cannot do everything does not mean we shouldn't do something. The battle ahead is fierce but we have the Victor on our side and His Kingdom will know no end. Jesus has given us the battle plan in His Word and the empowerment in His Holy Spirit to complete it. Even small changes can produce huge results!

If a home is dysfunctional there will be little positive fruit produced within its walls. The opposite is also true - if a home is in its proper function, great fruit can come forth. A divided home will be a time drain on just about everyone resulting in many counseling hours, discipline and relationship issues with the children, and little ministry benefit to anyone else.

On the other hand, a strong marriage, healthy relationship between children and parents will not be a drain but a life-giving resource. Most pastors know this, yet how much of our ministry plan really addresses these truths? What part of our budget do we devote to strengthening the home structure? Perhaps we need to reorient our thinking and strategy.

For illustrative purposes let me give you just a few Scriptures and then include some action points that can be incorporated into any teaching. If we are going to attack the problem of home destruction, then we must begin to address the issue on a regular basis.

Adding marriage seminars and Sunday School classes can help, but in addition, we should make sure all our teaching ends up having practical application in the home and this will produce long term change.

Let's Go Deeper

As pastors and teachers there is limited time to drive home the point of the message given, so we must make sure that those that listen to the message make the connection to real life, and that begins in the family.

## Examples

God has chosen to reveal Himself to His creation in the family model, and the family example is used throughout the Scripture. God chose to be known as "Our Father," and not as Emperor of the Universe, President in charge of Human Relations, or CEO of Everything. God certainly could have chosen any title or model He desired, but He chose the family model. God is our Father, Jesus is the Son and our Brother, and we are born again into a huge Family and now have millions of brothers and sisters. All of this was God's idea and we should begin to focus on why He chose this illustration.

**Action Point:** Spend some time developing the concept of family from an eternal perspective. Answer the question as to why God picked this model instead of any other, and why does it matter. Sprinkle into your teaching time the concept of family and how these relationships should function. The Bible is a family-centric Book from cover to cover, why? Communicate that Adam and Eve were the first marriage, Jesus was born into a family and so are we when we are born again, and we all are heading to a Wedding Feast at the end of time, why?

> "Hear, O Israel: The LORD our God, the LORD is one. You shall love the LORD your God with all your heart and with all your soul and with all your might. And these words that I command you today shall be on your heart. You shall teach them diligently to your children, and shall talk of them when

## For Our Consideration

> you sit in your house, and when you walk by the way, and when you lie down, and when you rise. You shall bind them as a sign on your hand, and they shall be as frontlets between your eyes. You shall write them on the doorposts of your house and on your gates. Deuteronomy 6:4-9

The parents are given the charge from God to love Him, learn His commands, and to teach them diligently to their children. Why? God tells the parents to talk about these things morning, noon, and night. Put them on your hands and foreheads so everywhere you look, you can't help but see them. When you leave your home and when you return, see the commands of God. Should we help parents with this God-given task? If we should, how are we doing so?

**Action Point:** Begin to talk about what God requires parents to do with their children during your sermons specifically thinking about the passage in Deuteronomy 6. Add points regarding marriage, interpersonal relationships at home, how the life-giving Spirit can impact a home, and how the Scripture always points to change in the person from the inside out. Challenge parents to begin to make Christ the center of the home, not religion or some form of godliness, but a personal relationship with Christ. Begin to communicate regularly that true Christianity should be evident in the home first, and not just at Church.

> And I declare to him that I am about to punish his house forever, for the iniquity that he knew, because his sons were blaspheming God, and he did not restrain them. Therefore, I swear to the house of Eli that the iniquity of Eli's house shall not be atoned for by sacrifice or offering forever.
> 1 Samuel 3:13-14

This dreadful encounter was between God and a little child named Samuel. God used Samuel to pronounce judgment on His prophet Eli due to his fathering failures. Eli knew his sons were sinning yet refused to deal with the problems.

**Action Point:** Is God really that concerned about how parents discipline their children? What ramifications are there today when we fail to train and restrain our children? These concepts can be added to just about any sermon or lesson dealing with holiness, discipline, parental responsibility, and ministry. Eli lost the priesthood because of what he did not do! Do the parents we address understand how God views our failures to properly train the next generation?

In the New Testament, examples abound that can be used to stress the importance of Christ in the home. Qualifications of elders listed in Timothy and Titus contain rich material for stressing the importance of a functioning home. Paul's lists of sins in Romans 1 and 2 Timothy 3 include rebellion against parents right next to murder and every horrible sin imaginable and pastors can make the connection between these sins and the home. Ephesians 5 and 6 clearly list out the roles of each family member and are worthy of much study and teaching time. Even how not living in an understanding way with his wife can hinder a man's prayers is covered in Peter.

The topics of marriage, sexual sins, being single, walking in love (what better place than the home to learn to practice this!) learning to walk under authority, esteeming one another, and the list could go on for many pages, are all there for the taking.

Each of these can be developed into full teachings or simply added here and there to reinforce whatever message is being delivered. It

## For Our Consideration

will not be too big of a stretch to take almost any message and find a practical application for or in the home.

> And he will turn the hearts of fathers to their children and the hearts of children to their fathers, lest I come and strike the land with a decree of utter destruction." Malachi 4:6

This passage ends the Old Testament and leaves a startling reminder of the consequences of the destruction of the family. Are we already seeing its fulfillment in our day? God desires to turn hearts back to the home, and so should we. In the same book of Malachi, God also states that husbands are to treat their wives well, that He hates divorce and that He wants godly offspring because of marriage! We can and should teach these truths to those under our care.

Teaching is one of the primary methods of communication between pastor and sheep, and therefore that time should be used to clearly explain what God desires. The family relationships, both marital and parental, should be emphasized often if we hope to reverse the current trends of destruction. It can be done, but it will not be if we do not reprioritize the importance of the family.

### Beyond the Pulpit

Sermons and teachings are necessary but we should not stop there. Seminars can be added to encourage marital and parenting success, excellent resources should be provided to assist those that struggle, and personal accountability should be incorporated into the life of the Church.

Know well the condition of your flocks, and give attention to your herds, Proverbs 27:23

This verse is not just intended for shepherds and sheep, but for parents and pastors. We must have personal contact to know our flock well. How do we know what they are thinking and doing if we never have time for anyone under our care? Pastor's schedules can be so filled that there is little time for personal relationships, but should they be? Families can run in multiple directions and never have time together, but is this healthy?

Time is a commodity that can only be spent once. How are we doing in this arena? Are we investing in the matters that really matter? Perhaps an honest time of prayerful evaluation needs to occur before the Throne of Grace. Are we doing what we should be doing to reap the greatest benefit of all we are doing?

Parents need to be challenged to spend time together and with their children. Pastors and leaders need to do the same. Our schedules need to be evaluated in the light of what really is important, and discipleship must be way up on the list.

**Action Point:** Prayerfully and ruthlessly go through your schedule for the next month or two. What meetings, events, or activities could be removed and the time better used elsewhere? If it is important to invest in the family, how much time is devoted to doing so during this time? How much time is in the schedule to develop your marital and parental relationships at a deeper level? How much should there be? What are you willing to do about it?

Movements have come and gone over the last 40 years that emphasized small groups. This trend seems to be on the upswing again, and they are a powerful tool to help men and women in the arena of marriage and family. These groups work well because they are wide open regarding format and they can delve deeply into topics that are not possible during classes and sermons. Personal

## For Our Consideration

relationships and accountability develop by spending time together in these gatherings. These groups present a wonderful opportunity for the pastor who wants to promote discipleship. Books can be discussed, probing questions can be developed, and teachings dissected at a deeper level, all take place in this format. What an opportunity to challenge fathers to step up in their leadership in the home. Mothers can be encouraged, young people can be given direction, and families can be reinforced and strengthened through this ministry vehicle.

As relationships develop by spending time together, one natural byproduct is accountability. When men interact with men, and the ladies spend time together relationships form. As these develop, contact between one another takes place outside of the meetings and it becomes easier to detect problems in their infant stage rather than after they blow up. How many marriages could have been saved if the root problems were known to several others prior to the destruction? If there had been a group of support people around praying and talking to the couple, would it have made a difference?

**Action Point:** Are you using small groups in your church? Why not try scheduling a time or two with the express point of discussing a topic like fatherhood, or marriage, or parenting, and see how it goes. Perhaps a book discussion night could be attempted. Maybe a small group could gather to watch a marriage or parenting seminar on video. The number is not as important as the hopes of making a difference in real lives. With so much to gain, what have you got to lose by trying?

What would happen in your church if the men began to take responsibility for their own family's welfare? What if they were the primary teachers of the Scripture in the home? What if they really began to pursue an understanding of Ephesians 5 type love that Paul says is God's command? Is this even possible and if so, is it desirable? Absolutely on both counts! Not only is it possible, it is the Scriptural pattern.

Husbands are told to love their wives, wives are told to respect their husbands, and children are told to obey both. Should we hold them to any less standard? Shouldn't we be those that encourage them to walk in obedience to these Scriptural mandates? Shouldn't our ministry be primarily focused on helping men and women, boys and girls walk in obedience to the Scripture? What do we need to change to arrive at this conclusion?

Beyond adding a family oriented flavor to our teachings, and incorporating small groups of some sort, there are other avenues that can be pursued. Remember, the goal is to reverse the destructive trends of divorce and the young people rejecting their parent's faith to the tune of 70-90%! This is no small challenge or goal, but one we must undertake now!

### Pastor's Role

Pastors need to make a philosophic shift away from activity coordinators to a more Biblical pattern. The primary verse dealing with the job of the pastor is:

> Ephesians 4:11-12 – And he gave the apostles, the prophets, the evangelists, the pastors and teachers, to equip the saints for the work of ministry, for building up the body of Christ…

David Guzik's Commentary states – equip means "to be put right, the idea of mending a net, or fixing a broken bone." New International Bible Commentary – "The word equip conveys the idea of a harmonious development in which all parts are brought to a condition of being able to perform according to their created purpose."

Equipping, training, perfecting, are all various translations of this word regarding our life call. The idea is that as under-shepherds, we are to be about the business of correcting what is wrong in doctrine, theology, and thought patterns encompassing orthodoxy and orthopraxy and to strengthen and encourage what is healing and redemptive.

The family is in desperate need of being put right, in dire need of mending, and could also use some harmonious development! As pastors, we need to consider what we are doing in how we structure our church to fulfill the command to equip those that follow us.

The currently accepted age-segregated church model runs deep considering it only came on the scene a few decades ago. Prior to the 1960s and 70s, most of churches functioned the same way from the inception of the Church in the book of Acts. The family was intact and the pastor expected his message to be carried out by his listeners during the week. The parents were primarily charged with making sure the children were under control and were developing spiritually.

Somewhere during the advent of the modern movement towards accepting the generation gap theory, the Church adopted the view that the family should be broken down into parts so they could receive effective ministry. Children needed to be separated away from the parents so they could be given teaching at their level, and young adults should be isolated into their own peer grouping. How has this been working? 70-90% of the recipients are walking away from the Church and their faith.

Perhaps we need to reconsider our methods and models. If the destruction of the family is an issue, and it is, and, if young people walking away from the faith is problem for the future, and it certainly is, then we should consider a complete evaluation of what we are doing, including our ministry model. Perhaps some new ministry positions should be considered to help stem the tide of family destruction. Consider the following list of tongue-in-cheek titles:

- Staff in charge of strengthening the father in his leadership role in the home
- Pastor in charge of training husbands to love their wives as Christ loved the Church through dying to himself
- Malachi 4:6 curse avoider trainer
- Encouraging the wives and mothers in their Biblical mandate counselor
- How not to destroy your own home by your words consultant
- How to be more Christ-like with those that know you best pastor
- Family devotions to implement the pastor's message during the week advisor
- Marriage Stability and Longevity Coordinator
- Divorce prevention pastor
- Reducer of Hypocrisy in the home consultant
- Preparation for being a godly spouse trainer
- Teenage rebellion avoidance ministry leader
- Sibling relationships enhancer
- Helping young people make wise, godly decisions under their parents' authority director
- Giving single adults a purpose in life by serving others leader

## For Our Consideration

- Grandparents as support to parents and not undermine minister

I'm sure you could think of a few more.

Research indicates that we often spend a great deal of time and money on recovery programs but not all that much on prevention. While parking ambulances at the bottom of the cliff is helpful, stronger guardrails at the top would also seem in order. If we keep on doing the same things we have always done we will keep on getting the same results we have always gotten. That simply is not an option.

Another aspect of the fight to redeem the family is to rethink how we go about "ministry." What would be better for your church, for you to come up with a multifaceted outreach program that attempts to be all things to all people, or for individual families to be released into a far reaching ever expanding ministry outreach?

I would choose the latter for several reasons. First, the burden carried by the pastor would be significantly reduced. Second, the family, and the father will grow far more by planning and leading an outreach themselves, than simply attending one. Third, the family will gain in cohesiveness and strength as they accomplish a project together. Finally, there will be no limit to the creativity and growth of ministry because each family is unique in mixture and vision.

As pastors reconsider departments and activities to evaluate their overall effectiveness in accomplishing discipleship, the method is just as important to review. By scheduling a multitude of events to provide ministry opportunities for the family, are we helping or hurting our goal of redeeming the family? Are we adding to the division already taking place or helping to heal the breach? Perhaps another method could be considered.

## Let's Go Deeper

As an alternative to the traditional approach of the church staff and leaders scheduling events, perhaps families could be encouraged to reach out in a way that fits their gifts and talents. As marriages are healed and parent-child relationships grow, the next progression should be outreach. What would happen if the pastor asked each head of household to prayerfully plan an outreach for their family that is specifically geared for their own family? Some suggestions to consider:

- If a family is musical, perhaps they could contact a local nursing home and offer to perform. The father could act as the moderator and share a brief word from the Scripture.
- If the family likes hospitality perhaps they could schedule an open house for their neighbors with an outdoor skit, movie or backyard Bible study.
- If a family has a bent towards service they could contact local or regional parachurch organizations and offer to assist somehow. Voice of the Martyrs, for example, provides housing for groups to come in and work for up to a week at a time.
- If a family loves to do chores or outdoor work, pick the ugliest house in the neighborhood and make contact and offer to serve by cleaning or painting.

Hospitals, retirement homes, inner city ministries, pro-life groups, homeless shelters, prayer groups, political groups, and the list could go on and on all need help. The family is only limited by imagination and the leading of the Holy Spirit to find an outlet for ministry.

For Our Consideration

    Pastors that release their people into service will have a church full of people that love Jesus and families that are devoting their lives to something of eternal value. Sure beats counseling families in turmoil.

    I trust something of value was discussed above and that you will prayerfully consider it. Perhaps you know a pastor that might benefit from reading this section? Please feel free to share!

# Practical Family Discipleship Tools

Every follower of Christ is called to make disciples as part of the Great Commission. God has also ordained that each person is a part of a family structure of some sort and this provides a perfect training ground to put this command into practice. Our goal is to reach as many people for Christ as possible and to help them grow to maturity in their relationship with Him.

God has provided people in each of our lives that we can invest in, beginning with those closest to us. As we learn how to disciple those directly under our care, we will develop a skill set that can then be expanded to a very hurting world outside our homes.

Most of us are aware of the dismal statistics regarding the destruction of the family via divorce and the high percentage of young people rejecting Christ shortly after they leave the home. This tidal wave of failure must be addressed or we are in great danger of losing the bulk of an entire generation. Rather than just complain about the problem we want to move into solutions and becoming proactive.

Each person has a limited amount of time, and time is a resource that can only be spent once. In Economics class in college, the instructor introduced to us the concept of "Opportunity Cost." This professor illustrated the concept with this sentence,

> "The cost of a McDonald's hamburger is not just the cost of the burger, but everything else we could have spent the money on."

## For Our Consideration

This sentence also rings true with our schedule and daily decisions. We can only spend an hour once and the cost is not only what we did with the time, but everything we could have done with it. We are stewards of time as well as money and we need to consider how we spend our non-replaceable resource called "time." What are we investing in? Discipleship should be high up on the list!

Many families are not placing as high of a priority on discipleship as they could or should. Perhaps the reason is that they feel they are doing enough by sending the children to a youth group or Sunday School class. Maybe there is a lack of understanding regarding the severity of the need and responsibility. In addition, some may lack the instruction or ideas of how to go about the process. The truth is that sending the children to a few hours of spiritual instruction a week, while helpful, is not enough to overcome the onslaught of evil and pressures from our world system. Additionally, our schedules must be reviewed to make sure that they are under the Lordship of Jesus Christ, and whatever is not, needs to be removed.

What follows are multiple suggestions and ideas to help overcome a lack of knowledge or fear of how to disciple someone. Not every idea will work or even need to be implemented, but almost everyone can and should do something to disciple those under their influence.

Everyone is different so a "one size fits all" approach does not work in the Kingdom of God. Below are some suggestions for each basic type of family unit. The goal is to begin the discipleship process if we have not, and if we have begun, to learn even more tools to assist in the journey of discipleship. We learn at home so we can make a greater difference as we step outside of them.

### Singles

I want you to be free from anxieties. The unmarried man is anxious about the things of the Lord, how to please the Lord. But the married man is anxious about worldly things, how to please his wife, and his interests are divided. And the unmarried or betrothed woman is anxious about the things of the Lord, how to be holy in body and spirit. But the married woman is anxious about worldly things, how to please her husband. 1 Corinthians 7:32-34

Being a single adult provides the greatest freedom to serve Christ. The opportunities to travel, keep a flexible schedule, and develop a personal relationship with Jesus will open many doors for evangelism and discipleship. As a single adult, there is time to study the Word of God, listen to teachings, read, and serve without the time constraints of being married or raising children.

If used properly, this period of life can provide the greatest opportunities for investing in others. So many single adults waste this stage of their life worrying about what they do not have (being married) instead of enjoying what they do have, an abundance of time to further the work of the Kingdom!

If you are a single adult, stop and take an inventory of the people in your life. Whom would the Lord have you invest more time in? Is there someone at work/school that is hurting or going through a difficult time? Perhaps other single friends need help or desire to grow spiritually. Would the Lord want you to consider leading a Bible or book study, prayer meeting, or beginning a service project to assist someone in need?

For Our Consideration

Every situation can turn into a discipleship opportunity as you bring Christ into the time spent together with others. As you fill up your spirit with excellent teachings and your private devotional time, the Lord will provide others in your life so that you can share with them what you are learning.

One group to consider investing in are those that are younger than you. If you are a single adult, there are most likely younger people that look up to you. Siblings or other young people in your church or social networks often idolize the single adult, and this provides an excellent opportunity to invest in the next generation. Leading a Bible study or simply spending time with younger people can pay tremendous dividends for the Kingdom of God.

To realize how important this is, just remember how you felt when your older sibling or perhaps some other older young person reached out you. If that did not happen in your life, remember how you felt because it did not happen! You can make a difference in many people's life if you invest your time properly. Prayerfully consider the tools in this book, and how you could use them in your current relationships, and then marvel at what doors open to you as you seek the Lord!

If you will prepare yourself by study, prayer, and an investment of time, God will open doors for you to serve Him in marvelous ways.

A young lady named Sarah was twenty-eight when she was married. Her older sister was married at age 20 and her younger brother at 21. Sarah wondered why she had not been asked to be married, struggling with what was wrong with her. Her parents shared Paul's exhortation recorded in 1 Corinthians 7 and she choose to invest her time in serving others while she waited for marriage.

Let's Go Deeper

During this time, Sarah traveled to China and worked in an orphanage, taught English in a high school, and could share her life with many foreign students.

She went to cosmetology school to learn a useful skill and she used this service to assist low-income families and continues to do so today. In her local church, she became "Aunt Sarah" to many young girls, ages 10-20 and invested her time in discipling them. Sarah could often be seen before or after a church gathering surrounded by young girls hanging on her every word. She chose to invest herself in others rather than thinking solely about herself or what she was missing.

Eventually, God brought in a wonderful young man that swept her off her feet and they were married. At Sarah's wedding, she had 40 young ladies singing as a choir and there was not a dry eye in the house. Sarah used her singleness to help disciple many others and only eternity will reveal the full impact of her choice. Sarah chose wisely, and so can you if you are single...invest in others and God will grant you the desires of your heart as they align with His. (Psalm 37:4)

As this Sarah's father, I could not be prouder of her!

## Husband

Paul stated in the verses above that once you are married you no longer live your life for yourself. There is now a spouse to consider and this will radically change how you will live the rest of your days on earth. Marriage is a tremendous blessing as well as one of hardest jobs in the world in which to excel. The Apostle Paul gives detailed instructions regarding marriage in Ephesians 5:22-33:

## For Our Consideration

> Wives, submit to your own husbands, as to the Lord. For the husband is the head of the wife even as Christ is the head of the church, his body, and is himself its Savior. Now as the church submits to Christ, so also wives should submit in everything to their husbands. Husbands, love your wives, as Christ loved the church and gave himself up for her, that he might sanctify her, having cleansed her by the washing of water with the word, so that he might present the church to himself in splendor, without spot or wrinkle or any such thing, that she might be holy and without blemish. In the same way husbands should love their wives as their own bodies. He who loves his wife loves himself. For no one ever hated his own flesh, but nourishes and cherishes it, just as Christ does the church, because we are members of his body. "Therefore, a man shall leave his father and mother and hold fast to his wife, and the two shall become one flesh." This mystery is profound, and I am saying that it refers to Christ and the church. However, let each one of you love his wife as himself, and let the wife see that she respects her husband.

While not necessarily politically correct in our day, this is nonetheless the Word of God and must be considered prayerfully by every Christian married disciple. Beyond the specific instructions on how a marriage should function - husband's' loving their wives by laying down their lives for them daily, and wives making sure they respect their imperfect husbands, some key insight is given into discipleship.

Husbands should be helping to sanctify their spouse by making sure she is "washed in the Word of God." The "in the same way" part of this Scripture passage gives insight for the husband on how to help disciple his wife.

This may be intimidating to some men due to their wives being older in the Lord or perhaps not very receptive to the husband's leading, but the command is still there. Men are to learn to die for their wife, just as Christ did for the Church, and men are to make sure the Word of God is central in their homes.

Making the Lord the center of the home is a daily decision and a never-ending process. What currently dominates your home? The TV, Facebook, sports, or Christ? Husbands must be men of the Word to share the Scripture in their homes - Jesus said that out of the abundance of our hearts our mouths speak (Matthew 12:34), what is coming out of our mouths?

Making changes is not impossible, but must be a willful decision if they are to occur. If most meals are eaten together, (which they should be if they are not) then this time allows the husband to lead in a prayer of thankfulness for the food and for the one that made it.

In addition, this time could be used to bring up a discussion about what was read in your private devotions or perhaps what you believe God has shown you during the day. Open-ended questions could be asked about a verse of Scripture or some potential problem the two of you are facing.

Open-ended means a question that cannot simply be answered with yes or no answer. These type questions are more of the "what" or "why" type questions. "Why do you think God allowed this to happen to Joe and Mary?" Or, "What do you think God is trying to tell us about my job situation?"

## For Our Consideration

You don't have to reinvent the wheel or be super creative. Try suggesting reading a book or listening to or watching a Christ-honoring program together and then discussing it.

With the advent of the internet, there are unlimited resources available for you to consider if it is your desire to help your spouse grow in spiritual maturity. Biblically, husbands must take the lead in discipleship and God will give you the ideas and grace to do so if you will ask Him for it.

Another factor to consider is the tremendous power that is released by praying together with your wife.

> Again, I say to you, if two of you agree on earth about anything they ask, it will be done for them by my Father in heaven. Matthew 18:19

A husband that leads his wife in consistent prayer will increase her respect for him exponentially. Prayer allows for a deeper level of communication and will help to center the home in Christ. Even if the wife is not comfortable praying aloud, or for that matter the husband either, praying together will help both grow spiritually. It may be awkward at first, but the comfort level will come and the home will change under the husband's leadership.

Discipleship may happen by chance but it has a far greater potential to happen with a plan. If you seek the Lord about your responsibility and prayerfully ask Him for direction, He will give it. God brought your spouse into your life for a reason and part of that reason was for you to care for her, nurture her, and help her grow in spiritual maturity.

## Wife

A wife plays a crucial role in helping her husband grow and mature in the Lord (discipleship). She can build him up and help him become a strong man of God, or help to destroy him.

Solomon, who knew a little bit about wives, states it this way:

> The wisest of women builds her house, but folly with her own hands tears it down. Proverbs 14:1

> An excellent wife is the crown of her husband, but she who brings shame is like rottenness in his bones. Proverbs 12:4

Proverbs also states, "Life and death are in the power of the tongue," (Proverbs 18:21) and a wise wife will understand that what she says to her husband will help or hinder his maturing.

If the wife is older in the Lord, she should encourage her husband's growth by gently sharing insights she has learned from the Lord, and encouraging any efforts the husband displays in spiritual leadership. The principle is to fan into flame any spark, not to pour water on it because it is small. The wise wife will praise and encourage her husband when he leads in prayer or Bible study and resist the temptation to comment about how immature or short it may have been. Husbands often have fragile egos and they need their wife's support, not criticism. Men do not like to be "slapped" or put down by their wife's comments and will often retreat into work, sports, or hobbies when they do not feel respected.

If the wife is younger in the Lord, she should encourage her husband by asking him questions and thus helping him to reinforce his leadership role. Something rises in a man when he feels like he is fulfilling the role of being the leader, and this will spur additional desire for growth. A wise wife will help her husband become the man of God she desires rather than tear him down verbally.

In addition, the wife needs to be careful when discussing her husband with others. She will "bring shame" to him by exposing him to ridicule or by not protecting his reputation. Solomon stated that this will result in "rottenness to the bones," and this is an apt picture.

When a man finds out that his wife is talking about him behind his back to others, he feels undermined and the foundation is attacked. Bones hold the frame of our body up and by shaming her husband, she is causing damage to the structure. If she is complaining about his lack of leadership or perhaps some personal fault, once he knows that he is the subject of the discussion with others, all motivation to change has been lost.

Love covers a multitude of sins and so will a wise wife. The husband that trusts in his wife will grow into a much better leader than the one that does not.

If both husband and wife will seek to be mature and to continue to grow in their own discipleship. they will ultimately end up assisting their spouse. The husband and the wife play a major role in the discipleship process to one another, and when a child arrives, the roles even expand.

### Married with Children

When God blesses a couple with children (through either childbirth or adoption), the discipleship opportunities expand. In addition to what was stated above about the husbands and wives, now there are additional lives involved. The same principles apply whether there is one child or a dozen regarding discipleship opportunities. The more children the greater the possible impact. Regardless of family size, each couple will have to adjust their lifestyle once a child or children arrive. The first requirement for godly parents is to accept the Biblical assignment regarding children:

> "Hear, O Israel: The LORD our God, the LORD is one. You shall love the LORD your God with all your heart and with all your soul and with all your might. And these words that I command you today shall be on your heart. You shall teach them diligently to your children, and shall talk of them when you sit in your house, and when you walk by the way, and when you lie down, and when you rise. You shall bind them as a sign on your hand, and they shall be as frontlets between your eyes. You shall write them on the doorposts of your house and on your gates. Deuteronomy 6:4-9

> Fathers, do not provoke your children to anger, but bring them up in the discipline and instruction of the Lord. Ephesians 6:4

God has delegated the training of the children to their parents. This is a phenomenal sentence if we consider the ramifications of it. God has entered into a partnership with parents and He expects them to fulfill their roles. The Lord has built into every Christian family the opportunity for hands-on discipleship practice. As a unified team, husbands and wives begin the process of training a child in the ways of the Lord. This will help prepare both the parents and the children to reach out to other potential disciples. In addition, if the parents do

## For Our Consideration

a good job discipling those in their own homes, the destructive trend of faith rejection can be turned.

We have already mentioned making sure that both the husband and wife are growing spiritually in their own walk with the Lord, and this remains a focus after children arrive. Now the discipleship process needs to be enlarged to include the child(ren).

This can be accomplished in a variety of ways, a few of which have already been mentioned. First, the family schedule needs to be evaluated to assure that where the time is being spent is the most beneficial place. If it is not, then change must be made and the sooner the better. Second, mealtime offers a wonderful opportunity to bring Christ and the Scripture into the daily lives of each family member. Discussions can be planned or spontaneous, but make sure the Lord is a central figure in the conversations. Depending on ages of the children, topics can range from interpersonal relationship challenges to character development. The Scripture provides every answer to all questions either directly or in principle. Therefore, we must make sure that the Word of God is the center of our homes and always the ultimate resource for our answers.

Fathers can lead devotions around the meal table, in the living room or bedroom. These can be as deep as the level of understanding of the children. Bible stories can be read and discussed. Leading questions can be asked regarding moral choices or characters' actions, and a lively discussion can be achieved. The goal is to provide an atmosphere where Christ is central and the Word of God is valued. In addition, insights can be shared from the daily devotions that each parent or child recently received. The Psalm or Proverb of the day also provides an abundance of material that can be read and discussed.

The materials and ideas for a good discussion are only limited by the imagination.

Family worship times can help provide a growing discipleship environment in the home. If someone plays an instrument, chorus books or hymnals can then be used to lead in songs. If no one plays an instrument, then MP3 players and CD's abound that contain wonderful worship songs to be enjoyed in the home. Worship is supposed to be a part of every day and not relegated to Sunday services only and leading our children in worship will help keep Christ as the center of our homes. The children need to see the reality of our walk with Jesus to want to follow in our footsteps.

### Here are some other ideas to consider prayerfully

Mothers or fathers can read excellent books aloud to the family and then discuss them. These can cover any genre and could include classics like *Pilgrim's Progress* or *Pride and Prejudice*, fictional or actual history, end times thrillers, and a host of other type books. The book is not as important as the time spent together. Every discussion should focus on growing in Christ and obtaining a better understanding of how to walk with Him in our daily lives. The characters actions and thoughts can be evaluated and then their lives become object lessons to impart spiritual truth into our everyday lives.

Family prayer meetings can be called during times of crises or when the Lord's specific direction is needed. Praying together and recording the request and the answer will help solidify the reality of Christ to the children. These times will often provide opportunities to explore issues like patience, waiting on God, what happens when God says, "no" to our prayers, etc. These are basic discipleship training issues. We teach our children to pray by praying. They will ultimately "catch" what is important to us by what we did, not necessarily what we said.

DVD's or movies can be watched and evaluated from a Biblical perspective. We are not to be naive or unaware of our adversary's schemes, (Ephesians 6:11) and we should help our children process the entertainment they watch so they are growing in discernment as they mature. (Hebrews 5:14) Every book, movie, and song has an author and they had a reason for writing what they did. These things may be germane in nature, but there is a spiritual side to everything and we must train our little disciples to grow in discernment.

Like any other discipleship relationship, the spending of time together is critical. A great deal of impartation and spiritual life takes place as you spend time doing the normal family activities. What is done is not as critical as the fact that a large amount of time is being spent together. Every parent looks for teachable moments, and the majority of these happen as large chunks of time are spent together. Very few people in nursing homes regret not spending more time at the office yet often regret that they cannot spend more time with their family. We can only spend time once, choose wisely.

### Single Parents

In our current society, divorce is rampant and this has created a large group of single parents. Both men and women are now attempting to raise their children without a spouse to assist. Children often fall through the cracks of the broken home. As the single parent attempts to maintain a job and eventually seek another potential marriage partner, the children can be overlooked. Time is required and reprioritizing the schedule must be considered for the sake of the children. It is not their fault that the marriage fell apart, and they should not be deprived as a result. Single parents must attempt to fulfill the role of discipler even though they are now doing it alone. In fact, it is even more critical since the home is broken in two.

A single parent still should invest in the lives of their children in the arena of discipleship. Reading books, praying together, Bible study, home worship, church membership, and such are needed for children of a single parent home. Children still spell love - t-i-m-e.

If the couple was Christian and divorced, the message has already been given to the children that the parents' Christianity was powerless to stop the divorce. This hurdle must be overcome in the discipleship process with the children. Even more time will need to be given to explain the marriage failure and why God did not intervene to prevent it. These issues provide a great opportunity to teach about forgiveness, patience, endurance, and many other desirable spiritual qualities.

Whether male or female, the single parent will need to supplement their discipleship process of their children with godly role models. The single parent will have to seek out others to include in their life to replace the spouse that is no longer there. Small groups, church involvement, gender specific clubs or sporting programs can all assist in this process. The goal is to present to the child(ren) others that are excellent examples of Christianity and invite them into the process of discipleship with your children. Strong, godly friendships, extended family, and a committed church body can all help to stem the damage caused by divorce.

## Summary

The family unit is an excellent training ground for discipleship. It is often the most important, as well as the most overlooked regarding its potential. God created the family structure and He gave explicit

## For Our Consideration

details explaining how He expects it to function. If the Christian families would do a better job at discipling the children under their roofs, we would begin to see a reversal of the devastation of the family unit, the Church, and the nations. In addition, the large number of young people rejecting Christ as soon as they leave high school would begin to reverse. God spoke through the prophet Malachi the following:

> And this second thing you do. You cover the LORD's altar with tears, with weeping and groaning because he no longer regards the offering or accepts it with favor from your hand. But you say, "Why does he not?" Because the LORD was witness between you and the wife of your youth, to whom you have been faithless, though she is your companion and your wife by covenant. Did he not make them one, with a portion of the Spirit in their union? And what was the one God seeking? Godly offspring. So, guard yourselves in your spirit, and let none of you be faithless to the wife of your youth. Malachi 2:13-15

The family unit is designed by God to propagate not only children but future disciples of Christ. Parents are given the honor and responsibility, from God, to invest wisely in the children under their care. While some of this process of discipling can be delegated to others to assist, the parents are still the ones that God will hold responsible for the discipleship. This is an awesome responsibility and the potential is amazing. God will empower and give grace to those that seek Him and walk in obedience to His commands. This includes the command to make disciples, beginning in the home.

The natural outworking of this process is forward looking. While it may seem that investing so much in the family is working against the spreading of the Gospel, the exact opposite is the truth. Since studies reflect a huge percentage of young people walking away from the faith, whatever investment is necessary to stop this bleeding is well worth the effort. If the 70-90% leaving the faith could be kept, or significantly reduced, the long-term results would be overall growth of the Church at large.

In addition, as families begin to heal, refocus on Christ, and walk in discipleship, outreach will increase. A great deal of time and energy is currently being spent on recovery programs in the Church, but little on prevention. As marriages spiral into destruction, young people walk away in rebellion, and the overall condition of the family deteriorates even further, the Church and communities struggle to pick up the pieces. If the tide of family destruction could be reduced significantly, these burdens would be relieved.

Functional families can generate significant energy for the propagation of the Gospel, while dysfunctional ones drain it. Functional families require far less resources from the already overburdened churches and can be released sooner into ministry. Healthy, growing, discipleship oriented families will help reproduce more of the same kind, whereas, dysfunctional ones also reproduce more of their same kind. Which one offers the brightest hope for the future?

Since our goal is to walk in obedience to Jesus' final command - go and make disciples, then the home is the first opportunity to learn how to walk in obedience and perhaps is the best place to invest for long term growth potential.

For Our Consideration

# A Bible Study on Authority

Authority is a word that sends the heart of every rebel into spasms, yet, the Scripture has a great deal to teach on the topic by direct command and inference. Consider this seminal section from Paul's letter to the Romans.

> Let every person be subject to the governing authorities. For there is no authority except from God, and those that exist have been instituted by God. Therefore, whoever resists the authorities resists what God has appointed, and those who resist will incur judgment. For rulers are not a terror to good conduct, but to bad. Would you have no fear of the one who is in authority? Then do what is good, and you will receive his approval, for he is God's servant for your good. But if you do wrong, be afraid, for he does not bear the sword in vain. For he is the servant of God, an avenger who carries out God's wrath on the wrongdoer. Therefore, one must be in subjection, not only to avoid God's wrath but also for the sake of conscience. Romans 13:1-5

All authority finds its origin in God, and it is God's primary way of ruling His creation. God has established four different realms of leadership and authority; governments, families, churches, and employers. Each institution is independent and ultimately accountable to God for their actions. The head of the family answers directly to God as does the president, boss, or pastor.

Each realm of authority mentioned has its own jurisdiction and must not intrude into other realms. Biblically, the family has the widest level of authority and the church, the government, and the employer must not interfere unless there are sin/safety issues involved.

To illustrate, consider that God had given the right of rulership to both Eli as a father, and Saul as the king of Israel. In their positions, they could rule as they pleased, but they did have to be accountable to God for the way they handled their leadership positions. The Scripture shows us the outcome of their rulership, and in both cases, the result was failure.

The right to rule is God given, and subjection/submission is God's plan and purpose for individuals who are under authority. I believe our understanding of this concept, and subsequent actions taken towards those in authority, is an excellent barometer of our spiritual maturity.

This view of authority is not a preference, but a conviction. Understanding authority and walking it out is foundational to Christianity. This cannot be separated from our Christian thinking any more than my skeletal or digestive system can be removed from my body. This is a major function of the Kingdom of God and its neglect and abuse has done great damage to the Body of Christ. There simply is no room in God's Kingdom for rebellion, lawlessness, and anarchy.

In Matthew 8 Jesus is asked by a Roman centurion to heal his servant. We are very familiar with the story so I will not relate all the details. Jesus offers to come with the man, but the man tells Him do not bother, just say the word and my servant will be healed. His reasoning for this understanding is what interests me. The centurion understood the principles of authority. After he explains why he does not need Jesus to go with him, Jesus marvels and says, "I have not seen such great faith in all of Israel." Why didn't Jesus say, "great understanding of authority?" It seems that living under authority and walking out our daily lives with a biblical understanding of its workings, equates to faith. This Roman understood that Jesus was the One in authority and His word would accomplish what He said it would.

Being under authority in every area of our lives takes great faith, and demonstrates the reality of our belief system. Submission is a word that awakens negative reactions in people. Some instantly go to dominance or doormat, however, the word really means, "being willing to line up under." In other words, an act of my free will to freely choose to follow someone else.

No one can really force submission. We can force external behavioral change but we cannot control the inner workings of anyone. We all understand the saying, "I am sitting on the outside but I am standing up on the inside." I can outwardly comply without ever bending my will inside. Submission means that I willingly lay down my will for another. Therefore, submission to authority takes a great deal of faith and without faith, it is impossible to please God. Ultimately, voluntarily placing yourself under a God-given authority is an act of faith in the sovereignty of God.

The truth of what we believe about authority will be revealed when there is a crossing of wills. Submission is something that we can say we like or agree with, but the test will come when someone in authority crosses our will. Then it will be evident what we really believe!

With that backdrop let's move into a brief study of the Scripture. We will begin in the Old Testament first, and while this is not a complete list of verses, we can certainly gain some insight. Before we begin, we must understand that in the Old Testament there is a great deal of material presented with little commentary on whether the behaviors presented are good or not. What we are looking for then, are principles, not necessarily rules regarding authority. Secondly, many of the men in the Old Testament lived for generations and the overall societal structure was patriarchal with the fathers even commanding adult children and their families. I am not for reinstating trans-generational authority, but I am for reestablishing a proper understand of Biblical authority.

**Old Testament Scriptures**

In Genesis 16 we encounter the story of Sarai and Hagar. Sarai had talked Abram into a plan to help fulfill God's promise to produce an heir that involved marriage to Sarai's slave. After the plan was executed, Sarai became extremely jealous and began to abuse her slave. Hagar and her son fled and was close to death when an angel appeared to her and had this discussion:

> The angel of the LORD found her by a spring of water in the wilderness, the spring on the way to Shur. And he said, "Hagar, servant of Sarai, where have you come from and where are you going?" She said, "I am fleeing from my mistress Sarai." The angel of the LORD said to her, "Return to your mistress and submit to her." Genesis 16:7-9

For Our Consideration

God had plans for this child, as well as Abram and Sarai, so this slave was told to return and submit to a harsh master. We are to submit to authority even if we do not like the way we are treated. I am not saying that we must stay in a dangerous or abusive situation, but we simply cannot run away every time there is hardship. God usually has a plan that is way beyond what we can conceive.

> For I have chosen him, that he may command his children and his household after him to keep the way of the LORD by doing righteousness and justice, so that the LORD may bring to Abraham what he has promised him. Genesis 18:19

God chose Abraham and instructed him to train (command) his household in the "way of the Lord." In addition, there is the clause, "so that," which would certainly seem to indicate a conditional aspect to this promise. What if Abraham failed in his God-given task? Would God have not brought Abraham into his promised land if he failed to train his family? We do not really know, but we can at least understand how important it was to God for Abraham to invest in the generations that followed. God expected Abraham to exercise authority in training his family to follow in the ways of the Lord.

In Genesis 19 we read the story of Lot and his encounter with the angels getting ready to destroy Sodom. I will not dwell on the details of the account, but simply point out that Lot, and his adult-age daughters, were taken out of the city. These young ladies were betrothed to men, but the men did not come with them. At the father's command, and the angel's insistence, only these three were spared. Lot exercised authority over his family.

Let's Go Deeper

While on the topic of Old Testament parents exercising authority over their adult children, Genesis 21, 24, 28, and 34, all contain stories and examples of parents selecting mates for their children. Again, I am not advocating that we return to that practice, but I am simply pointing out how normal it was for the one in authority to do so. Parents exercised great authority over their children even to the point of selecting their life partner. Tremendous faith would be required to trust that the one in authority was choosing wisely!

In Genesis chapters 42-48, we see Jacob the patriarch commanding his adult children to go to Egypt for grain. The men end up finding Joseph their brother (though they do not initially know him) that they sold into slavery many years before, and then must beg Jacob to send their other brother (Benjamin) down with them before they can get more food. Jacob exercised tremendous authority over his family, and they honored his wishes.

In the time of Moses, his authority was directly given from God. His task was to rule over and lead a huge number of people that had lived for generations as slaves in Egypt. The struggles were vast, and the people were very difficult to lead. Consider this passage and think about the concept of delegated authority from God to man.

> So Moses and Aaron said to all the people of Israel, "At evening you shall know that it was the LORD who brought you out of the land of Egypt, and in the morning, you shall see the glory of the LORD, because he has heard your grumbling against the LORD. For what are we, that you grumble against us?" And Moses said, "When the LORD gives you in the evening meat to eat and in the morning bread to the full, because the LORD has heard your grumbling that you

> grumble against him— what are we? Your grumbling is not against us but against the LORD." Exodus 16:6-8

The principle to consider is when those under authority grumbled against those in authority, they were not simply complaining about the human, but against God! We must be very careful to control our frustration at those in leadership positions, for all authority ultimately comes from God's hand.

Part of what God provided for this group of suddenly free slaves, was order. A slave in Egypt would have lived a lifestyle very like an abused dog in our day. After four hundred years of neglect and subjugation, this mass of humanity was set free in a single day. As this mob roamed around in the desert, it would be necessary to establish some common understanding of societal decency and morals.

God provided Moses with detailed instructions concerning relational issues, religious requirements, and many more laws than we can look at in this study. For our purposes, we can look at one of the "big ten." The Ten Commandments are easily recognizable and most folks have at least heard of them, if not read them at some point in their lifetime. It is interesting to me that the first four deal with our vertical relationship with God and the last six how to get along with our fellow man. The middle one specifically addresses the parental relationship.

> Honor your father and your mother, that your days may be long in the land that the LORD your God is giving you. Exodus 20:12

The land was everything to the people of Israel and God directly tied their possession of it to how they dealt with the first authority figure in their life. In fact, in the next chapter of Exodus, if a son or daughter attacked their parents or even cursed them, the punishment was death! God obviously placed a premium on honoring the parental position.

While there are hundreds of Scriptures we could look at in the Old Testament, time simply will not allow. In Numbers 16 Korah and his entire family was killed for rebelling against Moses. In Numbers 30 a daughter's vow can be disallowed by her father. Deuteronomy 21 describes how a rebellious son should be dealt with by the leadership. Later in Samuel, both Eli and Samuel were rejected by God for failing to restrain their own children. King David demonstrated the proper way to handle authority by not taking Saul's life, and the improper way to deal with sin in his household. The references could continue for pages. We have not even opened the Book of Proverbs which is full of statements regarding listening and receiving instruction from those in authority. The point should be clear – God raises up people to positions of authority and He does not take kindly to those under that authority resisting them. God has established order and He requires His people to line up under authority.

## New Testament Scriptures

Every possible relationship is dealt with in the New Testament regarding authority. Man to God, spouses, parents, employers, civil, and church, all involve people and there is a God-ordained order to each of them.

First, God deals with each of us as His legitimate children.

For Our Consideration

> And have you forgotten the exhortation that addresses you as sons? "My son, do not regard lightly the discipline of the Lord, nor be weary when reproved by him. For the Lord disciplines the one he loves, and chastises every son whom he receives." It is for discipline that you have to endure. God is treating you as sons. For what son is there whom his father does not discipline? If you are left without discipline, in which all have participated, then you are illegitimate children and not sons. Besides this, we have had earthly fathers who disciplined us and we respected them. Shall we not much more be subject to the Father of spirits and live? For they disciplined us for a short time as it seemed best to them, but he disciplines us for our good, that we may share his holiness. Hebrews 12:5-10

God demonstrates His authority over us by executing discipline in our lives as loving father should. In fact, a mark of our adoption is the very fact that we are punished by our Authority, for if we are not, then we are not truly valued. I won't belabor the point that God is worthy of our honor, worship, and submission, so let us move on to the other realms of authority that everyone encounters.

### Government Authority

In addition to the Romans passage at the beginning of this study, there are several others that relate the same principle of submission to government authority. Please note that each of the writers lived under absolute dictators when penning these commands.

> First of all, then, I urge that supplications, prayers, intercessions, and thanksgivings be made for all people, for kings and all who are in high positions, that we may lead a peaceful and quiet life, godly and dignified in every way. This is good, and it is pleasing in the sight of God our Savior, who desires all people to be saved and to come to the knowledge of the truth. 1 Timothy 2:1-4

Paul states that how we live under authority has a direct impact on the measure of peace and quiet we have in our lives.

> Remind them to be submissive to rulers and authorities, to be obedient, to be ready for every good work, to speak evil of no one, to avoid quarreling, to be gentle, and to show perfect courtesy toward all people. Titus 3:1-2

Paul instructs his young charge that we need to be and remain submissive to authorities and to be perfectly courteous toward all. Quite a challenge considering the current political climate we find ourselves in!

> Be subject for the Lord's sake to every human institution, whether it be to the emperor as supreme, or to governors as sent by him to punish those who do evil and to praise those who do good. For this is the will of God, that by doing good you should put to silence the ignorance of foolish people. Live as people who are free, not using your freedom as a cover-up for evil, but living as servants of God. Honor everyone. Love the brotherhood. Fear God. Honor the emperor. 1 Peter 2:13-17

Peter was not exactly a spiritual lightweight in his own right and he agrees with Paul – submit to those in authority. Peter even added, "honor the emperor," and I am sure that was quite a challenge to those living under Roman oppression. Even given the circumstances of being a conquered, oppressed people, Peter did not back off the command. The rulers were entitled to honor and respect because of their position, not based on their ability, actions or personality.

### Family Authority

The first authority structure everyone encounters is the family. God has clearly established a structure within the family and has specific commands for all members. Many of these have been rejected in our day and we are paying a huge price for these choices.

There seems to be only three family categories mentioned in the Bible, husband, wife, and children. There is no age limit mentioned in any passage regarding children, and there is no category called "young adult," or "single adult." "children" covers both male and female until they began their own home and leave the parental authority.

> Wives, submit to your own husbands, as to the Lord. For the husband is the head of the wife even as Christ is the head of the church, his body, and is himself its Savior. Now as the church submits to Christ, so also wives should submit in everything to their husbands. Ephesians 5:22-24

Almost every man alive knows these verses and if they cannot find them in the Bible, they at least know they exist! God did instruct Paul to write them and they are there from His hand. Therefore, they must be dealt with and not simply rejected because of our society. God's plan from the beginning was for the man to be the head of his family.

The chapter goes on and explains how the man is to rule and if he begins to grasp the depth of God's command, he would most likely reject it! The point of this discussion is not a detailed examination of this chapter, but to simply point out that there is an authority structure. Wives are commanded by God to willingly line up under their husband. A frightening prospect, however, remember it takes faith to be under authority!

Paul restates this command in his letter to the Colossians:

> Wives, submit to your husbands, as is fitting in the Lord. Colossians 3:18

Husbands are accountable to God for the usage of their authority, and they are repeatedly instructed to love those under their care. Not just any kind of love, but the exact type of love the Christ demonstrated when He willingly embraced the cross. This is a death-to-self type love that only comes from God's grace. Husbands are not dictators ruling over their spouse, but Christ imitators embracing His cross daily.

Children are specifically addressed in several passages.

> Children, obey your parents in the Lord, for this is right. "Honor your father and mother" (this is the first commandment with a promise), "that it may go well with you and that you may live long in the land." Fathers, do not

## For Our Consideration

> provoke your children to anger, but bring them up in the discipline and instruction of the Lord. Ephesians 6:1-4

> Children, obey your parents in everything, for this pleases the Lord. Fathers, do not provoke your children, lest they become discouraged. Colossians 3:20-21

These two sections of Scripture are clear as to the role of children and includes some warnings to the fathers. If children desire to do what is right and please the Lord, obeying their parents is the first step.

The current generation is leaning towards rejecting honoring parents, lining up under their authority, and many parents simply are too busy for their children, thus causing them to end up discouraged or angry.

Two other considerations regarding fathers and their children should be considered before we move on. First, how a man leads his family directly qualifies or disqualifies him for other leadership positions.

> He must manage his own household well, with all dignity keeping his children submissive, for if someone does not know how to manage his own household, how will he care for God's church? 1 Timothy 3:4-5

In this passage, and in Titus, the qualification of elders is spelled out. One of the only requirements that has added detail is the one dealing with the man's parenting skills. If this man failed when his children lived under his direct leadership, how will he possibly lead

Let's Go Deeper

the church people that he exercises far less authority over? A good question to be pondered in our day.

The second issue to consider regarding fathers and parenting is the ramifications of failure. The apostle Paul is famous for his lists. Several long sentences populated with horrible sins are found in his writings. Space limits our developing these listings of sins, but notice that in both, "disobedient to parents" is listed right next to some horrible crimes!

> But understand this, that in the last days there will come times of difficulty. For people will be lovers of self, lovers of money, proud, arrogant, abusive, disobedient to their parents, ungrateful, unholy, heartless, unappeasable, slanderous, without self-control, brutal, not loving good, treacherous, reckless, swollen with conceit, lovers of pleasure rather than lovers of God, having the appearance of godliness, but denying its power. Avoid such people. 2 Timothy 3:1-5

> They were filled with all manner of unrighteousness, evil, covetousness, malice. They are full of envy, murder, strife, deceit, maliciousness. They are gossips, slanderers, haters of God, insolent, haughty, boastful, inventors of evil, disobedient to parents, foolish, faithless, heartless, ruthless.
> Romans 1:29-31

Children become disobedient to parents because the parents allow it. It is not popular in our day to even discuss the topic, but Paul (under the inspiration of the Holy Spirit) lists disobedience to parents with all manner of evil. Parents must teach their children to honor and respect them.

## Church Authority

The next realm of authority deals with the church realm. God's Kingdom is one of order and authority for without these anarchy reigns. The Kingdom of God is built on a different value system than the world, so the leadership is supposed to be servant oriented, not led by greed or ego. However, even those leaders that are not perfect are entitled to submission from those that are under their authority.

> Obey your leaders and submit to them, for they are keeping watch over your souls, as those who will have to give an account. Let them do this with joy and not with groaning, for that would be of no advantage to you. Hebrews 13:17

> So I exhort the elders among you, as a fellow elder and a witness of the sufferings of Christ, as well as a partaker in the glory that is going to be revealed: shepherd the flock of God that is among you, exercising oversight, not under compulsion, but willingly, as God would have you; not for shameful gain, but eagerly; not domineering over those in your charge, but being examples to the flock. 1 Peter 5:1-3

> Let the elders who rule well be considered worthy of double honor, especially those who labor in preaching and teaching. 1 Timothy 5:17

I will not take the space necessary to detail all the verses, but Biblically, elders were to assure that there was doctrinal purity and no willful sin in those that were under their charge. Discipline could be exercised on unruly members including public humiliation and excommunication for those that refused to come under discipline. Accusations against elders had to be weighed carefully, and rewards await the faithful church leader.

The main point is that there is a realm of authority within the church structure and those that lead should have followers that are willingly lining up under their leadership.

## Employer Authority

The final realm of authority deals with employers. The Scripture does not have a great deal to say directly to employers and employees, but there are some principles that are clear. We are to be good workers giving a full day's work for our pay (Colossians 3:23). We are to work or we do not eat (2 Thessalonians 3:10). Employers are to be fair and not cheat their employees (Jeremiah 22:13).

In addition, if we move the discussion to slaves and masters, we would find an abundance of verses dealing with how to walk in this relationship. The one in authority was to be non-abusive and the one under authority was to serve with a right spirit. The point for us to remember is that our bosses are authorities in our lives and are therefore entitled to our willingness to line up under them.

I have not presented an exhaustive listing of Scriptures dealing with this topic, but certainly enough to give us an overview of the Biblical stance on the topic of authority. From this overview, several things become clear: God has set up an authority structure that

## For Our Consideration

includes family, government, bosses, and the church. Each of these structures has a realm and most of us are living under multiple ones at any given time in our lives. We who are dwelling under these structures have a responsibility to willingly line up under the authority. When we refuse, we are resisting God's plan and order.

There are times of course when we must refuse to submit to authority. If the authority is asking us to sin or to violate God's Word in some fashion then we must not obey. However, we must be ready to suffer the consequences of this disobedience when we choose not to submit. If we are in an abusive situation and we can escape, we should. The Apostle Paul told slaves to bear up, but if they could get free, do so (1 Corinthians 7:21).

Even in difficult situations, the commands given are often "to bear up under," rather than "flee from." It seems that God is not nearly as concerned with what we go through as He is with our response to what we go through. In all He allows us to experience, His chief concern is that our attitudes become Christ like, not that we necessarily have an easy path.

God repeatedly instructed people to bear up under bad or even abusive authority to accomplish a greater goal. For example, Hagar, King David with Saul, Joseph served a wicked Pharaoh, the prophets served wicked kings, Daniel was a leader in a wicked government, Jesus said to render unto Caesar (not exactly a nice man) what was his, Jesus also said to do what the religious leaders said, but do not imitate their actions, Paul said you should not revile a high priest (even a corrupt one) and wrote all those verses dealing with submission to authority, while in a Roman prison.

If you find yourself in a very difficult situation, remember that those under authority have the God-given right to appeal to the authority,

Let's Go Deeper

and then to go over the authority's head to God with any decision they feel is unjust. Daniel and his three friends appealed to the king for an exception to his dietary law. Esther approached the king to plead for her people's life (and this was at the direction of her uncle that raised her as his own daughter) because she knew this verse:

> The king's heart is in the hand of the LORD; He directs it like a watercourse wherever he pleases. Proverbs 21:1

We can ask God to change the authorities heart as He desires. We can have faith that the Almighty, Sovereign God can change any circumstance in an instant when He desires and if He has not changed it then He has something else for us to learn.

The question arises as to when do I outgrow the need to submit to authority? The simple answer is, never.

> Young men, in the same way be submissive to those who are older. All of you, clothe yourselves with humility toward one another, because, "God opposes the proud but gives grace to the humble." Humble yourselves, therefore, under God's mighty hand, that he may lift you up in due time. Cast all your anxiety on him because he cares for you. 1 Peter 5:5-7

> Submit to one another out of reverence for Christ. Eph. 5:21

The "all of you" and "one another" in the verses means all of us! There is never a time when we are not under some type of authority, and most times, we will be under several different ones. We are not a lawless people demanding our own rights, but we are servants of the

## For Our Consideration

Most High God bowing before His will. That will is most often revealed by and through His delegated authorities.

The ultimate issue is one of the heart. Am I willing to submit to someone other than myself? Am I willing to allow God to work in my life and the lives of those in authority to accomplish His plan and purposes, or will I demand my way and perceived rights? Will I be willing to bear up even under an unjust authority for the sake of the Gospel, or will I demand my rights to my will and pleasure?

By demanding my own way, most of the time I will cause damage to multitudes of people and God still will have to work on my selfishness and pride through another situation. A good principle to follow is that if my authorities in my life are not in agreement with my actions and desires, then I need to wait and submit to them until they agree or my desires change.

Being under authority takes great faith in God, not the authority, for the authority gets that authority from God, and God can change them, remove them, or harden them at His command. Selfishness and demanding my rights are not a fruit of the Spirit, but humility and submission are a very good reflection of my spiritual maturity.

If I will humble myself and submit to authority (in all areas of my life) then the Scripture teaches that:

- Things will go well with me – Ephesians 6: 2-3
- As a child, I will be a delight to the Lord - Colossians 3:20
- I will avoid fear of judgment and condemnation – Romans 13:3
- I will have a clear/good conscience – Romans 13:5
- I will have a good testimony with others - Hebrews 13:17
- I will bring glory to God – 1 Peter 2:18-19

- God's name will not be blasphemed – 1 Timothy 6:1
- I will receive clear direction – Proverbs 6:20-22
- I will learn discretion – Proverbs 6:23-24
- I will gain discernment – Proverbs 15:5
- I will receive praise – 1 Peter 2:13-14
- I will escape destructive pride – 1 Timothy 6:2-4

In conclusion, one of God's primary tools to shape us, change us, and reveal our true heart motives, is the authorities in our lives. God has placed them and allowed them for His purposes. With faith and humility, we can walk through any difficulty that may arise. Ultimately how we respond to the earthly authority provides an excellent picture of how we are responding to our Heavenly authority.

For Our Consideration

# Parental Authority

Having looked at authority in general, this study develops the domain of parental authority. While there is some overlap with the previous study, there is also a great deal of information that is unique in the pages that follow.

Parental authority, what is it? It's a topic of much debate and discussion these days. What does it look like for me as a parent or as a young person specifically in relationship to being part of choosing a marriage partner?

It really doesn't matter what people think or surmise, it only matters what God says regarding this subject. My theology comes from searching the Scripture and deciding what I believe the Word of God is saying. It should be developed from a diligent search of the Word and a conviction which I believe to be from the Holy Spirit for my life.

The customs and people of the days of the O.T. were different than ours in America, but there are basics that don't change. Perhaps something like a floor plan. How I paint, the carpet I choose, or the pictures and furniture may vary from yours; but the floor plan is the same and it stays the same.

The Patriarchal system had its issues, and some in our day have attempted to reinstate it. I am not one of them! I believe what Paul wrote about being a new creation in Christ. Men and women have differing roles, but equality is not an issue. (See Galatians 3:28)

## Let's Go Deeper

The Old Testament and New Testament give us different perspectives, but a lot to chew on. I believe that the Bible clearly gives examples regarding parental involvement and authority in general.

It is my belief that the concept of authority is foundational to every area of my walk. When Jesus stood amazed at the centurion's understanding of authority and said in Matthew 8:8-10 "I have never seen such great faith in all Israel" it makes me think it takes great faith to believe and to walk out authority in any area of our life. And it is important!

This is not a preference, but a major system within the Body of Christ. Understanding authority and walking it out is foundational to Christianity. This cannot be separated from our Christian thinking any more than my skeletal system, or digestive system can be removed from my body. This is a major system of the Kingdom of God.

I realize that we don't live in the days of the Old Testament, but principles regarding parents being involved can be seen throughout. There was no specific rule stated, "Dad's the authority here…" it was just an accepted part of their culture. And there is no way that anyone could have come in and told them otherwise.

In the New Testament, the writers addressed authorities and it seems they take for granted that everyone already new and understood the basic principles from the O.T. There was little reason to explain… it was a given. They just added to the already standing foundation of parental authority.

I believe that this is God's design and not my own. He set things up this way with different levels of authority as the structure.

It is His way of ruling His creation, and what He has instituted. And so, we must start with the clear understanding that God has

## For Our Consideration

established different realms of leadership and authority. Governments, families, Churches etc.

Each realm of authority is independent of the other and directly accountable to God. The head of the family answers directly to God as does the President or a Pastor. Both the Governor and a Father are answerable to God. For example Eli as a father, and David as the King of Israel.

God has given the right of rulership to these positions. They can in one sense rule as they please, but they will one day be accountable to God for the way they handled their leadership positions. The right to rule is God given and subjection is God's plan and purpose for those individuals who find themselves under authority.

With that as my back drop let's look specifically at parental involvement in the lives of the people of the O.T. working my way through to the N.T. I hope to see if God's view of "the right of rulership" fits into my life. If by chance it doesn't, I pray that my life will change, as I know that God's word is not wrong.

One difficulty with simply listing Scriptures is that there is often little detail given regarding the culture and times when these actions were taken. Historical events are given with very little comment regarding whether the actions taken were correct, righteous or wicked.

For the record, I am not endorsing a return to any of these customs necessarily, simply suggesting that we study them to glean principles and see how the people acted in their day.

Please look up each Scripture, read the context and consider my comments that follow.

## Let's Go Deeper

Genesis 18:19 - God chose Abraham so that He would direct and command his children and household after him to keep the ways of the Lord. I guess God wanted a strong man that would command, like in an army. It was his right to rule.

Genesis 19:8 - Lot had two daughters pledged to be married. Yet he, as the father, had the right to rule his girls and to send them out to the wicked men of the city. There is no record of objection anywhere. The sons-in-law to be were not their authority yet. This seems to be an abusive authority to say the least, yet the mindset appears to be taken for granted, "What Dad says goes."

Genesis 16:6-9 - Scripture states that Sarai was an abusive authority, yet the angel of God tells Hagar to go back and submit to her master and mistress. Submission seems to be the issue not being mistreated.

Genesis 21:21 - It was normal and part of the culture to choose your son's wife. Parents had the power, and the right to rule. Hagar took a wife for her son as well.

Genesis 24:3-4 - Isaac was at least 40 years old and he gave no objection to having his dad send his servant to choose his wife. This was a normal process for obtaining a bride.

Genesis 24:50 - Laban and Bethual answered for Rebekah "Here she is, take her and go" she apparently had no say in the matter. When her Mom and brother didn't want her to leave they asked her to stay ten more days and they asked her what she thought in verse 57, but this had nothing to do with her marrying Isaac. She didn't appear to

## For Our Consideration

have any say in the matter, she was pledged to be his wife, period! They had made the decision because they had the right to do so.

Genesis 26:34 - Esau choose for himself without any advice and it was a disaster all the way.

Genesis 28:1-2 - at the age of at least 40 years old Jacob is commanded by his father to go to Laban and get a wife from his family. Jacob gives no objections. The word says he *obeyed* his father and mother in verse 7.

Genesis 34:4-6 - Shechem has violated Diana yet his father goes to Jacob and asks for her hand for his son. These people were not Israelites, yet they understood the right of the father as the ruler of the home.

Genesis 42:1-2 - Jacob orders his grown sons to go to Egypt and refuses to let Benjamin go who is at least 30 years old. It was the father's right to command adults.

Genesis 43:8-11 - Judah, who is maybe 15 years older than Benjamin, has to appeal to his dad and convince him that Benjamin must go with them down to Egypt.

Exodus 2:21 - Jethro gave Moses his daughter in marriage.

Exodus 16:8 - God states that when the people grumbled against Moses they grumbled against HIM. Wouldn't this be true against any leadership position when God has given the right to rule? There are

Let's Go Deeper

proper ways to appeal and deal with things we don't like and to not be divisive and/or grumble. God certainly frowns upon complaining.

Exodus 20:12 - Now the law arrives and honor your mother and father is right in the middle presented as the 5th commandment. Written for all ages to be read and never be forgotten.

Exodus 21:15, Deuteronomy 27:16 - If you attack or curse your parents you must be put to death or stoned. This was a law from the throne of God.

Exodus 22:16-17 - If a man seduces a girl he must pay and marry her, unless her father absolutely refuses to give her in marriage. Daddy had the final word and the right to rule…this was also one of the laws.

Numbers 14:29-30 & 21:5-7 - Joshua and Caleb are the only ones who didn't grumble and rebel against Moses and God, and they are the only ones who get to enter the Promised Land. This is clear regarding how God feels about speaking and acting against an authority which He has put into place and had given the right to rule.

Numbers 16:27 - God judged Korah and his family for leading a rebellion and gripping against Moses. The earth opened and devoured them and their belongings.

Numbers 30:3 - When a young woman living in her father's household made a vow, and he doesn't like it, he can forbid it and disavow it, as could a husband. She was under submission to either her dad or husband.

For Our Consideration

Deuteronomy 7:3 & Judges 12:9 - Daughters were to be given away by someone.

Deuteronomy 2:18 - If a man had a stubborn and rebellious son that would not listen to them who was a drunk and a profligate they were to stone him. Obviously, he had to be an adult to be a drunkard.

Judges 11:29-39 - This daughter was willing to give her life rather than to dishonor her father, she could have run away. A tragic story yet demonstrates the relationship between a father and daughter.

Judges 14:1; 15:2 - Samson tells his parents to get him this girl for his wife. Why didn't he just go get her himself? Because he honored the fact that God gave parents the right to get wives perhaps?

I Samuel 17:25 - The reward was the daughter. He had the right as dad and king to give her to whomever he wished.

1Samuel 18:17 - Again the daughter is given away without any apparent say in the matter.

1 Samuel 3:13 - Eli was rejected by God because he did not restrain his adult sons clearly failing in his responsibility.

It seems clear from this small sampling of verses; the parents were to be a part of getting and giving their children in marriage. They were to rule their homes and their adult children would listen and honor their parents. God's law repeated this in many ways. God never accepted or encouraged rebellion in any form.

Another reference to rebellion versus honoring can be seen in David's relationship to King Saul. This is the correct way to deal with an abusive authority. He would not touch him, but let God take care of him. This took great faith, patience, and endurance on David's part.

In the New Testament, we rarely see stories of how the family relationships function, but certain principles didn't change. Fathers are still the head, children were still told to obey, and adult children were still instructed to honor their parents.

Matthew 15:3-6, Mark 7: 8-13 – Jesus severely rebukes the Pharisees because they have let go of the command regarding honoring their parents, so they could do what they wanted to do with their money.

Romans 1:29-30 – A list of depraved deeds belonging to ungodly people is given and being disobedient to parents is included. It must have been unheard of to disregard or disobey parental involvement like a large percentage of our culture does. We think it is normal, God lists it among evil behavior.

Ephesians 5:21- 6:4 - Paul addresses how we should live as believers - submitting to each other and under authority. Wives, husbands, children and slaves, who else is there?

Colossians 3:18-21- Provides rules for holy living. Children are to obey and honor, and fathers are told not to exasperate their children by being unreasonable, or embitter them.

## For Our Consideration

2 Timothy 3:2 – Again, a list of the horrible ways that people will be in the last days. Being disobedient to parents is among them.

1 Timothy 3:4-5, Titus 1:6 – These are lists of qualifications for being an elder. He cannot have children that are disobedient. Disobedience is an issue with God and against His purposes. Fathers have the right to rule their homes and children should consider it their spiritual duty to obey.

Philemon 8 – Paul tells Philemon that in Christ, he could order him to do what is right. But instead, he will appeal to him. There is a realm of authority that Paul has, but he chooses to exercise that authority with kindness and gentleness, appealing to him instead. Maybe fathers need to remember this in dealing with their adult children.

Hebrews 13:17 - Obey your leaders for they do give an account. Parents will give an account of how they rule their homes and children. This should put the fear of God in all of us as parents.

1 Peter 2:11-13 – We are to be aliens and strangers in the world. We are to abstain and live such good lives among the pagans that they will see our good deeds. One good deed in verse 13 is to submit for the Lord's sake to every institution among men. This would clearly be children to parents especially when disobedience is named as a wicked, sinful desire in Romans 1:29.

1 Peter 5:1 – Elders are to serve and young men are in the same way to be submissive to those who are older, and clothe themselves with

humility. Young men should be submissive, not demanding boastful or proud, but humble and servants to others.

Jude 1:6-13 – Jude is describing certain godless men who have changed the grace of God into a license to sin. He compares them to Korah's rebellion and how they also rejected authority. There are authorities and we should take care to respect those in places of authority lest we be compared to Korah.

God has set parents in the place of authority. Rebellion and disobedience is wrong. Each family has the right to choose and rule as they seek God and do what they deem correct for their family.

If abuse is involved then get out and seek help. However, short of abuse, every family will walk out their God-given mandate and order in slightly differing fashion. We are to learn to respect, love, and encourage one another in such matters.

Parents were granted broad authority by God and will be held accountable for their usage of it. Children were instructed to obey and submit and this includes prayerfully appealing to parents when believed to be in error.

God came up with the family concept and He has provided the guidelines and rules for its function. While we may disagree over the details, we would be wise to go to the Word of God and let the truth be our guide in how we live our lives.

For Our Consideration

# Called to War – A Spiritual Warfare Discussion

I personally don't make iron clad doctrines based upon one Scripture, but only when the truth surfaces many places. If it is an important concept then most likely the same thing will surface in multiple locations from multiple authors- these Scriptures included are instructions from Jesus, Paul, Peter, James, and John, so I feel pretty good about this one that I had the opportunity to share with a group of pastors.

**Scriptures to Consider**

Be sober-minded; be watchful. Your adversary the devil prowls around like a roaring lion, seeking someone to devour. Resist him, firm in your faith, knowing that the same kinds of suffering are being experienced by your brotherhood throughout the world. 1 Peter 5:8-9

Submit yourselves therefore to God. Resist the devil, and he will flee from you. Draw near to God, and he will draw near to you. Cleanse your hands, you sinners, and purify your hearts, you double-minded. James 4:7-8

You are of your father the devil, and your will is to do your father's desires. He was a murderer from the beginning, and has nothing to do with the truth, because there is no truth in him. When he lies, he speaks out of his own character, for he is a liar and the father of lies. John 8:44

See to it that no one takes you captive by philosophy and empty deceit, according to human tradition, according to the elemental spirits of the world, and not according to Christ. Colossians 2:8

Whoever makes a practice of sinning is of the devil, for the devil has been sinning from the beginning. The reason the Son of God appeared was to destroy the works of the devil. 1 John 3:8

...and give no opportunity (place or jurisdiction- think beachhead!) to the devil. Ephesians 4:27

Put on the whole armor of God, that you may be able to stand against the schemes of the devil. Ephesians 6:11

These verses have some common points:

- We have an enemy and he wants to destroy us or these verses are meaningless.
- Contrary to popular teaching the devil is real, or Jesus spent a great deal of time dealing with fantasy. (In the NT - Devil 31 references, Satan 34, and demons 73 times mentioned)
- The devil's primary weapon is composed of lies, schemes, and deceit.

## For Our Consideration

- We, as God's children, have a responsibility to resist and not to yield to our foe, and God has provided us with a defense to help us succeed.

Fathers, pastors, and leaders are in a battle that includes among other things, fighting personal depression, discouragement with people, pride, arrogance, and sexual temptation.

Most of us know people and probably pastors that have given (I carefully use this word instead of fallen) into adultery. The destruction has been immense and the pain inflicted relationally is almost incalculable.

One does not simply fall into sin by accident, i.e. oops, just walking around minding my own business and now I am in a hotel room with someone other than my wife! But it is a series of willful choices to walk down a path of destruction. Proverbs 7:6-27. Written by a man very familiar with sexual issues experienced both personally and generationally, shouts of process and poor decision making.

The Cost is High: sin will take you further than you want to go and cost you more than you ever imagined.

I served as the executive pastor for 11 years with a gifted pastor of a 3,500-member church and leader of about 50 churches in our group. May 19th, 1993 after praying with his wife in the morning, he ran off to Florida with his book editor and people asked how did this happen? My answer was, he made a series of small, very bad choices. He did not simply get up one day and decided to throw away a lifetime of work.

Deception was of course involved, but frontal attacks typically do not work, so subtle, little compromises gradually are allowed and then like the sheep to the slaughter we walk down the path of destruction.

It's the little foxes that spoil the vine. (Songs of Solomon 2:15) Or as I like to say, "we are all one or two bad decisions away from a great deal of trouble."

If you have been around for long you probably have your own tales of woe. I have dozens but will spare you the gory details. It is sufficient to understand the trail of heartache and destruction that follows in the wake of giving into sexual sin via adultery, porn, or premarital failures. (I have included at the end of these notes a listing from Randy Alcorn's perspective)

If a leader is involved, then the leader's reputation is tarnished and his ministry is typically destroyed. His family is often devastated as well either through divorce, children rejecting the Gospel, or at best, a shadow of mistrust hovers for the remainder of his life.

Those that were under the teaching of the leader are shaken to the core. If THIS man fell, what hope do I have? The sheep are often scattered and wander around and I have to think that at least part of the judgment on this action includes seeing the ramifications of it on the innocent.

In the case I just mentioned, the church shrunk from 3500 and 50 churches to zero churches and a church that now is about 400-500 and on its third pastor since he left. This pastor, who did come back to town, repented and was able to salvage his marriage. Since he was very well known due to being on TV and the radio, he would have people come to him on the street and cry, curse, and verbally attack him for his failure. Woe to the shepherds that scatter the flock! I spoke with him shortly before his death and he was still weeping and grieving over his moral failure and its fallout.

Another ramification of this type of failure is that the world loses even more respect for the Church at large. This pastor's actions made the front page of our local paper. Those that do not know Christ expect us to maintain a higher standard than they do! As Nathan told David after his sexual failure with Bathsheba:

> However, because by this deed you have given occasion to the enemies of the LORD to blaspheme, the child also that is born to you shall surely die. 2 Samuel 12:14 (NASB)

Our behavior can give the enemies of Christ a reason to blaspheme, God forbid! We who took a stand for Christ have now tarnished His power and name in the eyes of the world. We do not have to think too hard to remember national leaders failing morally and the fallout from those actions.

The cost of giving into sexual sin is huge, yet those in the Church continue to run into it. Families are destroyed, churches and ministries are reduced to scorn.

> For this purpose he was hired, that I should be afraid and act in this way and sin, and so they could give me a bad name in order to taunt me. Nehemiah 6:13

The devil laughs, loves to tempt us, see us fall, give us a bad name, and gleefully mock us for it.

### Let's Fight to Win

1. Planning will not guarantee that we will not fail, but failing to plan will not help in any fashion. Being prepared always helps, while attempting to make rational decisions in the heat of the moment may not happen at all! Realize the reality and intensity of the struggle. Do

not be ignorant of the schemes of our foe. There is a time to stand and fight and there is a time to flee. This is one of the only sins we are told to run from:

> Flee (to seek safety by flight) from sexual immorality. Every other sin a person commits is outside the body, but the sexually immoral person sins against his own body.
> 1 Corinthians 6:18

2. Do not be casual about this area for we are living in a battle zone! The Scripture told us to be: sober-minded, be alert, resist, do not be taken captive, don't give a place for the devil, and put on your armor to stand against the schemes - these imply that we can be casual, unaware, lax, compromise, captured, and unprepared.

3. Put on the armor and use the weapons God has provided for us.

A. Take our thoughts captive to the obedience of Christ. 2 Corinthians 10:5 more in a moment on this one. I cannot control which birds fly over my head, I can control what I allow to nest in my hair.

B. If our enemies main weapon is lying, we must fight it with truth. Thy Word is truth. We need to fight the lies presented by our foe with the truth engrafted in our hearts and minds. We must be people of the Word filling our minds with truth often!

C. Do not ignore or deny the reality of the struggle in your own life or the life of the men you walk with. Get help and get it now. Sin loves the dark, get it into the light.

D. Starvation is the only long-term effective tool. Quit feeding it. The intensity will lesson as times passes, but not if we keep feeding it.

For Our Consideration

    E. Develop a strategy ahead of time and use it. For me, prayer targets work well. Basically, when confronted with a mental or visual temptation, think of someone that would do great damage to the kingdom of darkness if they were saved and begin to intercede for them every time temptation knocks on your mind. Others use Scripture quoting, singing, whatever, but be ready! Plan, be ready for a counter attack.

    4. Be aware of those around you and learn to grow in discernment. If there really is a devil and if he really wants to destroy us and our families, do we not think that there are spies and double agents? Don't be naive. Listen to the women in your life for their cautions - your wife and daughters can detect sensuality in other women probably better than you. Better to be cautious than foolish. Most normal folks won't be upset with your taking precautions.

    5. Take precautions and avoid even the appearance of evil (1 Thessalonians 5:22). If we allow ourselves to be put in places where accusations can occur, even if innocent, great damage will take place. Billy Graham would not go into a public restroom alone!

### Let's Get Practical

    1. Do not put yourself or your family in compromising positions with the opposite sex. The difference between good kids and those in trouble is one thing - parental supervision. Christians' children still have hormones and they still play doctor. Allowing our wife or daughters to spend time with men can lead to problems and failure. Physical contact, extensive talking, skits, musicals, spending large amounts of time in close proximity with the opposite sex can lead to failure so be careful.

2. Be careful with touching other women via hand holding or extended frontal hugs. Do you really need to feel her breasts against your chest? What is going on inside her head as your arms are around her or as you are squeezing her hand? We do not want to be a stumbling block.

3. All sin first begins as a thought. Philippians 4:8 is an excellent filter for our thought life and entertainment choices - GIGO - old computer talk - garbage in garbage out.

> Finally, brothers, whatever is true, whatever is honorable, whatever is just, whatever is pure, whatever is lovely, whatever is commendable, if there is any excellence, if there is anything worthy of praise, think about these things.

4. For me, I do not meet alone, ride with, or talk very often alone with women other than my wife and daughters. I never go to a woman's house alone. Engaging in communication with women opens the door to fantasy. Many good sisters in the Lord tend to elevate leaders and we are not wise if we help them entertain that illusion. If the talking gets personal involve your wife or hand off the counseling to an older woman via Titus 2:3-5. Our protector gene kicks in quickly, be careful.

5. If you are struggling with a particular woman, break it off now. Tell someone that you can trust and become accountable. Accountability works only if you want to be accountable. If you don't stop, you will fall and live with regret.

6. Is it easier to avoid or to overcome temptation? I prefer the first option. Take practical steps to avoid temptation and accusations. Keep the door to your office open. Install glass in it. Don't office alone.

## For Our Consideration

Move your computer to a place where it can be instantly seen by all when they walk by or enter. If we really want to be free and remain free, we can be. Practice the "Law of First Glance." Do not buy into the lies of our culture - "I just appreciate God's beauty," or "I am just window shopping." "No harm in looking." Yes, there is. We undermine our wife's self-image and we model to others that lust is okay. It's not. When with other men watch what they watch to get an ideal of their struggles. As someone said, "Let our wife or children catch us doing something good when they enter our room!" Find us on our knees.

7. Make sure we know well the condition of our flock, beginning with the sheep at home.

    A. Is your wife struggling in this arena? How about your children? Are you observant as to signs of wandering? Our wife and children also have a bull's-eye on their backs. Your wife or child getting involved in immorality will destroy your credibility and hinder your ministry as quickly as you falling.

    B. Social media is quickly becoming the number 1 mentioned reason for divorce. Do we know what our family is doing on Facebook or one of the hundreds of others? Do we have access to passwords, emails, texts, chat conversations, etc.? If not, why not?

    C. Do we know who our family is hanging out with and what they are talking about? A wise man walks with the wise but a companion of fools comes to ruin. Prov. 13:20

    D. Are we taking responsibility for how our wife and daughters are dressing? Do we really want other men to stumble over them? How about our sons? Are they flirts? Are they being trained to protect women or to walk down the path of destruction?

    E. Will we ask the tough "why" questions? Why do I like/want to look at other women? Why does my wife or daughter want to dress that way? What condition is my heart really in? How about my family? Do I really hate this sin? Why not?

8. The above points (7) can be expanded to include the men we work with, our fellow elders, and those under our care. In addition, we must be working with the men, both married and single, to assist them in this arena in their own families. Positive peer pressure is good!

9. Failure is not the end but a chance for a new beginning. If you have failed, seek the Redeemer for His mercy, grace, forgiveness and a new beginning! We all fall, for a righteous man, falls seven times, but he gets back up, let's just fall in the right direction and on the highway of holiness!

> The steadfast love of the LORD never ceases; his mercies never come to an end; they are new every morning; great is your faithfulness. "The LORD is my portion," says my soul, "therefore I will hope in him." Lamentations 3:22-24

Amid complete judgment and national failure of Israel, God says such things! He loves you and wants to restore you. Do not run from the only solution there is, for this too is a trick of our enemy. We approach a throne of grace by the shed blood of Jesus!

For Our Consideration

## Let's Get Personal

If you have fallen or are trapped then consider the following shared by my good friend named Eric:

- Being genuinely honest with yourself about your sin. You are not likely to get help until you are ruthlessly honest with yourself and God about your present condition.
- Who else knows about your struggle? If no one, then you have neglected some of the most basic avenues of deliverance, including the counsel, prayer and the reproof of your Christian brothers and even the elders of the church. If you have been seeking deliverance over a long period of time, but have failed to bring others in for fear of losing reputation, position or ministry, you may be missing the very means God intends to set you free. If your crying out to God for victory over a sexual bondage has failed to free you, God may well be waiting until you bring others in - even at the risk of embarrassment, exposure, and loss. Proverbs 28:13 Whoever conceals his transgressions will not prosper, but he who confesses and forsakes them will obtain mercy.
- Seek some accountability. This can be an on-going aid to increased moral freedom.
- It MAY even be necessary that you go to your wife and rectify any breaking of your vows. This is certainly something you must pray about, but the alternative MAY be going the rest of your marriage while hiding something that touches the very core of your intimacy. This should be considered with a great deal of prayer and counsel.

## Summary

We are in a battle but we are not unprepared, for we have all the tools necessary to walk in victory. We are told to not be ignorant, be on guard, and to be diligent. We will encounter this battle practically every day of our lives personally and certainly in our families and with those under our care. God knew this and He has promised us help through the power of the Holy Spirit and through His Word. May we walk in the truth and remain faithful. May we help those that we care for to be prepared and to learn how to win this battle!

The Apostle Peter gives me great encouragement:

> His divine power has granted to us all things that pertain to life and godliness, through the knowledge of Him who called us to His own glory and excellence, by which He has granted to us His precious and very great promises, so that through them you may become partakers of the divine nature, having escaped from the corruption that is in the world because of sinful desire. 2 Peter 1:3-4

Personalized List of Anticipated Consequences of Immorality - Randy Alcorn http://www.epm.org/blog/2009/Jun/26/counting-the-cost-of-sexual-immorality

- Grieving my Lord; displeasing the One whose opinion most matters.
- Dragging into the mud Christ's sacred reputation.
- Loss of reward and commendation from God.

- Having to one day look Jesus in the face at the judgment seat and give an account of why I did it. Forcing God to discipline me in various ways.
- Following in the footsteps of men I know of whose immorality forfeited their ministry and caused me to shudder.
- Suffering of innocent people around me who would get hit by my shrapnel (a la Achan).
- Untold hurt to Nanci, my best friend, and loyal wife.
- Loss of Nanci's respect and trust.
- Hurt to and loss of credibility with my beloved daughters, Karina and Angela. ("Why listen to a man who betrayed Mom and us?")
- If my blindness should continue or my family be unable to forgive, I could lose my wife and my children forever.
- Shame to my family. (The cruel comments of others who would invariably find out.)
- Shame to my church family.
- Shame and hurt to my fellow pastors and elders.
- Shame and hurt to my friends, and especially those I've led to Christ and discipled. List of names:
- Guilt awfully hard to shake—even though God would forgive me, would I forgive myself?
- Plaguing memories and flashbacks that could taint future intimacy with my wife.
- Disqualifying myself after having preached to others.
- Surrender of the things I am called to and love to do—teach and preach and write and minister to others. Forfeiting forever certain opportunities to serve God. Years of training

and experience in ministry wasted for a long period of time, maybe permanently.
- Being haunted by my sin as I look in the eyes of others, and having it all dredged up again wherever I go and whatever I do.
- Undermining the hard work and prayers of others by saying to our community "this is a hypocrite—who can take seriously anything he and his church have said and done?"
- Laughter, rejoicing and blasphemous smugness by those who disrespect God and the church (2 Samuel 12:14).
- Bringing great pleasure to Satan, the Enemy of God.
- Heaping judgment and endless problems on the person I would have committed adultery with.
- Possible diseases (pain, constant reminder to me and my wife, possible infection of Nanci, or in the case of AIDS, even causing her death, as well as mine.)
- Possible pregnancy, with its personal and financial implications.
- Loss of self-respect, discrediting my own name, and invoking shame and lifelong embarrassment upon myself

If we really considered the above from Randy Alcorn, we would flee and not give into temptation in this arena. The pain is real and so is the destruction. I pray we would stand as men of God complete in the power of Jesus, ready and able to do battle for the Kingdom.

For Our Consideration

# Spiritual Incrementalism Part One

Many of us bemoan losing our society to wickedness. We see the direction that our nation is heading and we grieve. We did not lose everything overnight and we will not gain it back that way either. We gain or lose ground by inches. I believe this is also true in our walk with God.

Let's define the term incrementalism:

**The method used in which desired changes are implemented gradually or in small steps instead of giant strides.**

After we are saved, the Bible uses the term "walk" to describe our journey. Most of us would agree that the life we live after we meet the Lord is a day by day experience. This walk has been described as a marathon and not a sprint. The Bible presents our journey this way:

For we walk by faith, not by sight. 2 Corinthians 5:7

But I say, walk by the Spirit, and you will not gratify the desires of the flesh. Galatians 5:16

I therefore, a prisoner for the Lord, urge you to walk in a manner worthy of the calling to which you have been called. Ephesians 4:1

# Let's Go Deeper

This sampling of verses indicates that our walk is by faith, can either be in the Spirit or in our flesh, and that we can walk in a worthy manner, or not depending on what we do.

We walk in a direction each day. I also understand a bit about losing a day or even a season through illness, depression, or a major trial. We certainly can get turned around so much we don't even know which way is up, let alone forward. The direction is not always clear, though it is clearer than we think sometimes.

God's view of us is important to understand in our journey. One of the primary pictures used in the Scripture referring to you and I is that of sheep. We are the sheep, God is the Shepherd.

> All we like sheep have gone astray; we have turned—every one—to his own way; Isaiah 53:6
>
> The Lord is my Shepherd; I shall not want. Psalm 23:1
>
> I am the Good Shepherd. The Good Shepherd lays down His life for the sheep. John 10:11

Each of us are sheep, God's words not mine. Sheep tend to stray and wander. From what I read, sheep don't really back up well, they tend to become entangled in thorn bushes, they often put their heads down and just wander away from the flock. Sheep are led not driven, and the picture of the Lord being our Shepherd is one of the most familiar ones in Scripture.

Because of our sheep nature, many times we turn away from God's revealed will, His Word, His leadings, and follow our own choices and self-dominated instincts. I am sure that this year was a year that was

## For Our Consideration

both successful and full of failure in this manner. It is easy to get distracted or to not pay attention to the Shepherd.

As we mature, we desire for our walk to be more Christ-like, our choices to be grounded in wisdom, maturity and to demonstrate growth. I am not the same man I was when I began this journey. By God's grace, I will not be the same man when I finish it. My desire is to walk on, live a life pleasing to the Lord, to complete the works that He has planned for me, and those arrive day by day.

With these two thoughts in mind – we gain and lose ground in small increments, and that we are sheep, how should we enter a new year?

We need to understand two principles – God is good, and He expects us to do something with our choices. First, we are told in the Scriptures, almost 200 times, that God is good, has steadfast love, unending mercies, and is great in faithfulness.

Consider these familiar passages:

> The steadfast love of the Lord never ceases; His mercies never come to an end; they are new every morning; great is Your faithfulness. Lamentations 3:22-23

Amid extreme judgment on the nation of Israel, the weeping prophet Jeremiah shares these deep truths about our God. In addition, Jeremiah instructs us what to do about them.

"The Lord is my portion," says my soul, "therefore I will hope in Him." The Lord is good to those who wait for Him, to the soul who seeks Him. It is good that one should wait quietly for the salvation of the Lord. Lamentations 3:24-26

Let's Go Deeper

We are told to wait upon the Lord, seek Him and do it without complaint, or quietly. We learn to wait in trust realizing that the Lord is our portion, or He is enough for every need, desire, dream, or problem.

When we look to the Lord, we will quickly realize that many times we have made wrong choices. We soon understand that we have followed our own way, have not sought His will first and with all our heart, soul, mind and strength. We, like all sheep, have wandered away from the Lord in some fashion.

So, we look to the Lord and we realize that we need to do something. This something is almost lost in our day, but I assure you it is a frequently used Biblical word representing a necessary action. The word is repent, which means we change our minds, our actions and the direction we are walking.

This concept, while not especially popular today, is the first step to spiritual growth and change. Consider just a sampling of verses:

> Repent, for the kingdom of heaven is at hand.
> Matthew 4:17(b)

> So they went out and proclaimed that people should repent.
> Mark 6:12

> Repent therefore, and turn back, that your sins may be blotted out, Acts 3:19

> No, I tell you; but unless you repent, you will all likewise perish. Luke 13:3

## For Our Consideration

> Repent and be baptized. Acts 2:38
>
> He commands all people everywhere to repent, Acts 17:30
>
> …remove your lampstand if you don't repent. Revelation 2:5

Day by day, and moment by moment we are faced with two possible directions. If we want to grow in spiritual maturity we begin by repentance. We walk away from our wandering, our sinful choices, and yielding to our own will, and we return to the Shepherd. Repentance was the message of the early church and it should be ours as well.

If we keep walking in the wrong direction no matter how much we care, no matter how fast we may be going we will never get to the desired destination. The only way is to repent – to turn around and walk in a different direction.

And, because of our repentance, we are commanded to bear fruit, and to understand that it is because of God's kindness that we are drawn to change our mind:

> Or do you presume on the riches of His kindness and forbearance and patience, not knowing that God's kindness is meant to lead you to repentance? Romans 2:4

God is kind to us and wants us to repent, to align our will, minds, and actions with His. God loves us so much that He will not leave us wandering, sinning, and hurting ourselves for long. His kindness will draw us, convict us, and even put great pressure on us to return to

Him. God sent His Son to redeem us from our sin and our own choices, and it begins with repentance.

Every breath we have is a gift and a new chance to walk in a way worthy of our calling. We do not have to remain trapped, guilt ridden, and walking in the wrong direction. God's grace, mercy, love and the Holy Spirit are available for us to choose a different life and path. God loves you and I so much He sent Jesus to pay the price for our sin.

We enter this forgiveness by confessing and repenting. If we want to grow, to learn to know the Shepherd better, to hear His voice, we must return to Him.

If you think we have nothing to repent of, I would beg to disagree. The Scripture lists many sins that believers commit. Here is a partial list to consider:

- Pride/Arrogance
- Envy
- Deceit
- Judgmentalism
- Phariseeism
- Hate
- Bitterness
- Unrighteous anger
- Selfishness
- Lust
- Coveting
- Greed
- Gluttony
- Sensuality
- Fraud/Flirtation

## For Our Consideration

- Hypocrisy
- Laziness
- Disobedient to parents

This list does not even include taming the tongue and sins of omission – failure to do the right things. If we honestly reflect on our lives, we will agree with God's Word – all we like sheep have gone astray. We must return to the Great Shepherd, and the doorway is repentance.

I understand that there is grace and that we are forgiven for our sins. Paul understood those concepts as well I assure you, yet he still wrote out those lists of sins that believers commit.

Repentance is not all there is, but it is a necessary starting point on our spiritual journey. If we want to be in a different place spiritually at the end of next year, we need to do something different than we did this year. Grasping the need to repent and make better decision is a good launching point.

In the next part I will explain what we should be doing, so if you read this far, hang on…for now, I would suggest some quiet time with your Shepherd and His Word to reflect.

# Spiritual Incrementalism Part Two

Just to review my definition of incrementalism:

**The method used in which desired changes are implemented gradually or in small steps instead of giant strides.**

In part one we focused on two concepts – we are sheep and we tend to wander off, thus the need to change our mind, or to use the Biblical word – repent.

We gain or lose ground in small steps. If we are walking in the wrong direction, no matter how sincere or good we may feel about the direction, we are going the wrong way. We must turn around.

When we turn around we begin to head the right way. We learn to hear the Shepherd's still, small voice. Our actions change. John Baptist put it this way in Matthew 3:8 – "Bring forth fruit with your repentance." Being born again should result in a visible, discernible change of our behavior.

So, what does the right direction look like if we turn around? What is it that sheep that are following the Shepherd's voice do? While each of us is unique there are general principles we all follow.

We must learn to slow down and look at the Shepherd. If we are wandering off because we take our eyes from Him, it would seem wise that we should change that behavior and gaze upon Him. We must learn to listen to His voice. We must make room for Him to speak into our lives.

## For Our Consideration

Most of us seem to need noise. We get up, plug in, turn on, and begin to chatter. Throughout our day we avoid quiet. Silence is deafening to our generation. Being still and quiet is scary to some, yet we are told to be still and know that He is God.

> Be still, (relax, let go,) and know that I am God. Psalm 46:10

> For God alone my soul waits in silence; from Him comes my salvation. Psalm 62:1

We must learn to be quiet. We must learn to make time to interact with the Shepherd. We must be sheep of the Word. I know there are things to do. I know there are children, work, and distractions of plenty. That does not change the fact that we need to slow down, quiet our souls and listen. There are seasons, I understand that. We still need to do it. We grow one decision at a time. If we don't spend time with the Shepherd we will not know His voice. If we don't spend time reading His words, we won't know what to do or how to think properly. Our minds will not be renewed.

If you are struggling with this issue, try a noise fast, or a technology fast, perhaps a social media fast, maybe even an email fast, or if desperate, a sports fast. How about a just turn it all off and be quiet fast. We must renew our minds and fight noise/distraction clutter.

For the record, I like computers, smart phones, sports, etc. But I love the Shepherd and if I allow those things to squeeze His voice and His word from my life, I will simply wander away and become entangled in a mess. So, will you. Try to obey - 1 Thessalonians 4:11 and hear His voice - and to make it your ambition (strive earnestly) to lead a quiet life and attend to your own business and work with your hands, just as we commanded you, (NASB)

After our primary relationship with the Shepherd then we have other people in our lives. Most of us live with many people around us. Is that an accident or did the Sovereign God of the Universe decree it? Did God put those people in your life or not?

If He did, and BTW, He did, then He has reasons for it. I believe there are two primary reasons – first, we grow into maturity by learning how to interact with others -Proverbs 27:17 – Iron sharpens iron, and one man sharpens another.

Second, we are given the opportunity to fulfill the second greatest commandment, love your neighbor as yourself (See Mat. 22:37-39) We attempt to fulfill the first commandment of loving the Lord with all our heart, soul, mind and strength, by spending time with Him and learning to hear God's voice. We also learn to walk in obedience to what He says. We learn to fulfill the second one by how we love one another, which also fulfills the first one. John the beloved said this about love:

> If anyone says, "I love God," and hates his brother, he is a liar; for he who does not love his brother whom he has seen cannot love God whom he has not seen. And this commandment we have from Him: whoever loves God must also love his brother. 1 John 4:20-21

Day by day, often minute by minute, we are given the opportunity to grow in our walk with God because of the people in our lives. Many of us are married and God has provided a perfect opportunity in that relationship to help us learn servanthood, death to self, esteeming

## For Our Consideration

someone as better than our self, humility, long suffering, and overcoming all manner of sin.

Because many of us are married, we have produced children and we gain even more opportunities to grow in spiritual maturity. We learn how to serve, how to be careful with our words, control our anger, grow in self-control and all the other fruits of the Spirit – love, joy, peace, patience, kindness, goodness, faithfulness, and gentleness.

Those who are unmarried have parents, siblings, and countless others that they can learn how to grow in the Lord with. God has provided everything we need to learn to obey the two greatest commandments He gave to us. He loves us that much!

As we look to a new year and our desire to grow, to walk in the right direction, we know a great deal of what to do. Love God, love others.

As we leave our homes, we encounter even more people. Everywhere we go, there are opportunities to grow. Driving, eating, meeting, working, playing, social media, wherever we go, growth potential abounds.

Walking in the right direction involves choices that lead to action. Jesus put it this way:

> You are the light of the world. A city set on a hill cannot be hidden. Nor do people light a lamp and put it under a basket, but on a stand, and it gives light to all in the house. In the same way, let your light shine before others, so that they may see your good works and give glory to your Father who is in heaven. Matthew 5:14-16

We are light in the darkness. Light will be seen. As light, those in the darkness will look at us, and Jesus says they should see our good

Let's Go Deeper

works. We are to go around doing good works. We do not work for salvation, but because of it.

We are called to do good works:

> For we are His workmanship, created in Christ Jesus for good works, which God prepared beforehand, that we should walk in them. Ephesians 2:10

Each of us, for however long we live our lives post salvation, is called to fulfill the works God has for us to do. That work includes love.

In fact, the world will know we are His by how we love one another.

> A new commandment I give to you, that you love one another: just as I have loved you, you also are to love one another. By this all people will know that you are My disciples, if you have love for one another. John 13:34-35

Love is an action word. How we speak, what we do, how we serve all speak to the reality of Christ's Gospel changing power in our lives.

We do good to all men, especially those of the household of faith:

> So then, as we have opportunity, let us do good to everyone, and especially to those who are of the household of faith. Galatians 6:10

As we go around doing good, the darkness notices. They may not like it, they may, in fact, attack it, but they can't ignore it.

## For Our Consideration

Many believe that the believers were called Christians early on as a slam – little Christs…mocking, yet the darkness noticed. We love others because we are loved by Love Himself.

So, how do we enter a new year – I would suggest the following:

- Make time to listen to the Shepherd's voice
- Embrace growth potential through relationships beginning at home
- Do good to everyone, especially the household of faith

We can learn how to live our lives in a worthy manner. This is not all there is to walking in the right direction, but it is not less than this either. What will you do with this challenge? Is there something you can change in your schedule to include more Shepherd time? Is there something you need to do to improve the relationships in your life? Given the gift of today, is there something good you could do for someone?

If we keep walking in the same manner as we have been walking we will end up in the same place we are. That may be a good thing, or perhaps not. I do know that our lives will not change unless we begin to, or continue to walk in the correct direction.

# Spiritual Incrementalism Part Three

Here is my premise for these articles – making small intentional changes will bring about a huge impact over the long haul.

People who study such things, generally say it takes 10,000 hours to become an expert in a field of study or a new skill. While the debate rages concerning how accurate that may be, I know I will never become an expert in anything unless I make small, incremental decisions to become one. In fact, my day to day decisions have a major impact on where I will be when I get old…or older. We are where we are today because of our previous decisions.

Passing age 61, I can look back and see major forks in the road of life. Choices made have led to where I am today. Each day we face choices and many times it will be years before we see the full ramifications of the ones we make. Good or bad.

God says we are sheep. Sheep need to have a relationship with the Shepherd and to listen to His voice. We have been given the Word of God to have our minds and our spiritual senses trained, and we must make time in our lives to be quiet to listen. This is a daily decision that will have a major impact over the course of our life.

If we are walking the wrong direction in some aspect of our life, we must repent and turn around if we ever hope to change this.

Since we are looking at incremental change towards spiritual growth, I want to delve into an arena that I would normally avoid. My assumption is that you desire to grow, you want to please the Lord

## For Our Consideration

and you are open to learning, or you would not be reading this. If you do not want to be challenged, then please stop reading now. You have been warned.

I want to discuss the realm of obedience. We do not have to guess at most of what our Lord requires of us. The issue most of the time is not lack of understanding when we fall short, but lack of obedience.

Obedience is expected. Jesus put it this way:

> Why do you call Me Lord, Lord, but do not do what I tell you? Luke 6:46

> If you love Me, you will keep My commandments. John 14:15

> If you keep My commandments, you will abide in My love, just as I have kept my Father's commandments and abide in His love. John 15:10

Jesus sets the standard of obedience and He gives us commands to obey. We have looked at some already in previous blogs – love one another beginning with those closest to us. Embrace the cross and die to ourselves. Do good to everyone we meet, especially those of the household of faith. These are not a suggestion, but a command.

Day by day we build upon the foundation of Christ. We are saved, and we fill each day with the choices we make. The truth is that we rarely will see the full outcome of our decisions until a great deal of time has passed. We probably will never understand all the "why's" of God's commands because we are trapped in this time space world of ours. Perhaps in eternity, all will become clear.

## Let's Go Deeper

Walking in obedience is required in every area of our life. One area I have not shared much on is stewardship; however, how we handle the resources we receive from God is very important.

Every dime we have comes from the One who owns everything. The earth is the Lord's and the fullness thereof. Every provision in our life is the result of God's grace -including our finances.

Barna the pollster and others, state that a very small percentage of Christians tithe. These studies report that 5% of Christians tithe, and even in the born again/evangelical groups, the number only rises to 12%. My question is why is this number not 100%?

The Scripture is not vague about this:

> Honor the Lord with your wealth and with the first fruits of all your produce Proverbs 3:9
>
> To the Levites I have given every tithe in Israel for an inheritance, in return for their service that they do, their service in the tent of meeting. Numbers 18:21

Abraham tithed to Melchizedek hundreds of years before the Law was given to the Children of Israel. The Law simply formalized the process, but the intent for His people to be generous givers was always there in the heart of God.

In Matthew 23, Jesus pronounced the seven woes upon the Pharisees. There are some harsh words towards this group of men. In one place, Vs. 23, Jesus rebukes the Pharisees not about their tithing, but about their neglect of the weightier issues of the Law, like justice, mercy, and faithfulness. In fact, what Jesus said was, "you should tithe," but this fact is often lost amid the rebuke.

For Our Consideration

I won't print it out here, but go read Malachi 3:9-11. Most Christians have no problem agreeing with this prophet when he addresses divorce, the pursuit of godly children, returning the hearts of the fathers back home, and the wonderful truths regarding the Messiah, but we balk at the tithing section. Why?

God doesn't need the money, so what's the big deal? While I don't pretend to know all the answers, here are some thoughts to think about why believers are not the most generous givers on the planet.

Perhaps it is a lack of knowledge. I didn't know you should be a generous giver to the work of the Lord until someone told me about it.

Perhaps the reason people do not give is they have an obedience problem. The Scriptures are clear; God's people should be givers.

Perhaps people really do not understand that they are stewards and not owners. No matter how much we may have here on earth, we will leave all of it behind when we die. We are not owners, but we manage whatever we have at the Lord's bidding, and we will give an account to Him of how we did after this life.

If you don't like any of those reasons, try this one on. Perhaps we have an idolatry issue. Jesus said:

> No servant can serve two masters, for either he will hate the one and love the other, or he will be devoted to the one and despise the other. You cannot serve God and money. Matthew 6:24, Luke 16:13

Money is placed in direct contrast and conflict with the Lord as a potential master. An interesting choice. Jesus did not pick lust, pride or any other sinful failure, but money. Why?

## Let's Go Deeper

Apparently, money and God both want to be served. We must make a choice. Will we honor the Lord or will we honor the idol of money…not necessarily the picture of dead presidents, but what money does for us – security, provision, status, gratification of our flesh, etc. We can't serve both for one will rule, and one will receive our trust.

People argue and debate over whether we should tithe as a New Testament Christian. One thing is clear, most people are not doing anything, and that is a real shame.

Like most arenas, the New Testament standard far exceeds the Old Testament one. Money is no different. Consider Paul's words:

> Each one must give as he has decided in his heart, not reluctantly or under compulsion, for God loves a cheerful giver. 2 Corinthians 9:7

One reason God loves a cheerful giver is because it demonstrates a proper understanding of faith, our Source of provision, the temporary nature of our lives, and it is a part of our worship.

It has been said, and I have not verified it, that Jesus spoke more on money than heaven, hell, and a host of other subjects. I don't know if that is true, but my point is that if we want to grow in our walk with the Lord this year, it may very well begin with obedience – and, specifically in this arena of money.

Study it out for yourself. Ask the Lord to show you what your attitude towards money and giving really is.

Giving is one of the few areas where we are challenged to test God.

> Bring the full tithe into the storehouse, that there may be food in My house. And thereby put Me to the test, says the Lord of hosts, if I will not open the windows of heaven for you and pour down for you a blessing until there is no more need.
> Malachi 3:10

I have over the last forty-five years and I have always found that God is faithful. God does not need the money. It's our need that is in question; it's our spiritual growth and development. Will we decide today to begin to walk in obedience regarding this aspect of stewardship? If not, why not?

If we never start we will never arrive at our destination. We are stewards of Another's resources, and He expects us to handle them properly. Change begins with a decision, and since God loves a cheerful giver, why wouldn't we want that?

There is more that could be covered than these three articles touched upon, but these three are a beginning. I would challenge everyone reading this to begin here and build as you go.

Real change is possible if we begin. We can't do everything at once but we can do something and we should. Pick one aspect of these three articles and begin there. Real growth and change will happen as we begin to make small adjustments in how we actually think and live.

# Fatherhood Part One
# A Calling

The term "father" in our day is almost synonymous with lazy, ignorant, selfish, and out of touch with what is really going on in any given situation. While I do not watch the current crop of TV shows, it is impossible to avoid the onslaught against fatherhood. The sitcoms portray fathers as remote-control addicts with a low IQ, and completely ignorant of what their wise wife or teen is capable of grasping. The heroes of our day are usually more wicked than good and display little in the way of positive character traits. It is difficult to find a movie or TV show that presents fathers in a good light outside of Christian movies like Courageous. Why is this? Is it simply a reflective trend or an accident?

When I was much younger, fathers were presented as wise and understanding, displaying character traits like hard work, courage, and death-to-self for the greater good. Times have changed. Is Hollywood simply reflecting our culture or are they influencing it? Is the message that is subtle at times and sometimes not so much, really a fluke or is it part of something far more dangerous? For the record, I am not given to conspiracy theories by nature; however, in this case, I do not believe that this is random chance.

Jesus taught that a house divided against itself will fall. As the family continues to implode, I cannot help but think that this is the result of a concerted effort of evil. Most of us are painfully aware of the results of divorce, abuse, and the ever-increasing problems associated with the breakdown of the family. While it is easy to point out the

## For Our Consideration

results of the failure, the cure seems difficult to grasp. Even in the Church, it seems we have a hard time understanding this basic truth. A house divided will fall, and great will be the consequences of that fall. We are living in such a time.

While there are no simple answers to a complex problem like this, that does not mean that there are none available! If the breakdown of the family is causing so many issues to society at large, and to the Church closer to home, we should attack this problem with all our resources and not simply give into it. We should begin to evaluate what we are doing and why. Perhaps a different set of filters need to be considered in the church and home. I believe we need to place more emphasis on prevention rather than recovery.

The Church-growth movement has produced some very large churches with huge budgets. How is that working in restoring the family unit? Mission oriented churches are reaching the corners of the globe, are their divorce rates up or down at home? I am not against any method of reaching the lost or expanding ministry to a hurting world. What I am advocating is that if we know our adversary is being successful in destroying marriages and the basic family unit, perhaps we need to rethink where our priorities lay. Jesus said if we gain the whole world but lose our own soul, what have we really accomplished?

Given the well-documented fact that the Church at large matches or exceeds the divorce rates of the world around Her, perhaps we need to look inward for a bit. If the studies are true, and there is no reason to doubt them, that 70-90% of our young people walk away from the faith in their late teens, shouldn't we be concerned about what is going on in the home? What will happen to the next generation if we continue to walk down this path and do not stem the tide of family implosion?

I believe a restoration of the role of fathers is a critical part of the solution. In this series of articles, I will attempt to explain why and how this will help defeat the foe that currently is being very successful. Fathers play a key role in the family and we don't have to look any further than our own inner-cities to see the damage done by the father being absent. Even in homes where the father resides physically, while better than the ones without him if he is not actively engaged in the battle, the war will still be lost.

Something to consider as I close part one: out of all the titles that God could have chosen for Himself, He chose Father. Why? Why not, Chief Emperor of the Universe, of Executive Supreme, President of the Universe, or The Ultimate CEO. God chose a family term instead, father. Hmmm.

For Our Consideration

# Fatherhood Part Two God's Idea

I ended part one with this thought: "Out of all the titles that God could have chosen for Himself, He chose Father. Why? Why not, Chief Emperor of the Universe, of Executive Supreme, President of the Universe, or The Ultimate CEO. God chose a family term instead, father. Hmmm."

The Sovereign, All-Knowing, All-Loving, All-Wise, All-Powerful, and All-Everything Being we worship as God, chose a family identity to set up His Kingdom instead of any of the other choices available to Him. By God choosing to reveal Himself to us in this mode, He declared a powerful truth; family relationships are extremely important and central to His will!

In one of my seminary classes, I came across the "desert island principle." Briefly, this concept means to read the Bible as if you are reading if for the very first time without any other preconceived considerations. Imagine you were born on an island with no access to anything other than what was in your own little world of sand and coconuts. One day a book washes ashore, it is the Bible in your native language, and you read it for the very first time.

As you read this book what would you discover? How would your life be influenced by the stories and examples you encounter on the pages of Scripture? What would your theology look like as you finished it? While no one can possibly know all the answers to these questions, some things are pretty much a slam-dunk. One would certainly understand that there is a Creator and that He (not she or it) is actively involved in the lives of His creation. Page after page God reveals Himself in the stories of the characters in the Book. God is not pictured as some far-off deity, but an active participant in the affairs of creation. As the story unfolded and just when it seems hopeless for the humans yet again, God steps in with the ultimate revelation of Himself, Jesus Christ! We would also know that the ending is very good for those that are His.

What would also be clear is that the Bible is family oriented and based on relationships. In the Old Testament God worked with family groups, and in the New, He continued to work in families and expanded the concept to include a relational grouping called the Church.

This inspired Book reveals thousands of names of real life people and their family connections. As the story moves along in time from Creation to Revelation, God described His followers as being adopted into a family, having brothers and sisters everywhere, and the family model continues to stay central until heaven, when everything ends (or really begins!) with a wedding feast!

The current philosophy of ministry that permeates the modern Church is not one that would be discovered using desert island theology. What would be found is a family-centric mode of living with the emphasis of true Christianity being displayed in interpersonal relationships at all levels, and especially in the family. God cares very deeply for family relationships and this is the pattern revealed in Scripture.

If I am even remotely on target with what I have written so far, then the implications are huge. As families continue to spiral into destruction, the Church and Her influence hang in the balance.

## For Our Consideration

If we hope to stem this tide of destruction then some changes at the root level of our understanding will have to take place. Changes do not come easily, but if we refuse to even attempt them, then we will continue to walk down the path to failure. It seems to me, that we let what we cannot do, which is to change everything, hinder what we can do, which is to change something.

Part of the changes that I am recommending, is that we would begin to reverse the degradation and disdain for fatherhood and replace this with a more Biblical view. After decades of attack from radical feminism, it is almost to the place of embarrassment to express a simple Biblical principle of the husband being the head of the family. To agree with Scripture, that clearly reveals God in the male gender and man as the head of woman as Christ is the head of the Church, raises eyebrows in some, and even temper in others.

Since God came up with the idea of family He must have the perfect order intended, and as is His history with humans, He has revealed His will clearly enough to be obeyed. The revealed truth in the pages of our Scriptures point to male leadership and responsibility for the marriage and family. Men are required by God to lead their homes, and this lost teaching lies at the heart of the problem we are facing in our world today.

The Church of Jesus Christ needs men that will lead their families, love their wives like Christ loved the church, and invest in the next generation. Anything short of this is not what we find in the Scripture.

Pastors need to model, teach, and encourage the men to step up and resist the mode being forced on them by our culture. We, as men, need to reengage in our families and churches and cast-off apathy. We must resist the label placed on us as unimportant extras, and step into God's view of us and our job in the home, extremely important! We

## Let's Go Deeper

must look at our priorities and be willing to ruthlessly evaluate what we are doing and why. What really is important in the grand, godly scheme of things? How do we fit in as men, fathers, and grandfathers? What is our responsibility, and even a more probing question, how are those under our leadership and authority doing?

These questions must be pondered and answered if we are to begin to change the direction of our family, church, cities, and nation.

We cannot do everything but we all can do something. We must begin somewhere and we must start now. Pray, read the Scripture, and begin to implement what you find there. Find some other men to walk with, and begin to talk to your spouse about what is stirring in your soul. Seek the Lord first and all these other things will begin to fall into place.

Rise up man of God, your wife, family, and church are waiting!

For Our Consideration

# Fatherhood Part Three
# Love Your Wife

We cannot do everything, but we all can do something, and it should begin now. In my management training, there was a principle that was repeatedly driven into my head – do it now. This is true when handling paper; file it, delegate it, or take care of it, do not just shift it around in piles on the desk, and it is true in our pursuit of God and our calling. Do it now.

Apathy and procrastination are enemies of our success in our employment and in our homes. Mix in some fear, worry, and ignorance, and we can turn into a real mess! Thankfully, God specializes in cleaning up messes! God is a redeeming God and He will help us when we come to Him. This is true regarding sin, and it is true in our marriages and parenting.

At times, we take stock of where we are in our marriages, parenting and daily walk with God, and feel overwhelmed. So many areas need help we end up feeling hopeless. We look at the entire picture and see that so much work is needed; we end up not doing anything because we cannot do everything. This is a lie that keeps us from walking on with God. God is not overwhelmed and hopeless is not a word used about His children.

As we consider this topic of fathering, we can become discouraged. We are supposed to be the breadwinner, dynamic spiritual leader, prayer warrior, master repairman, financial wizard, and all-wise man of God walking in daily servanthood. Sometimes the pressure is huge, and our failures seem even bigger. So, what should we do, give up? Not an option.

Another statement driven into my brain from the business world was this one – "Anyone can eat an elephant, just do it one bite at a time." I do not know what an elephant tastes like, but I get the picture. These huge beasts can weigh up to six tons and that is a lot of happy meals at one setting! However, breaking down the meat into bite size chunks can and does take place. I do not have to eat the whole thing at one meal and I do not have to change everything to begin to make a difference in my marriage or family. I simply should take small bites and chew, and sooner or later, the elephant will be gone. Okay, later, but you should get the picture. If I never start chewing, nothing will ever change. I must not let the fact that I cannot do everything stop me from doing something.

Since we are discussing fathers, let me just pick one thing we men can work on every day. Consider this verse:

> Likewise, husbands, live with your wives in an understanding way, showing honor to the woman as the weaker vessel, since they are heirs with you of the grace of life, so that your prayers may not be hindered. 1 Peter 3:7

Learning to love our wives will help our children in many ways. As our children observe us, they will be learning valuable life lessons on marriage that will carry over into their own someday. As fathers, we will be demonstrating character traits like death to self, courage, deference, self-control, obedience to Scripture, and Biblical love. We will be training our sons how to honor women and our daughters what to look for in prospective suitors.

For Our Consideration

Another key is that our prayers will not be hindered, and who doesn't want that? How I treat my bride has a direct impact on my relationship with my Lord. God was very clear about this in this passage as well:

> And this second thing you do. You cover the LORD's altar with tears, with weeping and groaning because he no longer regards the offering or accepts it with favor from your hand. But you say, "Why does he not?" Because the LORD was witness between you and the wife of your youth, to whom you have been faithless, though she is your companion and your wife by covenant. Did he not make them one, with a portion of the Spirit in their union? And what was the one God seeking? Godly offspring. So, guard yourselves in your spirit, and let none of you be faithless to the wife of your youth. "For the man who does not love his wife but divorces her, says the LORD, the God of Israel, covers his garment with violence, says the LORD of hosts. So, guard yourselves in your spirit, and do not be faithless." Malachi 2:13-16

There is a great deal in this section as well as the entire book, but for our purposes just notice how the relationship with God is impacted by how we treat our wife. God refused to accept their offerings because of how they were treating their bride. God also states that He was seeking godly offspring and He says that how the man and wife interact has a bearing on this! Prayers being heard, offerings being accepted, and the producing of godly offspring are big issues, and worthy of my further study and time investment!

## Let's Go Deeper

After my relationship with God, the one with my bride is key. Effective fathering begins with loving my wife. Each man's wife is different but God is clear that the responsibility to love her is the husband's, and therefore we are all in the same boat. We, as men, must learn how to love the wife God has given to us. Fortunately for us, there are many resources out there that will enable us to take the first bite of the elephant known as loving our wife. If we never start we will never grow, our marriage will never change, and our children will be deprived of a godly role model to follow.

Here is what I am asking you to do – Ask God right now what He wants you to do with this and then begin to act, right now, today, soon, don't put it off. Next, get a book on the topic and read all of it. Perhaps you can consider asking someone you respect for advice on how to improve or to give you an honest critique of how you are currently doing. When ready, talk to your wife about your desire to grow and change, and be open to her suggestions, without being defensive or hurt.

Whatever you hear from the Lord or decide to do, implement something today, no matter how small. If we do not start we will never make any progress. The task is at hand and it is well worth our time and efforts. Grab a fork and dig in guys, start eating that elephant!

For Our Consideration

# Fatherhood Part Four
# Love Your Wife - What in the World does that Mean?

> Likewise, husbands, live with your wives in an understanding way, showing honor to the woman as the weaker vessel, since they are heirs with you of the grace of life, so that your prayers may not be hindered. 1 Peter 3:7

This must be one of the most difficult verses for me in the entire Bible! I understand the words Peter writes, but it is that command to "understand the wife God gave me" that often produces frustration. Society spends a great deal of time and money researching and then produces such wonderful study results, as "Men and women are different because they are born that way." Go figure, most six-year-olds could have told them that and saved millions of dollars! Christians simply read Genesis 1 & 2 and gain this deep insight.

Over the last 42 years of marriage, and 40 years of counseling, one complaint is consistent in marriage – "My husband does not talk to me." Most men, me included, simply do not understand what the women are saying. We men reply, "Of course I speak, we talk all the time, I tell her what is going on, how my day went at work, etc." Yet, the wife will often say that they do not talk.

What I am seeing in this communication battle between the sexes, is that while using the same words, the meanings are very different. Authors attempt to capture these differences in books like, *Men are* from *Mars and Women are from Venus*, or *Men are like Waffles and Women are like Spaghetti*, both of which I think were best sellers. At the risk of being corrected by any women readers, I will venture into what I think is meant by the ladies when they say we are not talking to them. Generalities are just that, general by nature and not everything will apply exactly to everyone, so relax.

Men tend to exchange facts when talking and women are looking for something deeper, like emotions and feelings. This is foreign to most men. Men will ask another guy about how work was today and he will hear a listing of facts. Had a meeting, completed a report, messed up on a project, missed a deadline, or whatever. The other guy nods and that is it. He may or may not ask for more facts about any of the information exchanged. The guys will walk away from the conversation feeling connected to the other guy because they shared some facts about their day. Women shake their head in disbelief at this reality that men live in.

The women get together and while there may be an exchange of facts, it does not stop there. Friends probe to the feeling and emotional realm. "Oh, you missed a deadline, how did that make you feel, are you okay?" "The boss was angry, did you cry?" "Were you angry with him?" "What are you feeling right now?" These questions rarely enter the mind of a male, and many women simply do not believe what I just wrote! I assure you, it is true. When my guy friend shares that the deadline was missed we may talk about what to do, or how to fix it, but rarely will a man say, "How did you feel when you missed it?" "Were you really upset? Did you cry?" We may get there by accident, but not usually on purpose. Give me the facts, just the facts. This is probably why most guys can quote sports stats quite naturally but often cannot remember what the last argument was about.

## For Our Consideration

Just because we may be wired this way does not mean we cannot grow and change. If Peter was correct, and how I live with my wife has a direct impact on my prayers being answered, I had better learn to speak woman. If my wife tells me, "You are not talking to me," I better listen up and figure out what she means, because I talk all the time, at least I share facts. "Woman speak" is a foreign language to men, but that does not mean we cannot learn how to speak it. I do, after all, know a few words in Spanish!

This is important to the topic of fathering because if our homes fall apart, our children will be vulnerable. One of the best things we can do for our children is to learn how to love our wife. Who else is going to teach our sons and daughters about how to have a godly marriage? They will see the reality of Christ in our homes, or not. They will learn firsthand the truth of God's Word in action, or not.

If we boldly proclaim the Lordship of Jesus, yet there is no difference in our marriages than those that do not know Him, what will our children really learn? Will they be drawn to a powerless Gospel?

Interviewing young people has confirmed this to me. Comments like, "They went to church and were even leaders, but our home was a mess." "Sure, they made us pray, read our Bible, and go to church, but they didn't practice what they preached." "They never had time for us; they were too busy playing church." "Jesus didn't help them, why should I follow that?" Ouch.

Children will catch much more than what we pitch to them with our words. What are they seeing in our lives at home? What message is being communicated each day to the children living with us?

## Let's Go Deeper

As a male, it is difficult to get in touch with my feelings about facts, however, if I want to love my wife in the way she needs, I will learn to do so. Instead of just talking in fact talk, I can learn to express what those facts mean to me if I think hard enough about it.

We all have emotions, even guys. We simply need to probe beyond the reciting of facts to find them. If your wife has told you that you do not talk to her, ask her if what I am saying is even remotely true. Then tell her how you feel about it!

For Our Consideration

# Fatherhood Part Five
# Priests and Prophets?

I was brought up in a religious tradition that included men in long black robes that lived in a cloistered life style, so whenever I hear the word, "priest" this picture enters my mind. The term prophet really does not produce a much better image. I have probably watched too many movies and whenever I think of a prophet, John the Baptist springs into my mind wearing his dirty robe, holding a shepherd's staff in his hand, and yelling at sinners with his booming voice. Okay, it's not really John the Baptist it's Charlton Heston pretending to be him, but you probably get the idea. What do these ancient words and roles have to do with me as a father?

My understanding of one that serves as a priest includes the thought of someone that stands in the place of another. In the Old Testament, there were many priests that served as representatives of the people. These men would offer the sacrifices at the altar, they would pray for, and as a representative of the people of God, offer the required sacrifice. Not everyone could approach the altar but only the assigned priest, and his duty was to represent the people to God.

In the New Testament, the office of priest was fulfilled in Christ. Jesus is now the Great High Priest that forever lives to make intercession for His people. In addition, He is now the one and only Way to gain access to God the Father. As believers, we no longer need a man to be between God and us as a representative, for in Christ, we may all come to the throne of God and find grace and mercy in our time of need! We do not have the time or space to develop the complete role of the priest, but we know enough to grasp some of what this means to us as fathers.

First, as husbands and fathers, we are to intercede for those under our care. We are to stand in the gap for them in prayer. We cannot take their place for Jesus is the only Substitute, but we are to minister at the altar on our family's behalf.

Each member of our family must have a personal relationship with Jesus and there is no way around that truth, for He is the only way to the Father, and His sacrificial death is the only sacrifice needed. But, still, we are called to pray for our families. This mystery around prayer is great, yet, we are to be men of prayer asking God to reveal Himself and His will to those under our charge. We pray for our family!

Second, we are called to have a personal relationship with Jesus that is visible to those under our care. We should be men of prayer, service, and students of the Scripture. What does our family see in our life? Do we lead them to the Throne of Grace in prayer? Are we going there our self? This is not meant to be a heavy rebuke, but which of us prays enough?

If God has called us to lead our families, we must be men of prayer to find out what He wants. We should be those that come before our God and wait, listening to Him to find out what His will is. We should be those that prayerfully read His Word to discover the direction He desires for us to take. We must be leaders that pray and lead others out of our relationship with our Lord.

Okay, I need to pray more, I get it. What about this prophet thing? Prophets in the Old Testament spoke for God to the people. In the New Testament, the role is still the same. Many may argue over what the title now means, and I will leave them to continue with the discussion. As fathers, the point is we need to be hearing from God as

## For Our Consideration

to what He wants us to do and how we are to live. We proclaim that we are His servants, so we should attempt to figure out what the Master wants from us, and to do with us.

As a pastor for four decades that has been heavily involved in family counseling, the number one cry I hear from the ladies is that they want their man to lead. The wife wants to know that her husband has a relationship with Jesus and that their man is walking in daily obedience. Submission is not a problem for a wife that knows that her husband is close to Jesus. On the other hand, it is a fearful thing to attempt to willingly line up under (submit to) a man that is not connected to Christ. While not true in every case, if the wife knows her husband is hearing from God, she will be more than willing to follow wherever he wants to lead.

As men, we are charged with raising the level of spiritual conversations and activities in our home. We should be the ones that are considered wise in the Scripture. We should be the ones that our children look to for biblical answers. We should be the spiritually mature ones in our homes. Should be and reality may not be the same, but we must have a goal. Like most men I know, I feel that I married up, way up! That does not mean that God does not want me to grow, mature, and lead, even if I believe my wife is far more mature than me in many ways. God wants me to lead and this will drive many a man to his knees, which is where a priest and prophet should be.

Our families are not demanding perfection, or at least they should not be asking for the impossible. Most of the time what they are asking for is quality time, a relationship with us, and the knowledge that we are connected to the Lord. We can give them that, and should. If you do not know where to start, pray.

Make some time to read the Word of God and then begin a discussion around the dinner table about what you read. Start slowly and encourage any little sign of interest you see. Maybe reaching under the covers at night for your wife's hand and praying together would be a good place to start. Perhaps kneeling beside your children's bed as you say goodnight and pray with them is the place.

You cannot steer a parked car so get it in gear and pull away from the curb, brothers. Priests and prophets are still in great need today.

For Our Consideration

# Fatherhood Part Six – What Am I Supposed to be Doing Again?

I have had many titles in my life – Husband, Father, Grandfather, Pastor, Doctor, Teacher, and to one friend of mine, Philosopher. I have been a CFP, CFO, CEO, CSO, Salesman, District Manager, Author, Elder, Deacon, and I suppose several others that have long been forgotten.

The one title, next to being a husband that I cherish the most, is father. Father is the same title that God used to identify Himself to His creation. The term father should imply a close relationship with his children. Father is a term that hopefully stirs up images of affection and strength. As I have shared in my previous parts, father is also a name under attack!

I understand that some reading this may not care much for the term father. Perhaps the one they knew was abusive, neglectful, or abandoned them. There is little I can offer in the way of comfort for this tragedy, but we can and must learn to walk in forgiveness, as well as to seek to redeem the title. God is our Father and He is perfect, regardless of how our earthly fathers may have disappointed or hurt us. God wants us to be different from those that may have failed us, and we certainly do not want to repeat the failure!

As we consider this subject of fatherhood, the question arises as to what we are supposed to be doing as fathers. Most do a pretty good job of bringing home a paycheck, and hopefully, after you read my last part, you are learning how to understand your wife a little bit better. But what else should we be attempting to do to make a difference in the next generation?

There are multitudes of verses that address this topic and I cannot possibly cover them all. Most of the verses from Deuteronomy 6, Proverbs, and the New Testament letters, speak of two main points – involvement and diligence.

While it is hard to nail down, studies show that the average father does not spend much time in personal interaction with his children, especially during the workweek. Some say as little as 1 minute a day and others up to 2 hours. The issue to me is not so much how much, but that we are spending time together investing in the relationship.

Having three children over the age of 35 that still talk to me, and want to be around me, is a blessing! We attempted to spend time together as a family and often forsook other distractions so we could. We certainly were not perfect, but being together was a priority. Is it in your home? Do you enjoy being with your wife and children? Jobs come and go and so do buddies, your children will be your children for life. Which ones get the most time and attention?

Other studies indicate that rarely in assisted living and nursing homes do the occupants wish they had spent more time at work or playing golf. What they regret is not spending enough time with their family. If your children are still at home, you have time to change! Please do not waste it.

The other issue I mentioned was diligence. God delegated the raising of our children to us and He expects us to do something with it. We cannot righteously give this task to someone else. Others may assist us, but they cannot replace us. We are the ones that God expects to train, discipline, and disciple our children. We must spend time

# For Our Consideration

with them and we must be diligent in our efforts to fulfill this God-given task.

Here are two verses to consider:

> Fathers, do not provoke your children to anger, but bring them up in the discipline and instruction of the Lord. Ephesians 6:4

> Fathers, do not provoke your children, lest they become discouraged. Colossians 3:21

Both familiar passages are addressed to fathers and both challenge us to not provoke our children. I guess that means we can provoke them by what we do or do not do. If we neglect them, abuse them, or abandon them, then certainly we will provoke them. Most reading this are not in that category, so how do we provoke them then?

There are many ways we can bring our children to frustration. We can consistently be inconsistent in our expectations. One day we demand a certain type of behavior and the next day we overlook it.

We can set unrealistic expectations of perfection for our children. A three-year-old is not fifteen, and a fifteen-year-old is not thirty. We can lie to them by making them promises that we never keep. We can be hateful and nasty to their mother.

We can live as a hypocrite. We can ignore them unless we are mad at them for not doing something. We can ignore their need for discussion and understanding. If we try real hard, I bet we could enlarge this list by personal evaluation of our own behaviors.

Children are extremely impressionable and we must be careful. I still remember talking to my father-in-law about his father. Jack was over 80 at the time and was still crying over his father's neglect. We say things like, "Children are tough, they adapt easily." Do they? Talk to anyone over the age of 60 and I bet they could still tell you of hurts, wounds, and disappointments from their childhood. Children will go on, they will forgive, but they will often carry the scars for life.

For this series, I want us to consider two things. First, are we involved enough with our family? Do we know well the condition of our flock? Are we spending time with them, not sitting around watching TV or playing video games, but talking, sharing, and listening to them? Are they more important than our job, friends, or personal desires? Perhaps if you are brave, ask your wife or older children what they think about this question. You might be surprised.

Second, do we really understand what God expects from us as fathers? Have we searched out the Scripture to see God's job description? Are we attempting to be diligent, not perfect, but involved and consistent? Have we delegated away our responsibility to someone else? Pastors, Sunday School teachers, education professionals, and others may all play a part, but God holds you and me responsible for those under our care. Are we involved and are we diligent? Will we be? If not, why not?

If you have messed up (and who hasn't?), there is always hope. Ask for forgiveness, and ruthlessly evaluate your schedule. Change often comes slowly, but it won't ever come if we don't see the need for it.

For Our Consideration

# Fatherhood Part Seven
# Take the Next Step

I awoke one day with this thought turning over in my mind. The ancient philosophers had a saying, "A journey of a thousand miles begins with a single step," and this is more than a truism, it is a reality. If we do not start, we will not ever arrive at our destination. No matter the length of the journey, a first step must take place. After the first one, multiple ones will follow or we will never arrive.

There is a tension between resting and working in the Scripture. We are saved by grace, yet we demonstrate this saving reality by how we work. We are not saved by works, but we will work once we are saved. Galatians and James are both in our New Testaments and both are the inspired word of God. Galatians focuses on saving grace alone and James says show me your saving faith by your works, so which one is true? They both are.

God wants us to strive to enter His rest regarding salvation, but we are to constantly be about His business while we maintain rest. We were not born again simply to punch our ticket to heaven or God would have been better served to take us there as soon as we were saved. God left us here after salvation with instructions to continue with the work He began.

As fathers and men, we are called to be about the Father's business beginning in our homes. We are charged with the leadership and responsibility of discipling our family as well as striving to enter rest. After a full day's labor, navigating the rush of traffic and carrying a variety of responsibilities in our employment, we still have the duty to be godly husbands and fathers. Sometimes this can be overwhelming.

We must make time somewhere in our day to be filled with the Spirit, receive a dose of God's empowering grace, and draw life from our Life Source, Christ. If we do not, we will not have the strength to do what we have been called to do!

Seeking the Lord is commanded in Matthew 6:33 – we are to seek Him first and to desire to further the work of His Kingdom in everything we do. This goal should be underneath all our endeavors. Easy to say, not so easy to do being human. Nonetheless, this must be our desire and goal no matter how many times we may have failed in its execution. This desire should also be behind what we are attempting to do in our families.

So, back to the title of this part of the discussion – what is the next step for you? Each of us is different and in a wide variety of places in our Pilgrims' journey to the Celestial Shores. Some of us have been walking for decades and others just now starting, however, the process is the same; take the next step. We all walk one step at a time. What is that next step for you? What is it that God wants you to do with your family? Excellent questions that only you and God can answer.

For me, God has asked me to move more into being more of a mentor. For my whole life as a pastor, I was always looking for the older man that I could connect with, to collaborate with, to learn from. As one of my friends so gently told me one day as I bemoaned my futility in this search, "Look in the mirror, you are the older man!" He is correct, I am the older man now, and as such, I have a responsibility to attempt to help others in their walk. My children are grown, my wife and I have been married for over 42 years, and I have been

For Our Consideration

pastoring our type of church for just about as long as anyone else in the country. It is time to step up to helping others.

How about you? Perhaps it is time for you to take the next step in your marriage or parenting adventure. Maybe this is the day to start praying with your wife. The next step might be to begin family devotions or reorganize the family schedule to allow for more time together. It might be about time to consider how to begin a family outreach of some sort, perhaps to a local nursing home, or to volunteer for a needy organization. The possibilities are endless, but they all begin the same way, one step at a time. Will you ask your Sovereign Lord what the next step is for you and yours? Your journey will be different than anyone else, but they all work the same way, they begin with taking the next step.

# Final Thoughts

Well, we have reached the end of our journey together. My prayer is that the time invested will be profitable for the Kingdom of our Lord Jesus.

We are all important to our loving Father and we all have a role to play while living on this planet. May the Lord grant you great grace and favor as you find your part in the journey. Ephesians 2:10!

Keep on walking in the Light. – Pastor Jeff

# Biography

Dr. Jeffrey Klick serves as the senior pastor at Hope Family Fellowship in Kansas City, Kansas, a church he, and a group of dedicated people, planted in 1993. Dr. Klick married his high school sweetheart, Leslie, in May of 1975, and they have three adult children and thirteen grandchildren.

Dr. Klick loves to learn and has earned a professional designation, Certified Financial Planner, earned a Master's degree in Pastoral Ministry from Liberty Theological Seminary, a Doctorate in Biblical Studies from Master's International School of Divinity, and a Ph.D. in Pastoral Ministry from Trinity Theological Seminary.

In addition to serving as senior pastor at Hope Family Fellowship, Dr. Klick is a consultant with The Institute for Church Management and serves on the Board of Directors for The Council for Gospel Legacy Churches.

Visit - www.jeffklick.com for more information.

# Dr. Klick's Other Books

**Pastoral Helmsmanship—A Pastor's Guide to Church Administration***

**Confessions of a Church Felon** – Protecting your Ministry from the Flames of Fraud*

**Courage to Flee, Second Edition** - How to achieve and keep moral freedom.

**Gospel Legacy: A Church and Family Model Reaching Beyond Our Generation**

**A Glimpse Behind the Calling: The Life of a Pastor*** - Written to help both pastors and those who love them.

**The Master's Handiwork – Your Life has a Purpose**

**Reaching the Next Generation for Christ: The Biblical Role of the Family and Church** - Detailed research on faith impartation to the next generation.

**The Discipling Church: Our Great Commission***

All books available at Amazon.com in print and Kindle formats.

www.jeffklick.com

*Co-Authored with other excellent brothers

Made in the USA
Columbia, SC
20 August 2017